Beyond Keynesianism

Beyond Keynesianism
The Socio-Economics of Production and Full Employment

Edited by
Egon Matzner
and
Wolfgang Streeck

Edward Elgar

Published by
Edward Elgar Publishing Limited
Gower House
Croft Road
Aldershot
Hants GU11 3 HR
England

Edward Elgar Publishing Company
Old Post Road
Brookfield
Vermont 05036
USA

British Library Cataloguing in Publication Data
Beyond Keynesianism: socio-economics of production and full employment
  1. Labour market
  I. Matzner, Egon II. Streeck, Wolfgang
  331.12

Library of Congress Cataloguing in Publication Data
Beyond Keynesianism: the socio-economics of production and full employ-
  ment/Egon Matzner and Wolfgang Streeck, editors.
    p. cm.
  Selection of papers presented at the Conference titled 'No Way to Full
Employment?' held in Berlin from 5 to 7 July, 1989, and later revised for
this volume.
  1. Full employment policies-Congresses. 2. Keynesian economics-
Congresses. I. Matzner, Egon, 1938- . II. Streeck, Wolfgang, 1948- . III.
Conference 'No Way to Full Employment?' (1989: Berlin, Germany)
HD5701.5.B49 1991
339.5-dc20   90-27736
                                                                  CIP

ISBN 1 85278 424 5

Printed in Great Britain by
Billing & Sons Ltd, Worcester

Contents

Part 3: On Effective Demand Conditions

Part 4: Towards a Context Enhancing Full Employment

Tables and Figures

Contributors

Eileen Appelbaum is Professor of Economics at Temple University, Philadelphia, USA and a Guest Fellow at the Labour Market and Employment reasearch area of the Wissenschaftszentrum für Sozialforschung, Germany (henceforth abbreviated WZB/LME).

Christoph F. Büchtemann is a Senior Research Fellow at the WZB/LME.

Gernot Grabher is Research Fellow at the WZB/LME.

Gerhard Hanappi is lecturer at the Institute of Economics, Technische Universität Wien, Austria.

Hansjörg Herr is Research Fellow at the WZB/LME.

Jan A. Kregel is Professor of Political Economy at the University of Bologna, and Professor of International Economics at the Bologna Center of Johns Hopkin University, Italy. From 1985 to 1989 he was a Consultant at the WZB/LME.

Egon Matzner is Professor of Public Finance at the Technische Universität Wien, Austria. From 1984 to 1989 he was Director of the WZB/LME.

Bernd Reissert is Research Fellow at the WZB/LME.

Ronald Schettkat is Research Fellow at the WZB/LME.

Günther Schmid is Director at the WZB/LME and Professor of Political Science at Freie Universität, Berlin.

Heinz-Peter Spahn is Professor of Economics at the Hochschule der Bundeswehr in Munich. From 1984 to 1989 he was a Senior Research Fellow at the WZB/LME.

Wolfgang Streeck is Professor of Sociology and Industrial Relations at the University of Wisconsin-Madison, USA, and a Guest Fellow at the WZB/LME where he was a Senior Fellow until 1988.

Michael Wagner is Director of the Institute for Economic and Social Research, Wien, Austria.

Acknowledgements

Most of the papers in this book were originally presented at the conference under the title 'No Way to Full Employment?' The conference took place in July 1989 at the Wissenschaftszentrum Berlin für Sozialforschung (WZB). Editors and authors are indebted to conference participants for invaluable comment and criticism. The contributions to this book contain results of interdisciplinary and comparative research achieved at the Labour Market and Employment unit of WZB during the period 1985 to 90.

In addition, we would like to thank the many people that made the conference a success and who made the production of this volume possible. Special thanks go to Amit Bhaduri for his intellectual support from the very beginning until the final stage of the work. We are also grateful to Patricia Blaas, Christl Degen, Thomas Ellermann, Hannelore Minzlaff, Sylvia Pichorner and Andrew Watt for lending the project their professional competence. Furthermore, the editors express their thanks and appreciation to the WZB for its support of this publication.

Egon Matzner and Wolfgang Streeck (eds.)
WZB, Berlin and University of Wisconsin - Madison, 21 February 1991

1. Introduction: Towards a Socio-Economics of Employment in a Post-Keynesian Economy

Egon Matzner and Wolfgang Streeck

As pathbreaking theoretical ideas migrate into the public consciousness and are adapted for practical application, they are bound to lose part of their characteristic complexity. The work of John Maynard Keynes gave rise to Keynesianism in the same way as, for example, Karl Marx prepared the ground for Marxism: both systems being simplified and homogenised praxeological constructs that abstract from the ambiguities, contradictions, and unexplored ramifications in the theories from which they spring, and disregard as confusing and unproductive the gaps, doubts, and open questions underneath the surface of the original theory's written text.

One way in which a complex theory may be simplified for public consumption is through transformation into constants of dimensions that the theory has, or might have, treated as variables. A condition under the purview of a theory that is turned into a constant can *for all practical purposes* be relegated into the background, becoming a fixed parameter that the simplified theory, or praxeology, does not have to take into account: since a constant does not change, it cannot make a difference. Often, major reorientations of theory and public policy begin with the discovery that something that has in the past been considered fixed and given, is in fact variable or has historically for some reason become so. Simplified, or codified, theories are particularly vulnerable to such discoveries, given that their very simplicity is derived from the fact that they by definition take a lot of things for granted. Typically, if a praxeology like Keynesianism gets into difficulties in this way, attempts are made to show that the original theory could in principle accommodate the liquidification of the respective parameter; that the author himself had at several occasions pointed out that matters would be different if the factor in question changes.

That furthermore his views on the subject had changed over time; or that he had intended to deal with it systematically but for some reason never got there.

This book's concern is with Keynesianism, not with Keynes and the 30 volumes of his *Collected Writings* - with Keynesianism as it had developed as a praxeological doctrine from the interwar period until, let us say, the mid-1960s. While the systematic structure of the 'General Theory' may or may not have anticipated the difficulties that Keynesianism encountered in the 1970s and 1980s, we will not in this volume try to establish to what extent Keynes can be held responsible for the 'crisis of Keynesianism' which, as is known, has a strong neoclassical core in the version of the 'neoclassical synthesis'. Exploring which part 'really' is causing the 'crisis' is not our concern here. Rather, we would like to limit ourselves to pointing out that in its heyday Keynesianism, with some grounding in Keynes original theory, had more or less tacitly become used to treating a number of important socio-economic conditions as given. These interdependent and interrelated elements can be conceived as a *socio-economic context*,[1] changes in which would tend to reduce the effectiveness of the previously successful praxeology.

In our view, there are essentially five conditions in the institutional structure of modern capitalist society that Keynesians had come to treat as given, unchangeable, and therefore largely devoid of practical interest. It is important to note that their elimination from the realm of the theoretically or practically remarkable need not be explained by a lack of intellectual effort or capacity. Rather, the constants in Keynesianism - that later, by becoming variables, were so seriously to undermine its praxeology - represented central pillars of the real world and the life-experience of a generation of economists and political decision-makers that had come of age in the 1930s and for which the world of the post-war settlement after 1945 constituted the paradigm of a, or the natural, rational, self-evident social order. The five conditions were:

1. A *social structure*, and especially a structure of the family, that allowed for an easy definition of the labour supply and, by implication, an unambiguous measurement of full employment. In a Keynesian economy, as in the European societies of the interwar period, the potential workforce consisted of all adult males who typically were, or were about to be, married and had to provide for a family. If less than, say, 95 per cent of this group were employed, the economy had unemployment. *Nota bene* that this society was enclosed in relatively tight borders, and long-distance migration on a large scale was unknown. In such a world, full

employment was far from being a moving target, and the labour supply effects of employment increases were negligible or absent.

2. A *labour market* that was *unproblematically flexible* in that there were *no strong unions* in the 1930s that could have pushed the wage above the market price of labour. Moreover, the *workforce* was *highly homogeneous*, in the sense that most people in danger of unemployment were manual workers willing to do any job at any wage that ensured their survival and that of their families (the typical worker benefiting from 'Keynesianism' can probably be imagined as a miner, between 20 and 65 years old, in a small English mining town). Although it is well known that Keynes regarded unions important for maintaining stable price levels by accepting productivity-orientated money wages, he thought sometimes that such a policy could be more easily implemented in a kind of authoritarian-corporatist tutelage with Mussolini's Italy being a case in point. In any case, given the general weakness of unions in the interwar period, not least in the United Kingdom, the problem was not regarded as systematically important, and did not become particularly relevant for 'Keynesianism' until the 1950s.

3. Processes of *structural and technological adjustment* on the supply-side that were *market-driven* and were unproblematical in the sense that they did not require *detailed* public intervention. Neither Keynes nor Keynesianism could, or for that matter wanted to, provide a systematic place for industrial policy. The existence and, above all, the satisfactory performance of *competition* in product markets regulating resource allocation was assumed largely without qualification. While the demand side of the Keynesian economy required strong and skilful public intervention, the supply-side remained the 'Kingdom of the bourgeoisie' (Przeworski and Wallerstein, 1982) and the terrain for the famous capitalist 'animal spirit'. It has also been argued that Keynesianism had a distinctive technological basis: that of large-scale, single-purpose machinery making for the superiority of mass production in markets that require political stabilisation (cf. Sabel, 1982). Today 'Keynesian' technology would appear to be replaced by microelectronic-based multi-purpose machinery which seems to have a decisive competitive advantage in more uncertain markets.

4. A *government*, or a *state*, of a *simple kind and structure* whose interventionist tools were limited to the areas of fiscal and monetary policy. Demand management, being essentially concerned with monetary and fiscal policy affecting expenditure, was something for a small number of experts entrenched in an élitist bureaucracy. Compare to this the enormously complex on-the-ground implementation mechanisms that are

needed for an active labour market policy or, for that matter, a sophisticated industrial policy - i.e., one that does not simply rely on transfer payments. *State capacity*, in other words, could largely be taken for granted once the centrist political consensus underlying Keynesianism had been established. Apart from the fine details of, for example, a central bank's open market policy - which, while they in themselves were certainly quite complex, could be dealt with inside small circles of experts, without direct interaction with 'clients' - there were no technical problems to Keynesian policies that would have required a rethinking or reorganisation of the state apparatus.

5. *National economies* that were contained within sovereign national borders and were therefore reasonably safely *closed off from their international environments*. Such external trade in goods and services as there was could without problems be conceptualised in terms of an external account which would never get large enough to be more than a marginal addition to what remained basically a domestic economy. Since the primacy of the internal economy is unquestionably assumed, the relevant economic aggregates are taken as a matter of course to be essentially controlled, or at least controllable, by national governments. Moreover, national economies were firmly embedded in an *international order* that managed whatever external effects there may have been between them. That order, too, was comparatively simple in that many fundamental problems of cooperation and co-ordination were taken care of by the overwhelming power of its major participant, the United States. Today's difficulties with international interdependence and the growing mutual penetration of national economies were clearly not an important issue before the 1970s.

Institutional and structural conditions of this kind, or rather their presumed fixity, enabled Keynesianism to do without sophisticated institutional analysis and to offer workable recipes for full employment without recourse to the national or historical peculiarities of the social and political setting in which it emerged. In this respect, if in no other, 'Keynesianism' was a genuine product of the discipline of economics. The general claim in this book is that as the implicit institutional assumptions of Keynesianism have become untenable, empirically founded institutional analyses of the employment problem have become necessary. Understanding employment and full employment now, once again, requires recourse to historically and socially grounded analyses. We should not continue to content ourselves with the economics but try to grasp what we call here the *socio-economics* not only of employment, but also of production.

To introduce our perspective, we would like to begin with a few examples responding, by and large, to the five points above.

1. The recent breakdown of most cultural and legal barriers to access to the labour market in most Western countries makes it immeasurably more difficult to define the *target* of full employment policy. Where high female participation rates, for example, are accorded greater social value, social and cultural change vastly increases the burden on full employment policy. Moreover, successful employment policy leading to increases in employment may have a positive ('imitation') effect on the labour supply and thereby generate further problems for employment policy. In such conditions, influencing the social valuation of paid employment can as such become a major way of reducing 'unemployment'. As far as comparative analyses of employment performance are concerned, taking into account the obvious differences in cultural values that are at least partly responsible for the differences in female participation rates between, say, Sweden and the Netherlands becomes a difficult and challenging problem.

Perhaps even more importantly, the removal of cultural restraints on the labour supply has made it possible to expand employment at low levels of productivity growth and even at declining real wages, with households *increasing* their employment participation in response to a declining wage level. In principle, reopening the frontier of the labour market through institutional and cultural change may, for all practical purposes, produce an unlimited labour supply. This allows fast growth at stagnant productivity levels, with a restoration of profitability and investment incentives at the expense of workers. It is especially enhanced if the mobilisation of women for the labour force is accompanied by the destruction of unions - two processes which may well reinforce each other in a relationship of mutual interdependence. Such a development - we are of course referring to the United States after 1980 - can be sold politically in the name, not only of full employment, but also of equal opportunity for women and, to a lesser extent, racial minorities and immigrants.

In so far as employment growth of this sort is in addition fuelled by government-led demand expansion, Reagan-style employment policy can be described as Keynesian. The label would, however, appear less than instructive. Compared, for example, to the expansionary measures taken by the Swedish government in 1932 - which were also Keynesian - the distinctiveness of the Reagan strategy lies in its *complementary measures on the supply-side*, such as redistribution of wealth from poor to rich, a dramatic rise in the wage spread, overall wage cuts, low investment in research and development and in skill formation, and the destruction of unions. More generally, the problem to which this kind of policy tries to respond is not unemployment but the desire to restore profitability without improving long-term investment and productivity growth. The US experience shows that full employment in this case does not necessarily indicate or promote international competitiveness; in fact the former may be gained at the expense of the latter, the political euphemism for this being structural change towards a so-called service economy which could more properly be called a 'servants' economy'.

2. With rising living standards and savings, strong social security systems and high levels of education, societies can afford, or will at least be inclined to try, to institutionalise social expectations concerning the *quality* and the kind of employment they are willing to accept. Unions are important mechanisms for generating and defending such expectations. A society that refuses to support low-skill and low-wage employment runs the risk of a specific kind of classical unemployment among unskilled workers whose productivity is lower than the lowest admissable wage. To avoid the consequence of social dualism and segmentation, such a society will have to demand of its government an employment policy that accomplishes full employment while respecting high general standards of social acceptability. A policy, in other words, that unlike traditional demand management is neither indifferent to what kind of jobs are being created, nor takes the existing distribution of human capital as given. Whether or not high-quality employment standards can in practice be maintained depends in part on the relative strength of conflicting social groups, and in part also on the capacity of labour market policy institutions to guide a panoply of market processes, in the labour market and elsewhere, in a compatible direction. Some societies, such as within the United States, may never have institutionalised expectations of this kind; or their social and political power balance may be adverse to them; or their public policy capacity may not be sufficiently developed to implement the required, complex labour market policy. Other societies, some of them in Europe, seem to have learned, more or less well, to eliminate involuntary unemployment in spite of 'rigid' social or cultural standards, relying on public intervention not just on the demand but also on the supply-side of the economy, so as to increase the demand of employers for high-wage and high-skill work beyond what the market would generate on its own.

3. The experience of the 1970s and 1980s has *undermined the credibility of simple economic models of structural change*, as traditionally accepted by Keynesianism. Under their rule, adjustment is optimal if firms are forced, or given the freedom, to follow market signals as closely as possible. Numerous studies, such as on the sources of Japanese competitiveness or on European industrial districts, have pointed to the contribution to successful adjustment of socio-economic contexts that are capable of suspending competition, mediating market pressures, facilitating cooperation and supporting long-term investment orientations. It is very clear that such contexts institutionalise and promote significant interventions in the operation of markets. In this sense, they constitute 'rigidities' that, in the framework of standard economics, would be expected to impede efficient resource allocation and adjustment, and thus to make an expansionary demand policy inflationary. In any case, since such institutions operate typically on the supply-side, their formation, cultivation or manipulation would almost by definition not be considered as an instrument of full employment policy.

An industrial policy that relies on non-market institutions to support effective structural change is not as easy to dismiss as one that, in the way that has given industrial policy its bad name, subsidises 'national champions' or declining sectors. In fact, it has been argued that market-driven and institutionally-guided adjustment processes are associated with different directions of industrial development, or production patterns, whereby those that result from pure market pressures may well be less economically competitive. To the extent that this is true, full employment policy, especially if it operates in an open economy and if it aims at long-term stable results, can no longer confine itself to traditional demand-side intervention supplemented on the supply-side, if at all, by a vigorous competition policy. Rather, the supplementation it would require would be an advanced, sophisticated type of intervention centred around the gardening of institutions that induce and enable firms to choose a high productivity, long-term competitive adjustment path over its market-driven alternative. Again, such intervention must be based on insights into the socio-economics of production systems that in the past were clearly outside the purview of standard economic theory.

4. Numerous studies have shown vast differences between national capitalisms with respect to the role and structure of the *state* and the way in which it intervenes in the economy. Not only do some states intervene more than others, but, perhaps more importantly, the styles and tools, if not the targets of intervention differ greatly, and so do the capacities of states with different institutional equipment to conduct particular policies

and attain specific objectives. This may not have been important for traditional Keynesianism with its very limited demands on state capacity. But where the institutional guidance of market processes affects the level and character of the employment that is generated, full employment requires more than just aggregate demand management plus flexible markets; indeed it may critically depend on the state being able to conduct, for instance, a fine-targeted active labour market or industrial policy. For this, the structure of public administration must be such that it can reach deep down into the networks that mediate exchanges in civil society, putting these to effective public use. Where the state is not well-equipped for this purpose, the conscious design or reform of appropriate state, or para-state, institutions may assume critical significance for employment policy. Moreover, the social networks with which effective institutional, or socio-economic, intervention must link up are mostly located on the supply-side, or in the production sphere, where they typically generate and enforce social or communitarian obligations that constrain market individualism. De-regulation, if it destroys such networks or severs their links with the machinery of public policy, may affect competitiveness and employment in a way quite different from what its proponents promise.

5. It is increasingly being realised that successful demand management in highly interdependent national, or rather post-national, economies that operate in an integrated world capital market is possible only through *international co-ordination*. The task of reconstructing the Keynesian macro-economy *as an international unit of political decision-making and collective action*, however, is one of institution-building, and standard economics has all in all very little to say on this subject. Indeed, not much is known generally on the prospects for effective, cooperative institution-building in an international setting characterised by enormous differences, and inconsistencies, in political power and economic performance, and by well-founded suspicions between the major players as to the others' trustworthiness.

Even less clear are the consequences of persistent failure of concerted action between rival economic blocs. One implication of an integrated world economy is that firms and industries now can in principle select their markets strategically - i.e., can actively try to find and choose the kind of demand that fits their structural capacities best, or alternatively reorganise such capacities in a way optimally suited to the requirements of desirable markets without being confined to national markets as they were previously. Internationalisation, in this sense, increases firms' range of strategic choices. Such choices, as has been pointed out, may be constrained by institutions and opportunities arising from the social system in which firms are embedded. Shaping the socio-economic context of firms' strategic choices in a way compatible with given social or employment objectives may therefore be a major tenet of an advanced post-Keynesian employment policy.

Moreover, what kind of opportunities and constraints a social system has to offer is likely to influence the amount and quality of the investment taking place inside its boundaries. With a worldwide capital market, different countries or cultures may compete for industrial investment by providing investors with an attractive public infrastructure and human capital supply. For example, by improving their infrastructures individual regions or countries could try to attract investment in highly diversified quality-competitive products, on the assumption that these will generate relatively safe, stable and well-paid employment. Public intervention in the production of supply-side collective goods may thus be an instrument of employment policy in an integrated world economy, especially as long as there is little prospect for successful international institution-building. Again, such intervention is widely different from the type of demand management that is usually associated with Keynesianism.

The premise of this book, then, is that the study of full employment can no longer do with the simplified image of production and institutions that has become characteristic of standard economics. Institutions in particular need to be moved from where they traditionally were in the Keynesian paradigm: in the unchangeable and therefore irrelevant background of theory and practice into the centre of concern where they become principal subjects of theoretical and practical interest. Without intending to offer a theory or unified methodology, the present book collects ideas and empirical material that might help inform more systematic attempts at a new *institutional economics* that, rather than trying to 'explain' institutions by neoclassical means, and thereby explain them away, takes them seriously *as non-economic social constructs with profound and manifold economic consequences* and as indispensable guideposts and stabilisers inside an economy that without them would be incomplete and functionally deficient. It is this programme which we broadly refer to, in the words of Etzioni (1988), as *socio-economics*.

Apart from their joint conviction that beyond Keynesianism there lies an institutionalist socio-economic theory of production and employment, the contributors to this volume share an interest in one particular country, West Germany (a country which, by the time this book will come out, will have disappeared into a larger entity, Germany). This interest is pursued in several papers by comparing West German economic performance with that of other OECD countries. West Germany, or Germany, is indeed a fascinating case for economic analysis. It is a country which is generally not well understood, and we suspect that this has something to do with the deficits of standard economics with respect to the understanding of social institutions. The German post-war economic 'miracle' has been interpreted, by many Germans and even more non-Germans, as a success story of market liberalism and supply-oriented economic policy.[2] This story was frequently held against the Keynesian convictions and practices that prevailed elsewhere in the West after the Second World War. (Japan, of course, was the other demonstration case of an economy that was highly successful without a declared Keynesian economic policy.) It is not for us to determine here the extent to which demand factors were instrumental in German post-war economic recovery, although they did, contrary to current orthodoxy, play a major role. Rather, it is the purpose of this volume to point out that the *institutional structure* of the supply-side of the German economy was and is quite different from what it would have to be to conform to the prescriptions of a liberal, free-market regime.

In a nutshell, West Germany was, and Germany will be, a political economy rich in 'rigid' non-market institutions such as strong trade unions, industry-wide collective bargaining, compulsory trade associations like Chambers of Commerce or Chambers of Artisans, a heavily and centrally regulated vocational training system, strong employment protection, statutory participation of workers, etc. Paradoxically from the perspective of standard economics, while all these institutions profoundly interfere with the free market, West Germany is one of the most competitive and prosperous modern economies. Indeed more detailed analysis has shown again and again that such institutions add to rather than detract from the German economy's competitiveness. As many of the chapters in this volume document, attempts outside or inside Germany to make a case for 'de-regulation' of other economies by pointing to the example either of Germany today or of the post-war miracle fundamentally misconstrue the way in which the German economy works. Such misinterpretations, intentionally or not, play to the prejudices of standard economics as a discipline for which national differences are irrelevant and competitive performance can result only from the 'free' functioning of markets. It seems that, more often than not, even German economists who should know better feel obliged to demonstrate to their peers in other countries that things are essentially the same here as elsewhere and that, to the extent that the German economy works better, this is because it comes closer to the universal model of free markets and unfettered competition. This is in many ways similar to the ritual attempts of some Japanese economists desperately trying to show that, for example, the Japanese labour market is really just a neoclassical market that functions in full harmony with the prescriptions of American human capital theory.

This volume differs from most books on the employment problem in its multi-disciplinary character. It collects contributions from various disciplines in the expectation that, in this way, the methodological restrictions inherent in any discipline can be overcome, and additional insights can be gained. Economists can learn from political scientists or sociologists about their 'black boxes' (Steindl, 1988, p. 350): for example, the production process. Or, social as well as political science contributions can explain the economic significance of social institutions or the implications of the 'undersocialisation' of economic models (cf. Granovetter, 1985). Social scientists, on the other hand, may learn from economists in the Keynesian tradition about the significance of macro-phenomena like 'effective demand', which cannot be established from micro-observations (cf. Bhaduri, 1986, p. 54). The contributions to this volume are thus organised under both disciplinary and transdisciplinary aspects.

Part 1 addresses the supply-side by developing a sociological approach towards organisational, technological, cultural and regional sources and preconditions of production and employment. In *Part 2* the impact of labour market and social policies is assessed by quantitative and qualitative methods used in the political and social sciences. *Part 3* addresses the demand side: it contains papers analysing the constraints and opportunities which fiscal and monetary policies have faced since the 1970s. *Part 4*, finally, is an essay towards a theory of comparative institutional advantage. In addition, it ventures suggestions for the making of a 'context' conducive to full employment. This part is to a great extent based on the arguments and the empirical evidence presented in the other contributions to this book.

There are two ideas behind this order of presentation: First, the argument moves from the part to the whole, from the micro- and meso-supply conditions through the (partial) analysis of labour market and social policies to the macro-aspects of demand at the national or transnational level. Second, special significance is attached to concepts such as 'supply' and 'demand', or 'policy' and 'institution', by combining them with the notion 'effective'. While 'effective demand' is well known from Keynesian theory, 'effective supply' is a rather novel concept. We consider effective supply as given if an increase in effective demand can be met by domestic suppliers in a competitive way. The concept contains thus both an *actual* and a *potential* dimension. Effective supply is hence not given, if an addition to effective demand increases merely imports and/or prices instead of domestic output and employment. In a similar way, policies and institutions can be analysed in terms of their *actual* and *potential* impacts. Effective policies and institutions are characterised by the extent to which they allow for a realisation of the potential inherent in a given context. In this way it should be possible to gain a better understanding of how 'the context' in which institutions operate and in which policies are applied influences their outcomes.

The study of institutions is the most important transdisciplinary element common to the contributions to this book. Institutions are, like technological devices, conceived as human artefacts. Irrespectively of how they may have emerged, by intention or spontaneously (cf. Hayek, 1978), they can be assessed in terms of their contribution to the solution of societal problems, be they economic, social or political. As institutions prove themselves as problem solvers, they also give rise to expectations regarding their problem-solving capacity. That capacity, its utilisation and the experience connected with it represent accumulated knowledge essential for effective institutions. Likewise, the erosion of their problem-solving capacity by changing circumstances will make institutional change (e.g., reform and replacement of an institution, or its decay and eventual death) likely. The results presented in this book, however, permit the conclusion that de-regulation, in the sense of substituting markets for non-market institutions, does not always entail the solution of societal problems. This is not to be understood as a plea for a freeze of the institutional or technological status quo. On the contrary, most advanced industrial countries have now entered an era of material maturity with high average incomes, a high level of education, and savings increasingly exceeding investment outlays. That they at the same time also tend to be often characterised by high unemployment points strongly to a need for institutional reform.

Among other things, this book is an attempt to explore the conditions under which a country is able to attain a high level of employment without recourse to 'social dumping'. This is only possible at a high level of competitiveness which in turn requires that the functioning of markets be supported and constrained by adequate policies and institutions. This approach differs fundamentally from that of the 'de-regulation school' that has become popular with the demise of Keynesianism. Our orientation is rather in the tradition of the English classical economists who, as Robbins has pointed out, were seeking a stock of institutions in which the pursuit of self-interest would create the 'good society'. Such an aspiration requires the conscious testing of social institutions, including markets, as well as of the policy instruments in use, and a continual revision of regulations (cf. Robbins, 1978, p. 42).

The present book can be perceived as a supplement to ideas inspired by Keynes which remained, however, neglected in much of Keynesianism and which post-Keynesianism has taken up only recently (cf. Shackle, 1972; Kregel, 1980; Hodgson, 1988). Essentially, the book's concern is with problems which Keynes outlined in his notes on 'The Long-term Problem of Full Employment' (cf. *The Collected Writings of John Maynard Keynes*, Vol. XXVII, 1980, pp. 320-50). As early as 1943, Keynes foresaw for a period of maturity a need for far-reaching changes of institutions and policies if full employment was to be achieved. Keynes envisaged the passage to maturity as taking place in the 1970s after the end of a period of reconstruction and following one or two decades of general expansion.

1. SUMMARY OF RESULTS

Chapter 2 is an attempt based on several strands of theorising and empirical research to establish the institutional conditions of a production pattern, called 'diversified quality production'. That pattern is argued to exist, to an important extent, in West Germany whose prosperity and competitiveness largely depend on it. In trying to determine the impact of supply-side institutional conditions on the possibility and viability of diversified quality production, *Wolfgang Streeck*'s paper deviates from the institutional minimalism of neoclassical theory and neoliberal practice, as well as from Keynesian-type recipes for state interventionism. The paper tries to show that, if market actors are always allowed to have their way, the result may in significant respects be economically suboptimal. Beneficial economic intervention is shown to entail not just the construction of opportunities for rationally-acting market participants, but also of constraints that prevent them from following perverse incentives that undermine the efficient functioning of the supply-side - or of 'effective supply'. Put otherwise, the paper emphasises a need for institutions capable of counterbalancing market imperatives and thereby preventing unregulated, or de-regulated market forces from undermining the economy's long-term competitiveness.

Regional growth (like in Baden-Württemberg) and decline (in old industrial regions in the Ruhr valley) are embedded in producer-supplier channels of a distinctive character. While the successful regions build upon an elastic network of ties which foster change, regional decline often goes together with a rigid pattern of producer-supplier as well as producer-buyer relations dominated by one or two large companies. Adaptation and qualitative change are absent and are often perceived also as a threat to the economic, social and political power structure of such a region. This is the theme of *Gernot Grabher's* paper (*Chapter 3*) which is based on studies of industrial restructuring in the Rhine-Ruhr area and in Lower Austria.

In *Chapter 4*, 'On the Institutional Conditions of Effective Labour Market Policies', *Günther Schmid* and *Bernd Reissert* present empirical evidence for their hypothesis that the size, quality and effectiveness of labour market policies depend on the institutional set-up through which the financial resources needed for them are channelled. In a six-country comparison *Schmid* and *Reissert* show that in most countries there is still room for institutional improvement and hence for reducing unemployment by active labour market policies.

In the scientific and political debate, a rigid regulation of the labour market is often regarded as an important reason for the non-clearing of labour markets. In *Chapter 5*, *Christoph F. Büchtemann* analyses the impact of the partial de-regulation of employment protection in West Germany, in particular by allowing firms to offer fixed-term employment contracts up to 18 months. On the basis of survey data and his own empirical research the author arrives at the conclusion that the contribution of concrete de-regulation in terms of *additional* employment has been rather modest. The expectation of a significant increase in employment resulting from labour market de-regulation cannot be substantiated in the case of West Germany.

The strong growth of employment in the US during the 1980s is often suggested as an example which European economies should follow. This refers in particular to the growth of service employment. *Eileen Appelbaum* and *Ronald Schettkat* take up this issue in *Chapter 6*. Their comparison shows that, in terms of employment shares, the patterns of industrial restructuring differ only insignificantly in the two countries. The variation, however, is dramatic if one compares the West German and US employment growth between 1979 and 1987: 15 per cent (14.4 million jobs) in the US and 2.8 per cent (0.7 million jobs) in West Germany. This difference is due to the low productivity of a great part of the new jobs created in the US. 'Rigidities' in West Germany did not prevent restructuring; they rather provided incentives for higher productivity increases and, consequently, higher wages and competitiveness than in the US at the cost of a more modest growth of total employment.

The emphasis in this volume on the institutional conditions of effective supply and effective labour market and social policies does not invalidate the significance of the principle of *effective* demand as established by Keynes and Kalecki. Effective demand (the sum of consumption and investment goods, of exports less imports and of public expenditure less taxes) which is necessary to provide for a sufficient number of socially acceptable and internationally competitive jobs requires a complementary institutional arrangement on the supply-side and support by labour market and social policies. Or, in other words, a well-adapted supply-side needs, to become fully employed and deployed, a macro-foundation in and through demand policies.

One of the consequences of the increasing internationalisation of capital markets has been the erosion of the efficacy of expansive fiscal and monetary policies. In *Chapter 7, Hansjörg Herr* comes to the conclusion that, in spite of the integration of world markets, there is still room for successful fiscal expansion. Highly-integrated international capital markets sometimes act as a constraint on national economic policy, but sometimes they create additional room for manoeuvre for fiscal expansion in countries whose currencies are in high demand by international asset holders. In four country studies (Japan, West Germany, France and the United States) it is shown that this room for manoeuvre has been insufficiently used in West Germany, which helps to explain its high and persisting unemployment.

One important idea for combating high unemployment has constantly been the plea for an international co-ordination of national fiscal and monetary policies. In *Chapter 8, Heinz-Peter Spahn* rejects such a proposal on the ground of objective as well as political difficulties which would make its implementation almost impossible and the outcome of co-ordination at least risky in terms of inflation. Giving priority to a stable value of the currency - in his case the D-Mark - over full employment, *Spahn* advocates for a 'monopolistic international policy co-ordination' instead of a bargained co-ordination - a position which comes close to that of the German central bank. He argues that such a monopolistic policy co-ordination could be achieved by an appreciation of the West German currency to be initiated by an increase in German interest rates. A stronger D-Mark according to *Spahn* would tend to reduce West Germany's trade surplus and thus increase domestic welfare instead of employment. At the same time the assumed reduction of the trade surplus would relax the international constraint on deficit countries. Such a greater room for manoeuvre could be used for fiscal stimulation.

Chapter 9 contains remarks by *Jan Kregel* on 'monopolistic policy co-ordination' as well as on some international consequences of German unification. In the first section Kregel discusses the feasibility of monopolistic international policy co-ordination by the Deutsche Bundesbank, as suggested by Spahn. He questions whether the intended effects could be realised by a revaluation of the D-Mark following an increase of German interest rates. Kregel argues that such a policy would rather tend to reduce aggregate international demand. It thus could intensify the imbalances and constraints inherent in the present situation. In the second section Kregel discusses the international economic consequences of German unification. An increase of effective demand in Germany, which is necessary for the urgent modernisation of the former GDR (as well as the other post-Communist countries), is likely to reduce unified Germany's foreign trade surplus. It will thereby increase the opportunity for fiscal expansion in deficit countries. The international net effect on aggregate effective demand is likely to be positive, if the Bundesbank abstains from a high interest rate policy. Pressure on the German price level which sometimes has been expected from overconsumption following the introduction of the D-Mark by 1 July 1990 in the GDR, has not arisen. Favourable international consequences of German unification may well improve the chances for a European Monetary Union and a single European currency.

How could the unutilised scope for fiscal stimulation which Hansjörg Herr found to exist in West Germany in the 1980s be used for increasing employment? *Gerhard Hanappi* and *Michael Wagner* suggest in *Chapter 10* an increase in public expenditures for industrial innovation. The impact of such a strategy for 'innovation-led employment growth' is estimated with the help of their simulation model Tandem-M - a model of the interrelation between investment, accumulation and absorption of innovation as well as labour markets in a system in which the state and the monetary sectors are endogeneous elements in an international economy. The impact of an (once for all) increase of public expenditure by 1 percentage point of GDP with additional funds for R & D promotion produces, in terms of Tandem-M, higher growth, a reduction of unemployment by 1.5 percentage points (or roughly 25 per cent in absolute numbers) in four years. The speed-up of inflation is rather moderate, the current account deteriorates and causes a slight rise of the interest rates. 'Innovation-led employment growth', perceived as a programme, integrates elements of supply-side (R & D promotion), and the demand side (public expenditure).

Chapter 11 on 'Policies, Institutions and Employment Performance' by *Egon Matzner* is an attempt to recollect the arguments and evidences presented in this volume around the concepts of *comparative institutional advantage* and of the *socio-economic context*. Both are indispensible for understanding and influencing the performance of production and employment of open economies. This is a conclusion which appears to be particularly important in times of dramatic changes in socio-economic contexts, such as the transformation of post-Communist economies or the establishing of the single European Market.

NOTES

1 More specifically, the 'context' of economic action consists of a combination of (1) signals emanating as relative prices, costs and incomes from market processes; (2) institutions and technologies which constrain as well as enable decisions, actions and outcomes; (3) policy instruments which influence (1) and (2); and (4) structures that can only be altered gradually (see Chapter 11, below).
2 Likewise, the return of high unemployment and of economic stagnation in the 1970s has been explained by the same school of thought by 'institutional rigidities', 'too high wages' and the subsequent deterioration of West German competitiveness caused by the welfare state and union power (cf. Fels and Fürstenberg, 1989).

REFERENCES

Bhaduri, A., *Macroeconomics. The Dynamics of Commodity Production*, London, Macmillan, 1986.

Etzioni, A., *The Moral Dimension. Towards a New Economics*, New York, The Free Press, 1988.

Fels, G. and Fürstenberg, G.M. (eds.), *A Supply-Side Agenda for Germany*, Berlin, Springer Verlag, 1989.

Granovetter, M., 'Economic Action and Social Structure: The Problem of Embeddedness', *The American Journal of Sociology*, Vol. 91, No. 3, 1985, pp. 481-510.

Hayek, F.A., The Errors of Constructivism. F.A. Hayek, *New Studies in Philosophy, Politics and Economics*, London, Routledge & Kegan, 1978.

Hodgson, G., *Economics and Institutions*, Cambridge, Polity Press, 1988.

Keynes, J.M., 'The Long-term Problem of Full Employment' (1943), *The Collected Writings of John Maynard Keynes*, Vol. XXVII (edited by A. Robinson, D. Moggridge), London, 1980, pp. 320-50.

Kregel, J.A., 'Markets and Institutions as Features of a Capitalist Production System', *Journal of Postkeynesian Economics*, Vol. III, No. 1, 1980.

Kregel, J.A., Matzner, E. and Roncaglia, A. (eds.), *Barriers to Full Employment*, London, Macmillan, 1988.

Przeworski, A., Wallerstein, I., 'Democratic Capitalism at the Crossroads', *Democracy*, July 1982.

Robbins, L.C., *The theory of economic policy in English classical theory*, second edition, Philadelphia, 1978 (first edition 1951).

Sabel, C.F., *Work and Politics*, Cambridge University Press, 1982.

Shackle, G.L.S., *Epistemics and Economics*, Cambridge University Press, 1972.

Steindl, J., 'New Lines of Research on the Question of Full Employment', in J.A. Kregel *et al.* (eds.), 1988.

PART 1:

ON EFFECTIVE SUPPLY CONDITIONS

2. On the Institutional Conditions of Diversified Quality Production

Wolfgang Streeck

1. INTRODUCTION

Little attention is paid in the Keynesian theory of full employment to the operation of the *supply-side* of the economy and to the social and political institutions required for its efficient performance. For Keynes, full employment was to be achieved through fiscal and monetary manipulation of aggregate demand at the national and, to some extent, the international level. The mechanisms by which supply was to respond to managed demand, and the process of demand management itself and how it was to be protected from interference by macro-irrational, particularistic political interests were not seen as problematic. It was only in the revisionist literature of the late 1970s, after the eclipse of Keynesian politics, that writers like Skidelsky (1979) pointed to the remarkably orthodox assumptions and requirements underlying Keynesian theory and practice: in particular, those of a 'free' and 'flexible' product and labour market being the optimal mechanism and a necessary precondition of efficient micro-adjustment on the supply-side; as well as of state institutions sufficiently shielded from popular pressure to be capable of making technocratic decisions solely on the merits of complex econometric analyses. If the blanks in the Keynesian discourse are taken, as they should be, as indicating agreement with the institutions and orthodoxies of the time, the conclusion appears justified that for Keynes, *the size of aggregate demand* was to be determined by a small group of technocrats while the *structure of supply* was to be left to the two, as it were, *minimal institutions* of standard economics: *competitive markets* and *managerial hierarchies*.

It seems that it was not least the political and economic traditionalism of its implicit assumptions that rendered Keynesianism so defenceless against the onslaught of supply-side economics in the 1980s. The discovery in the post-war period that the very practice of demand management had changed the 'rational expectations' of market participants and thereby 'distorted' the market (Brittan, 1978); that furthermore the 'flexibility' of markets, particularly for labour, had progressively declined due to institutional growth 'beyond contract' (Fox, 1974); and that macro-managerial decisions had become subject to and entangled in democratic electoral politics - inevitably shook the foundations of a theory of full employment that was for its practice dependent on both classical market economics and traditional codes of political authority and deference.

Keynesians, in spite of their 'Keynes-plus' rhetoric, found it hard to object to the call of the new supply-siders for a speedy restoration of state sovereignty, market flexibility and management prerogative. While they had placed their hopes on a different use of sovereignty, they had nothing to hold against their opponents' insistance that in a capitalist society state authority had to be protected from popular democratic dilution. They also, and more importantly, could not but accept the standard economic wisdom that only if firms are left alone by governments, and managements by their workforces, will they end up in the *market segments*, produce the *range of products*, adopt the *production technology*, develop the *organisation of work*, generate the *skills*, and pay the *wages* that will allow for full employment. Seen from the perspective of the late 1970s, the debate between Keynesianism and supply-side economics never went beyond the question of whether or not it was necessary, useful or possible for the national state *in addition* to provide for an adequate level of aggregate demand. To the extent that this, for all kinds of contingent reasons, had to be answered more and more in the negative, mainstream Keynesians had little with which to oppose the increasingly self-confident demands of their neoclassical opponents for de-regulation of product and labour markets and for a return to the *institutional minimalism* of market and hierarchy.

Deviating from the Keynesian as well as the neoclassical tradition, in the 1980s a number of social scientists and political economists began to develop a *social-institutional perspective on the supply-side* of modern industrial economies. Just as neoclassical supply-side economics, they emphasised the importance for full employment of the international competitiveness of a country's pattern of industrial output and industrial organisation. They also agreed with the, mostly implicit, claim of both economic camps that such patterns are importantly shaped by the social institutions within which economic action takes place. At the same time, they sharply rejected as simplistic and functionalist two fundamental assumptions that are explicitly or implicitly made by most economists of whatever denomination. They were that there is, at least in the long run, only one path towards competitive survival - one homogeneous 'best practice' without functional alternatives or equivalents, inside which national or regional differences are essentially insignificant - and that patterns of industrial output and industrial organisation ('production patterns', as we will from now on call them) are the more efficient, and therefore the more likely to bring about full employment, the closer the institutions that govern them resemble the *neoclassical minimum* of unregulated markets and unlimited managerial prerogative, complemented at most by a liberal (in the European sense of non-interventionist) and, in questions of property rights, non-majoritarian democratic state. While taking a firm supply-side view of the employment problem and its possible solution, contributors to the emerging new approach shared an unwillingness to accept a conceptual framework under which the only constructive contribution of politics to full employment would appear to be the dismantling of whatever socio-economic institutions exceeded the neoclassical minimum; one that relegates politics to the demand side where its residual function is to extract an equity price from an inherently efficient market economy in exchange for social stability and that carries with it the preconceived conclusion that a return to full employment requires above all unregulated markets and unlimited private hierarchies.

Central to the new political economy of the 1980s, then, was an attempt systematically to understand what could be called, with a recently fashionable expression, the *social dimension* of the supply-side. In various contexts and through alternative approaches, it tried to support claims like the following:

- that different institutional conditions may give rise to different *production patterns* that may represent *functionally alternative*, and sometimes *functionally equivalent, responses* to common economic challenges;
- that, to the extent that alternative responses are not equivalent in competitive terms, *institutionally impoverished economies* that rely solely on markets and hierarchies for the governance of economic activities *do not necessarily perform better* than societies where economic behaviour is more socially regulated;

-   that, quite to the contrary, *a repertory of social institutions that exceeds the neoclassical minimum* may in specific conditions make a *positive contribution* to competitive market performance;
-   that, in particular, certain highly-successful production patterns require for their emergence and survival *strong non-market institutions* that *modify and partly suspend individual market rationality and unilateral managerial control* and *thereby* make for higher efficiency;
-   that therefore public and private choices between high wages, stable employment, worker participation and social equity on the one hand, and full employment, monetary stability, competitiveness and efficiency on the other are *not nearly as simple* as suggested by standard economics in general and the supply-side economics of the 1980s in particular; and
-   that given the right kind of institutional regulation and political intervention, an *institutionally saturated and politically bargained pattern of production and employment* may be possible which may be highly *competitive* in an open world economy.

This paper is on the institutional preconditions of an advanced neo-industrial production pattern referred to as *diversified quality production*. Drawing on both empirical research and theoretical reasoning, it tries to specify a set of functional requirements that firms, and the economies in which they operate, have to meet in order for diversified quality production to thrive. The paper identifies three such requirements: a *congenial organisational ecology*, the presence of *redundant capacities*, and a rich supply of *collective production inputs*. It also tries to show that the functional requirements of diversified quality production can be met only to the extent that the economy in which production takes place *is at the same time a society* - i.e., is supported by an institutional substructure that exceeds the minimalist prescriptions of standard economics.[1] In essence, the paper tries to show that societies that want to exploit the employment opportunities offered by advanced forms of demand need to develop and cultivate a rich institutional structure capable of imposing enforceable social constraints on rational market participants, as well as of creating effective opportunities for them to restructure towards higher diversity and quality.

2. DIVERSIFIED QUALITY PRODUCTION

Beginning in the late 1970s, researchers in many countries took part in a worldwide attempt to understand the social origins and conditions of emerging 'neo-industrial' (Hirschhorn, 1984) production patterns. These had in common that they seemed to be able to attain superior competitiveness in world markets through sophisticated application of information technology, a diversified product range, and non-price-competitive marketing strategies, combining all these with high wages, skilled labour, and a flexible, non-Taylorist organisation of work. Due to different research experiences, points of access, and initial theoretical orientations, the new supply-side institutionalism developed along different trajectories, emanating in partly divergent and partly supplementary lines of work like the 'flexible specialisation' tradition (Piore and Sabel, 1984), the 'new production concepts' approach (Kern and Schumann, 1984), and others. The present paper is informed by the concept of 'diversified quality production' (Sorge and Streeck, 1988) which was proposed in an attempt to reconstruct the property space of the neo-industrialism debate so as to relate it more closely both to certain comparative empirical observations and to possibilities for political intervention under a full employment strategy for mature industrial societies.

The immediate origin of the concept of diversified quality production was in the analysis of alternative 'manufacturing policies' (Willman, 1986) associated with the absorption of new, microelectronic production technology. Three variables were found to be of importance (Sorge and Streeck, 1988): the degree to which products were standardised; the type of competition they tried to meet; and the volume of output. The first two factors appeared to be closely related in that standardised products are generally sold in price-competitive markets whereas customised products tend to be quality-competitive. This suggested a distinction between *standardised price-competitive* and *customised quality-competitive* production on the one hand, and *low* and *high volume* production on the other. Crossing the two dimensions generated four alternative product, or manufacturing, strategies two of which - the *low-volume production of customised quality-competitive goods* ('craft' production) and the *high-volume production of standardised price-competitive goods* ('Fordist' production) - were quite conventional. Indeed with some simplification one could say that before the advent of microelectronic technology, these would have been the only production patterns possible.

This comparatively simple picture was found to have become considerably more complicated as a result of technical change. For instance, new technology seemed to have lowered the break-even point of mass production, both enabling traditional mass producers to survive with shorter production runs and, perhaps, making it easier for artisanal low-volume producers to achieve economies of scale and enter mass-type markets. At the same time, the capacity of new technology for fast and inexpensive retooling seemed to have made it attractive for small component producers dependent on large assemblers to differentiate their product range and move into an advanced form of craft production, so as to reduce their exposure to price fluctuation and monopsonistic demand.

The most important impact of new technology on manufacturing strategy, however, seemed to be that it had created a new option for firms in the form of *high-volume production of customised quality-competitive goods*. In many manufacturing sectors, microelectronic circuitry had eroded the traditional distinction between mass and specialist production. The high flexibility of microelectronic equipment and the ease and speed with which it can be reprogrammed enabled firms to introduce a hitherto unknown degree of product variety, as well as product quality. The result was a *restructuring of mass production in the mould of customised quality production*, with central features of the latter being *blended* into the former and with *small batch production of highly specific goods becoming enveloped in large batch production of basic components or models*. This pattern was what came to be called 'diversified quality production'. It can be approached by firms through two different paths of industrial restructuring: by *craft producers extending their production volume* without sacrificing their high quality standards and customised product design, or by *mass producers moving upmarket* by upgrading their products' design and quality and by increasing their product variety, in an attempt to escape from the pressures of price competition or from shrinking mass markets.

Two empirical observations in particular made diversified quality production interesting. One was that its presence and absence seemed to co-vary with certain *national and regional differences in economic performance and competitiveness* which standard economics appeared unable to account for (Sorge and Warner, 1986). The leading case was the West German economy, both during the crisis and after, and, inside Germany, regions such as Baden-Württemberg where the highest average wages and the lowest level of unemployment in West Germany resulted from an export performance that included a positive trade balance even with Japan (Maier, 1987). Here, superior competitiveness coincided with a pattern of production, in part of long historical standing, at the core of which were customisation of products, differentiation of product ranges and high product quality providing shelter from price competition. Restructuring towards this pattern seemed to offer a promising strategy for other regions in Germany - and, by extension, for old industrial, high wage economies in general - that were at the time striving to protect their employment in the face of more volatile and crowded world markets.

Another point that stood out was that Germany in general and Baden-Württemberg in particular are *institutionally rich societies* where markets are deeply embedded in an array of cooperative, redistributive, and regulatory institutions (Sabel *et al.*, 1987). Detailed analysis in various studies gave rise to considerable doubts whether the performance of economies of this kind could, as standard economists would have predicted, be further enhanced by changes towards the institutional minimalism of neoclassical theory.[2] Quite to the contrary, there were numerous indications of a peculiar, complex interaction between diversified quality production and thick institutional structures, with the latter simultaneously being *sustained* by and *sustaining* the former. In particular, not only was diversified quality production not obstructed by social institutions, but there was reason to believe that *markets and managements on their own would be unlikely and frequently unable to generate that pattern*, and that if firms were reduced to their own devices the production pattern and the prosperity it had wrought *would be at risk*. This, at least, became one of the guiding hypotheses of much of the research on the institutional conditions for the supply of diversified quality production.

The concept of diversified quality production is just one of a number of attempts to make sense of profound transformations in the 1970s and 1980s in the structure and functioning of developed industrial economies. The fact that it took off from comparative studies of political economies like West Germany and, to some extent, Sweden seems to have entailed certain advantages for the understanding of neo-industrial production in general. Work on diversified quality production has always kept its distance to theories of industrial change that rotate around concepts like 'high technology', 'knowledge-based' (Hirschhorn, 1984) or 'post-industrial' (Jaikumar, 1986) manufacturing. While these no doubt point to important properties of neo-industrial production, their empirical references are primarily American firms or Japanese industries where trade unions are weak, politics is influential primarily by default or only in the form of MITI-style 'high politics', and *the social system of production* can either be taken for granted or, if at all, is treated as a matter of private, professionalised social engineering by and on behalf of unilateral management. The conceptual emphasis on product diversity and quality, by comparison, directs attention towards the shopfloor and the institutions and organisational forms that regulate and sustain complex manufacturing processes. In this sense, the concept of diversified quality production involves the programme of an *empirically grounded sociological production theory*. It is conceivable that the dominant concern in the study of diversified quality production with the 'low politics' of comparatively glamourless everyday institutions like industrial training systems and industrial relations, and with 'manual' work rather than university-trained engineers, represents a German bias, and indeed this preoccupation is shared by authors like Kern and Schumann (1984). But one might also argue that a production-oriented perspective has the advantage that it draws attention to important institutional conditions of successful quality-competitive performance whose discovery may be obstructed by excessive fascination with 'high technology'.

Differences and similarities between the various approaches to the study of neo-industrial production patterns result partly from different roads of empirical access and partly from different prejudices. Especially important for the analysis of diversified quality production was the rich and influential literature on *flexible specialisation* (Piore and Sabel, 1984). Among other things, research efforts on diversified quality production and on flexible specialisation have in common that they are ultimately *politically motivated*, in that their guiding interest is in the potential of advanced industrial production systems to underwrite an egalitarian society at a high level of welfare, with political democracy rooted in autonomy and participation at the workplace and in stable employment. They also attempt to transcend a merely redistributive definition of politics and political institutions in relation to the economy, trying to leave behind the traditional disjunction between economics looking after *efficiency*, and political or sociological analysis studying *equity*. Moreover, both are strongly and even primarily interested in the institutional underpinnings of neo-industrialism, and thus share the broad methodological programme of an institutionalist political economy.

But there are also major differences that have persistently stood in the way of merging the two concepts or simply taking over the more popular one. To the extent that originally, 'diversified quality production' was introduced polemically against 'flexible specialisation', this was primarily for the following reasons:

1. While Piore and Sabel (1984) locate their 'industrial divide' primarily in time - defining it in terms of a break in the historical continuity of industrial society in general - the study of diversified quality production placed its emphasis more on *synchronic differences* between social systems, in particular national and regional societies. It is true that the 'flexible specialisation' tradition recognises national, or spatial, variation in the degree to which 'Fordism' was able to supersede craft production. In the same way, the concept of diversified quality production is compatible with the notion that, due to evolutionary changes in the structure of demand, producers of customised quality-competitive products today have even better market chances than they had in the past. Still, the differences in emphasis are important. Obviously they go back to the fact that diversified quality production was 'discovered' in cross-national comparisons, in particular between societies like West Germany on the one hand and the United Kingdom or France on the other where the differences in production patterns are of long historical standing.[3]

2. The 'flexible specialisation' concept is coloured by the study of Italian small-firm communities from an American perspective, whereas diversified quality production, as indicated, derives much of its inspiration from the German experience. For the latter, the existence of highly competitive, highly flexible, and highly skilled and technologically sophisticated small firms, which is Piore and Sabel's formative empirical anomaly, is not surprising. In fact, the German artisanal economy - the *Handwerk* system - has all too often been taken for granted by German researchers (and unfortunately found *intractable* by most non-Germans). As a result, work on diversified quality production emphasises the extraordinary potential, compared to other countries, of large firms in Germany for customised, quality-competitive production, without always pointing out how much this is historically and economically owed to the legally protected presence of a large number of small artisanal firms. While Piore and Sabel do report 'flexible specialisation' in large German companies, they present this more or less as an odd exception, and the observation is neither explained nor systematically incorporated in the concept - the paradigm case of a 'flexibly specialised' economy remaining the Italian industrial district. This is why the flexible specialisation literature, quite unlike the concept of diversified quality production, was initially difficult to reconcile with certain central implications of the French Regulation School's competing concept, 'flexible mass production' (Boyer, 1987) - for example the expectation that there will continue to be significant economies of scale alongside the new economies of scope, or the assumption that there will still be important advantages to vertical

integration and large-scale organisation even where markets place a premium on diversity and quality.

3. Having grown out of the 'hard' German - as opposed to the 'soft' Italian - experience, the concept of diversified quality production has always kept its distance from the *communitarian voluntarism* that informs the more speculative chapters of Piore and Sabel's book. Diversified quality production is decidedly *not a new type of society* but a, in principle rather old, type of industrial output that today has come to be related to a particular kind of technology use. Unlike Piore and Sabel who see flexible specialisation giving rise to a high-technology version of Jeffersonian 'yeoman democracy', analysis of neo-industrial production patterns under the concept of diversified quality production does not entail Utopian expectations of a dissolution of large organisations in horizontal market relations between solidaristic free traders. Diversified quality production, as it exists in the real world, clearly does not require the disappearance of corporate hierarchies, but rather their containment and counterbalancing through institutions like, for example, co-determination.

4. Following from this, the most important difference between the two concepts may be that unlike flexible specialisation which often appears to be based primarily in communitarian-cultural-contractual-voluntary bonds, organised social conflict and 'hard' and formal institutions like trade unions, employers associations, the law and the national state continue to play a constitutive part in the generation and operation of diversified quality production. As will be pointed out below, diversified quality production has been found to thrive on the presence of competing and even incompatible perspectives and interests that may need to be accommodated through overt social conflict. In particular, it requires that the rational-individual pursuit of economic advantage be embedded in, and constrained by, institutionally enacted and enforced social obligations, on the assumption that the free, 'rational' decisions of individuals and organisations are by themselves insufficient for moving an economy-cum-society towards diversified quality production. The implied claim, of course, is that the 'softer', cultural mechanisms on which Piore and Sabel (1984) essentially rely to contain competition and enforce obligations in their industrial districts, will in reality not be able to perform that function, or will at least in the long run fail to ensure the reproduction of advanced neo-industrialism.[4]

The present paper makes the assertion that today's growing markets for diversified quality products can *only imperfectly* be served by an economy that is not also a society, i.e., that is not in a particular way regulated and supported by thick, non-economic social institutions. It also argues that among the possible institutional arrangements on the supply-side that may sustain diversified quality production are some that are highly compatible with traditional Social Democratic objectives like high wages, a low wage spread, workplace participation, and full employment. To make its case, the paper uses examples from different traditions of research on advanced industrialism, in an attempt to draw out, in an ideal-typical way, the institutional implications of a number of functional requirements for quality-competitive and customised production. In doing so, the paper uses the concept of diversified quality production generically to denote the full range of neo-industrial production patterns - as defined by their attempt to attain competitiveness through product diversity and quality - rather than just a large-firm version of 'flexible specialisation' or a set of certain German idiosyncrasies.[5]

3.   MARKET AND HIERARCHY FAILURE

The central claim of this paper is that a regime of free markets and private hierarchies is not enough to generate and support a pattern of diversified quality production, *a favourable product demand environment notwithstanding*. This is not to say that individual firms may not come to be diversified quality producers even in institutionally impoverished settings. However, it is argued that they will remain islands ('of excellence') in a sea of more traditional production and lower production competence, and it is likely that their performance will be less efficient and less stable than if they were part of a *general pattern*. By implication, in a neoclassical institutional environment, part of the existing demand for diversified quality products will remain unsatisfied due to a sluggish supply-side response, and employment opportunities offered by the evolution of product markets and demand structures will remain unexploited.

Diversified quality production is more than an individual commercial strategy. It is conditional on an *industrial order* (Herrigel, forthcoming), or a *social structure*, that can only partly, provisionally and precariously exist on a voluntaristic-contractual basis. Where it is fully developed, it is the outcome of a *collective, 'cultural' choice* (usually long-term, gradual, incremental in character) mediated by and crystallised in a set of *social institutions*. This is because, as we will argue in the present section, diversified quality producers thrive in an *organisational ecology*, or *community*, where other firms engage in the same kind of production;

they require investment in *redundant capacities* that are difficult to build as a matter of interest, and more likely to be created as a matter of obligation; and they depend on *factor inputs* that, if optimally provided, have significant *collective-good* properties.[6] Rational individualism of competing firms and unilateral managements is not an ideal decision-making mode for the *creation of community*, the *generation of excess capacity*, and the *provision and repletion of collective production factors*. Unlike the Fordist 'cathedrals in the desert' (Lipietz, 1980), firms in diversified quality production are neither self-sufficient nor can they in their own interest hope to become so; in fact, they perform best, i.e., serve their markets most successfully, if rather than relying on their 'private' *organisational endoskeleton*, they build on, submit to, and invest in a common, 'public' *institutional exoskeleton* to guide their decisions and facilitate their activities.

An important implication, again distilled from empirical research, is that neither *technological change* nor the *evolution of product markets* are by themselves sufficient to move industries into a diversified quality production mode, even if alternative production strategies are economically clearly less attractive. In this respect, the concept of diversified quality production takes on board the expanding literature in management science and organisational analysis on strategic choice, drawing on a realistic image of the firm as revealed by empirical research (like in Child, 1988). Far from determining firms' behaviour, technical and economic change are seen as having increased the range of, as well as the burden on, 'rational' managerial choices. While new technology and new demand structures create opportunities for firms, regions and national economies for blending specialist into mass production, they do not necessarily provide the rational motivations, irrational predispositions, technical capacities, and economic factor endowments required for this. Indeed, microelectronic *technology* has been found to improve firms' survival chances in quite different types of production and product markets, price- as well as quality-competitive. Similarly, while product strategies respond to the market, they are not determined by it. Firms have always had a degree of choice with regard to their own performance standards, and have differed among other things along organisational, sectoral and national lines with respect to the time they are willing and able to wait for investment to become profitable. Moreover, market signals are *never conclusive* partly because active marketing may be able to change them, partly because there are always different markets and market segments to select from, and partly because even the best marketing department cannot safely predict where future profits will be found, especially given today's *wider range of economic options complementing an increased menu of technical possibilities.*

Second, for a firm to be able to take up diversified quality production as its economically most efficient strategy, certain *factor endowments* may be required which firms on their own find hard to produce or procure since their provision depends on some form of co-ordinated collective action. Whether or not such *public production factors* can be generated may in turn depend on the presence of institutions that *resolve prisoners' dilemma-type rationality conflicts between and within the firms involved.* As has often been pointed out, individual choice may produce suboptimal results even from an individual perspective if there are no institutions that *protect rational motives for cooperative behaviour from rational expectations of defection.* To the extent that diversified quality production requires collective factor inputs, institutionally unfettered market-rational behaviour of the neoclassical type may stand in the way of a full use of product market opportunities for diversified quality production. A neoclassical institutional environment may thus prevent an economically optimal supply-side response to the evolution of demand even if the market opportunities on offer are correctly perceived.

Proceeding from literatures on regional economies (Sabel, 1989), industrial organisation (Piore and Sabel, 1984), national differences in work organisation and technology use (Sorge and Warner, 1986), and comparative industrial relations (Hotz, 1982; Streeck, 1987), there seem to be at least *three dimensions of market and hierarchy failure* with respect to diversified quality production, giving rise to a need for an institutional exoskeleton for rational individual actors not to be constrained by the limits of rational individualism. Each dimension stands for a category of functional requirements for firms trying to increase their *productive flexibility*[7] in response to new economic opportunities and technological possibilities, by blending craft into mass production:

1. THE REQUIREMENT OF A CONGENIAL ORGANISATIONAL ECOLOGY

Diversified quality producers seem to prosper in the presence of other, equally competent producers of the same kind. The problem here is one of creating and protecting a polycentric, decentralised pattern of *industrial organisation* that would be unlikely to originate and persist if markets and hierarchies were allowed to operate without interference. Under a competitive market logic, the prosperity of one firm is based on the elimination of other, competing firms; under a hierarchical organisation logic, it entails the inclusion of different levels of the production chain in one corporation and their subjection to centralised managerial control. Neither of these seem to be fully functional for diversified quality production where shorter (sub-) batches enveloped in long (sets of) batches, as well as higher quality standards, appear to put a premium on *strategic alliances and joint ventures* between firms at the *same* level of the product chain, and on *close, privileged and trust-based cooperation* between assemblers and suppliers at *different* levels. The reasons for this include high research and development costs due to more rapid product turnover and more specific product customisation, making it difficult for individual firms to maintain sufficient R&D capacities inhouse; as well as higher quality standards and advanced logistical methods requiring suppliers to be both technically competent and closely tuned into the operation of their customers.

High product diversity and quality sometimes seem to go together with an *attenuation of the distinction between firms and their competitors*, as well as a *blurring of the boundaries between firms and their suppliers* (Sabel and Kern, 1990). To the extent that diversified quality production is enhanced by a fluid, quasi-consortial pattern of industrial organisation - with joint ventures being set up, like building sites, for special projects, to be dismantled after their completion - firms in a given industry are at the same time competitors and potential allies. While competing in some areas, they depend in others on their competitors cooperating with them in good faith, as well as maintaining a level of technical and marketing excellence that matches their own. Firms' interest in the technological strength of their suppliers seems to account for the often described trend from *multiple-sourcing* from firms that were *not allowed* to work also for other customers, to *single-sourcing* from firms that are *encouraged* to improve their technological capacities by working for more than one client. The advantages of this new configuration seem to outweigh the risk of a firm's know-how being transferred to its competitors through a joint supplier, or of suppliers becoming so technologically powerful that they may move into their client's product markets themselves.

Markets and hierarchies are not well-equipped to govern the complex mixture of competition and cooperation required for diversified quality production since they do not help firms to act on their *self-interest in their competitors' and suppliers' competitiveness and well-being*. Where a firm's best interest is no longer in the competitive elimination or hierarchical incorporation of other firms, but rather in being part of a rich, diversified, polycentric economy, forms of governance are necessary that allow for cooperative upgrading of technological capabilities, and that protect the mutual confidence in each other's 'good will' that is central for holding down transaction costs and enabling firms to shift flexibly from competition to cooperation and back. Governance in diversified quality production, in other words, is the better the more it can help increase the number of potential strategic allies. This is particularly important with respect to small firms which, while they tend to find it comparatively difficult to attain a high degree of technical capability, appear particularly indispensable for productive flexibility.

For a pattern of industrial organisation in which large firms are to coexist and productively interact with a large number of technically and economically independent small firms, it is not enough for policy to remove barriers to market access. If this was so, small firms would be much more important in the British and American than in the German and Japanese economy. The fact that in reality it is the other way around has to do with a number of *status privileges* for small and medium-sized firms in Japan and Germany that are hard to reconcile with the principles of free competition and unlimited market access. Indeed, in an important sense it may be exactly the opposite that is necessary. Large German firms engaging in diversified quality production today benefit immensely from the presence in their immediate environment of a strong artisanal sector. Still, there can be no doubt that without the protective legislation that prevented and prevents large firms from entering artisanal markets, they would, like their British counterparts, long have wiped out their artisanal competition. Similarly, if small and medium-sized firms are to become full participants in diversified quality production, enabling institutional mechanisms are needed that provide for their upskilling through an efficient inter-firm transfer of technology and know-how. Such mechanisms may be implicitly or explicitly built into contracts between large and small firms; however, cooperative cultures and regulatory institutions *beyond contract*, like corporative associations of small firms under public facilitation (Chambers of Artisans, or of Commerce and Industry), or privileged market access for small firms that commit themselves to long-term investment in their technical capabilities, seem to be much more effective. Institutional mechanisms that overcome suspicion among competitors, insure firms against opportunistic defection of partners from implicit contractual understandings, and enable firms to invest not only in their own performance but also in that of other firms in their environment, thereby contributing to the collective good of a dense organisational ecology of potential strategic allies, are a major contributing condition of diversified quality production.

2.   THE REQUIREMENT OF REDUNDANT CAPACITIES

Diversified quality production requires not just high investment but also a type of investment that is likely to be undersupplied where economic rationality is not institutionally protected from becoming excessive, i.e., from turning into 'economism' or 'hyper-rationality'. Successful diversified quality producers seem to have an *investment function*, in the widest sense, that contains arguments that cannot easily be included in individual-rational calculations of 'return on investment'. This is because volatile markets and changing technological possibilities reward organisations with a capacity for *fast retooling* without loss of quality in response to unpredictable new demands. A central precondition for fast retooling is the *presence of generalised, unspecified, nondedicated, 'redundant' capabilities* that *can be put to many different, previously unknown uses* (Sorge, 1985). This applies regardless of the fact that diversified quality producers, as has been pointed out, often prefer to combine and recombine with others for specific projects, rather than produce everything inhouse. Indeed recognising fast-changing and highly specific market opportunities, identifying potential allies, and combining with others in interactive networks requires an *organisational intelligence* and *polyvalence* that is in itself a general, unspecific, 'reflexive' organisational resource (cf. Grabher, Chapter 3, below).

In firms that try to blend craft into mass production, a large share of their investment is only indirectly related to specific production purposes, and the causal chain between investment and return is longer and more difficult to trace. Investment in general capabilities for as yet undefined future purposes is not easy to justify for managements under competitive pressure, and is likely to be challenged by controllers and accountants as *excess investment*. It therefore runs a greater risk than more dedicated expenditures of coming under attack by higher levels of the managerial hierarchy if cost pressures rise. While large firms may sometimes be rich enough to resist economistic temptations, small firms find it particularly hard to build polyvalent, redundant capacities for production and, even more so, for design and marketing.

Redundant capacities are difficult to build in markets and through, or against, hierarchies, even if investing in them would open up superior market opportunities. To the extent that individually defined rational interests are not sufficiently instructive for investment in redundant capacities, following such interests may be the same as violating them. Examples of conditions of diversified quality production which involve the provision of *redundant capacities* and which therefore are more likely to be provided through *collective institutional obligations* than through individual-rational calculations, are:

(1) *Broad and high skills*. There is widespread agreement that a crucial resource for firms in technologically and economically volatile markets are *high skills* that are at the same time broad enough to allow for application to a wide range of rapidly changing, as yet unknown tasks. Skills are *broad* to the extent that they are *polyvalent* - i.e., not functionally dedicated to any specific purpose or activity. The most important polyvalent skill is the general capacity to acquire more skills (referred to in Germany as *Schlüsselqualifikationen*), with even less specific ('extrafunctional') attitudinal and behavioural skills like diligence, attention to detail, and willingness to accept responsibility in a group running a close second.

The problem with broad and high skills is that, whereas they seem to be best generated in a workplace environment, investment in them is not easy to justify for profit-maximising firms in competitive markets. The reason lies in a specific, intrinsic and inevitable 'fuzziness' of skill as a productive resource, which is especially in evidence for the kind of broad and flexible skills that are vital in periods of industrial restructuring and in production processes in which change is rapid and uncertainty high. Among other things, this fuzziness is apparent in the fact that both training costs and training returns are extremely *difficult to calculate*. Workplace training, especially if it is to be effective, inevitably shades into work and production, and its outcomes often and typically dissipate in the organisation and are impossible to trace precisely. As a result, where the costs and returns of training have to be explicitly calculated in order for the latter 'rationally' to justify the former, firms' human resource investment decisions are likely to be excessively, and irrationally, conservative. Indeed this may be the most important explanation for the fact that in institutionally 'thin' economies where training decisions are exclusively or primarily driven by market-rational economic motives, the supply of skills tends to be suboptimal for advanced industrial production purposes.

In diversified quality production, even more than in other production patterns, firms and managements find it hard to determine how much training is 'enough' training. What many of them know is that firms that create only those skills that they need, may well end up with less than they need. Cost- and profit-consciousness are more part of the problem than of the solution. When it comes to the creation of redundant capacities, it would appear that profit-maximising firms may have to be protected by cultural restraints or political regulation from their profit motive becoming overwhelming and depriving them of the capacity to generate profit from diversified quality production. While a culture of training conceived as education that values skills as such and apart from immediately discernable economic benefits would appear to be economically functional, institutions that impose on firms formal obligations to train can in part substitute for culture (for more on this, see below). The design and 'gardening' of such institutions constitutes an important function for public intervention in industrial skill formation as part of an affirmative supply-side policy.

(2) *A polyvalent organisational structure.* Much has been written in recent years on changes in the *division of labour* in response to new demands on organisations for higher product diversity and quality (for a synthesis see Gustavsen, 1986; as an example of an early, semi-popular treatment, Ouchi, 1981). If there is at all a common denominator in this literature - which runs the entire gamut from organisational and industrial sociology to the management press - then it is that for organisations to acquire a capacity for flexible retooling, *duplication and overlap* in organisational structures are, not a liability, but rather a crucial *productive asset.* This, at least, became the widely accepted explanation for increasingly frequent observations of empirical anomalies in the 'modern', functional differentiation paradigm of organisational structure, whose main practical application was Taylor's 'science' of industrial engineering.

The emerging orthodoxy in organisation analysis in the 1980s appears to be that organisational units - work roles, departments, organisations themselves - should *not be narrowly specialised* but should rather be *polyvalent*: capable, that is, of performing more than one operation, and of switching flexibly between different operations. The consequences of this for skill patterns have just been described. For organisational structures, polyvalence involves a *blurring of the functional boundaries between subunits*, with the effect that in the limiting case, subunits become able to substitute for each other by taking over each other's functions - although in most conditions functional overlap will be utilised primarily to facilitate non-routine cooperation. In both cases, the implication is that the organisation, in any given operational state, must have at its disposal potentially vast *additional* capacities that, while they may be employed for some future task, remain *unused in the background*. These capacities are, for this reason, redundant.

One development for which redundant capacities have been found to be of importance is the *erosion of the traditional distinction between direct and indirect labour* in the organisation of work on the shopfloor (Demes and Jürgens, 1989). In modern manufacturing plants, operation and maintenance of advanced equipment are often in the hands of the same, highly-skilled workers. This applies also to the handling of supplies and the feeding of machines on the one hand, and the programming and reprogramming of equipment and similar skilled functions on the other. Where new forms of group work are being used, it is often considered desirable that all team members should be able to perform all tasks assigned to the group, often including formerly managerial functions such as accounting or logistics. Simple 'direct' tasks are then carried out by workers who are far more skilled than would be necessary for such tasks to be satisfactorily executed.

Similarly, there is evidence that organisations engaging in product diversification for quality-competitive markets benefit from close, *synergetic cooperation between different functions*, or departments, especially sales, product design, production engineering, production management and personnel, as well as between various management functions and the shopfloor. *Functional interpenetration* complements and even supersedes functional differentiation where tasks cease to be highly routinised and need to be constantly redefined (Sorge, 1985), and where, as a consequence, the mutual obligations of organisational subunits have to be redefined from project to project. One central condition for this to be done efficiently is that each function understands the tasks and concerns of the others. Where this is the case, the organisation's internal structure can be flexibly rearranged to fit changing environments, *in the same way as consortia of independent, polyvalent firms can be formed and disbanded in response to fluctuating customer demands*.

A polyvalent organisation whose subunits are capable of flexibly crossing the boundaries of their assigned functions is expensive, and the return on investment in polyvalence is *difficult to establish*. This is why the de-Taylorisation of work organisation, profitable as it undoubtedly is for firms pressed for higher product quality and diversity, seems to proceed faster where there is additional and independent pressure for re-organisation of work, for other than economic reasons. In the same way in which institutionally-imposed obligations to train improve firms' skill base, legislation or industrial agreements mandating employers to enlarge and enrich job definitions may contribute to operational flexibility. In both cases, competitiveness increases as a result of *adjustments individual firms would or could not voluntarily have made*. Likewise, small firms that try to move from the position of dependent supplier to that of a diversified quality producer integrated into a network of joint ventures seem to need above all a set of polyvalent marketing, engineering and other capacities that they are often unable to acquire on their own; helping them become polyvalent would thus appear to be a major function of the institutions that support diversified quality production (cf. Grabher, Chapter 3, below).

(3) *Decentralised competence.* Another redundant capacity which is related to, but not identical with, organisational polyvalence is a *decentralised structure of decision-making.* In the same way in which investment in polyvalence runs up against market pressures for cost effectiveness, decentralisation of competence may interfere with the hierarchical principle of *unity of command* and may violate vested interests in the *integrity of managerial and proprietorial prerogative.*

Pressures for decentralisation in diversified quality production result from the need to adapt and readapt to an unpredictable market on a *routinised non-routine* basis. This requires lower hierarchical levels to have the *competence,* i.e. the authority as well as the cognitive capacity, to make fast and independent decisions. Recent writings on organisations suggest that high diversity and quality of output are difficult to attain in organisations that are run on a 'need to know' basis, since who 'needs' to know what is hard to establish under high task uncertainty. Similarly, the flexible regrouping of organisational resources in response to changing tasks appears to be facilitated by delegation of decision-making powers to the subunits by which tasks are carried out. This is the principle underlying the widespread interest in a reintegration of management and production, or *conception and execution.*

Building decentralised competence may appear as *excess investment* to the extent that it involves, as it does, the creation of high and broad, general skills. But in addition, managements asked to share information and authority with lower hierarchical levels may be afraid of *redundant competence* undermining swift acceptance of central decisions and delaying decisions generally. While the influence of quasi-political self-interests in managerial power and control can easily be exaggerated, as it appears to be in the Bravermanian 'labour process' theory, sharing competence with inferior ranks in a hierarchy is difficult. Especially where the costs and returns of decentralised competence are uncertain - as they typically are - there is likely to be a tendency for managements to be restrictive: to do less rather than more and keep to themselves as much as possible of what Karl Mannheim, has called *Herrschaftswissen.* Here, too, perverse incentives to cheat on one's own longer-term interests may easily become overwhelming. *Hierarchy failure* of this kind may be corrected, as Neuloh (1960) has found long ago when studying the impact of co-determination on West German coal and steel companies, by industrial relations procedures obligating managements to communicate their strategic thinking to workers representatives, *and thereby to themselves*, on a current basis and in advance of action being taken.

(4) *Social peace*. It has often been pointed out that a 'professional' work motivation and a quality consciousness among workers that do not need to be supported by specific monetary incentives or the possibility of negative sanctions are indispensable resources for what is here called diversified quality production. For this kind of *cooperative orientation* of workers to become available for a decentralised production process, a degree of mutual trust and loyalty between employer and worker seems to be required that can grow only on the basis of stable *social peace*. The latter, however, does not come to employers without costs, in both money and managerial prerogative. Moreover, even where the productive contribution of social peace is indisputable, its exact price is as difficult to calculate as are the returns on a firm's investment in social peace. This is why social peace, just as general skills, is fuzzy from a rational accounting perspective, and why rational managements tend to be tempted to invest less than they should invest in their own interest.

For a firm to have a sufficient supply of social peace when it needs it, it must be willing to incur potentially significant costs at times when it apparently does not need it. In this sense, investment in and cultivation of social peace creates a *redundant resource* which is exposed to the typical hazards of excessive rationality and short-term opportunism. In particular, if firms are free to select their own 'social peace equilibrium', they will often be tempted in competitive markets to exploit a temporary lapse in the market power of their workforce for short-term advantage - not least since firms know that their competitors are under the same temptation. As this, in turn, is unlikely to escape the attention of workers, the long-term result will fall short of the kind of 'high trust' (Fox, 1974) that appears to be such an important input in diversified quality production (Heckscher, 1988).

Being most of the time a redundant resource, social peace is more likely to be created as a matter of obligation than of interest, even though having it may very much be in a firm's interest. A case in point is co-determination in West Germany (Streeck, 1984a). Since co-determination increases labour costs and interferes substantially with managerial prerogative, its introduction was at every step resisted by employers. While there is little doubt that co-determination has contributed to the superior performance and competitiveness of German manufacturing in the (diversified quality) world market segments for which it produces, it is also obvious that German employers would not have adopted it voluntarily. Regardless of its beneficial economic effects, co-determination had to be *imposed* on employers *by law* so as to make it impossible for individual firms to 'cheat' on social peace in order to improve their competitive position. Moreover, the fact that co-determination is precisely *not* a voluntary arrangement, but is legally enshrined in what the Germans call a works *constitution*, ensures workers that it will not be unilaterally withdrawn in times of economic hardship, and thereby increases their trust in the fairness of the employer.

Social peace and the resulting mutual trust are often based in long-term employment relationships. Indeed, even in countries with flexible and easily accessible external labour markets, there are firms, often ambitious diversified quality producers, that commit themselves to stable employment for their workforces in exchange for their cooperation. Like 'unionism without unions', this may sometimes result in an effective pacification of industrial relations. However, as Dore (1988) in particular has pointed out, voluntary employment guarantees based on a firm's *enlightened self-interest* that are exceptions from a majoritarian pattern of flexible employment, tend on the whole to be less stable and less effective for worker commitment than, culturally or legally, *compulsory* arrangements that originate from institutionalised obligations and have to conform to a *general rule*. This is because in a voluntary arrangement, a possibility of defection remains always present in the background. Diversified quality production seems more likely to be enhanced if social peace is not generated inside individual firms with their own resources, but externally through a *collective institutional exoskeleton*. Again, privatised, contractual generation of redundant capacities appears inferior to publicly imposed and enforced behavioural obligations.[8]

3.   THE REQUIREMENT OF COLLECTIVE PRODUCTION INPUTS
Blending craft into mass production seems to increase the dependence of production systems on a range of factor inputs that have significant *collective-good properties*. To the extent that diversified quality production requires, as suggested by empirical research, a rich supply of *individually non-appropriable production factors*, industrial restructuring towards high levels of product diversity and quality is impeded by a neoclassical institutional environment that gives rational-possessive individualism precedence over collective, cooperative, and collusive action. A lack of appropriate non-market institutions on the supply-side may thus stand in the way of an optimal use of productive resources in response to rising demand for diversified quality production.

In standard economics, non-appropriable production inputs, to the extent that they are allowed for at all, are few in number and their supply is not in principle regarded as problematic. As a result they can essentially be neglected. The production inputs that count are assumed to be easy to appropriate and, therefore, to produce for and acquire through free markets. The few collective factor inputs that are needed can typically be generated through unilateral government provision - the only problem being to limit state supply to the very few resources that cannot be more efficiently provided by the market.

The analysis of diversified quality production casts doubt on these assumptions. First, it indicates an increase, with the evolution of production systems in response to more demanding markets, in the *relative dependence of private production and prosperity on collective factor inputs*. Secondly, it suggests that at least with some of them, unilateral state provision, like for example through the public educational system or through institutions of basic science and research, is less than ideal, and that *behavioural regulation of market participants* and the *creation of obligations for them may be superior modes of public intervention*. This is especially the case where *limited appropriability creates prisoners' dilemma-type problems* that require institutions capable of suspending competition and of protecting mutual expectations of *bona fide* cooperation. In particular, managing the complex mix of competition and cooperation between market participants needed for the provision of important collective factor inputs seems to demand a qualitative rearrangement and enrichment of organisational interfaces in the crucial zone between state and market that seems impossible to accommodate in liberal doctrine.

Possessive individualism of rational market participants creates shortages of major production inputs that are typically required for diversified quality production. Examples are:

(1) *Social peace.* Inside firms, as Fox (1974) among others has pointed out, trust cannot be hierarchically owned but has to be reciprocally and equitably shared. There also seem to be significant externalities between firms which make it more likely for any individual firm to achieve long-term peaceful labour relations if these exist also in other, neighbouring firms. As conflicts can spread from one firm to another, for example through competitive bargaining, firms cannot safely 'own' 'their' social peace, and their investment in it remains at risk. Moreover, firms that know that other firms may choose to cut costs by cutting their expenditure on peaceful labour relations, are involved in a prisoners' dilemma that may make them *adopt an irrational strategy for rational reasons*, chopping away at crucial conditions of their competitive capacity for diverse production at high quality levels. *Nota bene* the often

observed fact that strike rates are much lower in countries where social peace is jointly produced and, as it were, co-owned by employers negotiating at industrial or national level through strong employers, associations.

(2) *Competence*. In organisations engaged in diversified quality production, attempts to appropriate jobs through possessive job demarcations, for example by craft unions, depress productivity since they stand in the way of flexibility. Job ownership, defined as an individual or collective property right in a given organisational function ('competence'), is incompatible with group work or with functional interpenetration of tasks. Where organisational polyvalence and decentralised competence are desired, institutional arrangements have to be found that motivate investment in knowledge and authority with incentives other than the prospect of individual appropriation.

(3) *Ecological synergies*. By definition, a firm cannot own the community of firms of which it wants to be a member. The positive interest in the prosperity and technological capability of *non-appropriable competitors-cum-allies* cannot be acted upon through possessive individualism alone. Especially as industrial structures change to match the demands of diversified quality markets, the institutional embedding that they require seems to grow so complex that it can no longer, not even for pragmatic purposes, be treated as given or negligible. Instead, it turns into a collectively-owned production good whose provision is conditional on sophisticated institutional arrangements.

(4) *Knowledge*. Excessive consciousness of property rights on the part of firms may undermine and prevent potentially productive strategic alliances and cooperative relations. The blurring of inter-firm boundaries, both among competitors-cum-allies and between clients and their privileged single suppliers, inevitably entails a loss of control over intellectual capital. Similarly, technology transfer, conceived as investment in a congenial organisational ecology, directly involves a sharing of knowledge among potential competitors; it is therefore typically impeded by excessive property-consciousness. In terms of internal organisational structures, treating the knowledge vested in a firm as the hierarchical property of management prevents flexible decentralisation of competence as well as the creation of high and broad skills. Management concepts geared towards the achievement of high flexibility in response to fluctuating, diverse markets therefore emphasise the need for internal socialisation of knowledge, contesting members' and departments' claims to privileged or exclusive access to specific sets of information (see for example Peters and Waterman, 1982).

(5) *Skills*. Where workers may move from one firm to another, and where they do not feel socially obliged to stay with their employer all their working lives if he wants to keep them, firms will always have to be concerned that their investment in training may not be profitable for them since the worker may leave before the investment has amortised. Unlike in Japan, returns on training investment in Western firms *can never be safely internalised* as the skills imparted to a worker cannot be appropriated by the employer: if at all, they become the property of the worker. In effect, the fundamental uncertainty for employers recovering their training expenses in an open, contractual labour market turns skills, from the viewpoint of individual employers, into a *collective good*. By providing training, an employer adds to a common pool of skilled labour which is in principle accessible to all other employers in the industry or the locality, many of which are his competitors. While the individual employer may well recognise the importance of skilled workers for his enterprise, he also knows that if he incurs the expenses for their training, his competitors can easily 'poach' his trained workers by offering them a higher wage, with their overall labour costs still remaining below his. Since the rewards of his investment can so easily be 'socialised' whereas the costs remain his own, an employer in a competitive market will therefore be tempted not to train, or to train as little as possible, and buy in required skills from outside. As other employers are likely to perceive their situation in the same way as he, they will probably prefer not to train either. As a result, in the absence of regulation that suspends competition, there will tend to be an undersupply of skilled labour.

To increase their chances of internalising the returns on their training investment, firms may choose to limit their training efforts to workplace-specific as opposed to general skills. If what workers learn from their employer can be used only in their present place of work, 'poaching' becomes difficult, and the bargaining power of workers does not increase in proportion with their skills.[9] Such concerns over the appropriation of skills may, however, easily become excessive and counterproductive. An employer who is anxious not to give away too many transferable skills, may fail to create enough overall skills. More specifically, as has been pointed out, where skills are to be used to increase product variety and process flexibility, it is precisely general and not specific skills that are needed. In such a situation, possessive individualism, as with other collective goods, is bound to result in shortage of supply.[10]

4.   EQUITY AND EFFICIENCY

The dependence of diversified quality production on an *institutional exoskeleton* constitutes an open door for political regulation and intervention. In this sense, politics forms an integral part of the rich social dimension of diversified quality production.[11] Unlike in a neoclassical production regime where the only constructive contribution of politics to performance lies in the depoliticisation of the supply-side through the establishment and protection of the zero-institutions of market and hierarchy, diversified quality production presupposes an *affirmative polity* in which major conditions of competitive performance are, and have to be, collectively created and maintained. It is for this reason that diversified quality production may offer an opportunity for a supply-oriented 'new deal' between efficiency and equity.

Equity can make an important contribution to each of the three requirements for effective diversified quality supply, *congenial ecology*, *redundant capacity*, and *collective production inputs*. For all of them, *political redistribution* and *egalitarian supplementation* of initial factor endowments in favour of less well-equipped market participants may improve the performance even of those producers that were originally better endowed than their competitors.[12] For example, a more equal distribution of technological and design capabilities among firms than would emerge under a regime of competitive markets and unobstructed hierarchies *increases the number* of firms that may enter into joint ventures and strategic alliances with each other, and thereby extends each firm's range of strategic choices and alternatives. (This is the most compelling rationale for public or cooperative 'technology transfer' programmes being financed by taxing already successful firms.) The result is a collectively enlarged repertory of individual responses to volatile markets for customised goods, and a greater likelihood that opportunities for profit and employment offered by the evolution of product markets can be fully exploited.

Similarly, *redundant capacities* are by definition factor endowments whose acquisition and deployment is not (yet) indicated by immediate market pressures. This, as we have seen, is why rational actors normally have insufficient incentive to invest in them. In the absence of conclusive market signals as to where redundant capacities are best developed, their generation and allocation might just as well be determined by political criteria of distributive justice. The reason why political pressures for equality may be a superior way of motivating redundant capacity building lies, of course, in the intrinsic difficulties of rationally calculating expected returns on long-term investment in 'fuzzy' capabilities, and the resulting inconclusiveness of 'economising' as a principle of efficient allocation.[13] Similar problems also impede the production of *collective factor inputs*; here the contribution of politics to individual economic performance would appear to consist of either the authoritative provision of the required production factors, or of the creation of institutional settings that enable market-rational competitors to engage in cooperative non-zero-sum behaviour. In both cases, the indivisibility and non-exclusivity of publicly-provided factor inputs by definition entails an egalitarian redistribution effect. In addition, the furnishing of facilities to private gain-seekers by public authorities (of whatever kind) legitimates the latter charging a price for their services from the former through taxation. To the extent that public authorities are committed to equity as an objective in its own right, they may use the proceeds from the provision of collective factor inputs for further redistributive investment in an egalitarian organisational ecology or an evenly distributed pattern of redundant capacities.

It is important to emphasise that in the present context, equity and redistribution refer *not to entitlements for consumption*, but to *rights of access to and utilisation of productive capacities*. This is in line with, and follows from, the concern with the supply-side of the economy and the productive contribution of its 'social dimension'. In standard economics, of course, redistribution occurs primarily on the *demand side*, with - mostly negative - repercussions for the efficient allocation of production factors, especially in the labour market. Since suboptimal factor allocation results in an overall loss of welfare, political redistribution is essentially seen as a mistake - a 'justice illusion' comparable to the 'money illusion' in collective wage bargaining - which in the long run hurts everybody, including those that it presumably is to benefit. Keynesian theory, again in line with orthodoxy, also viewed egalitarianism in terms of access to consumption, and as a consequence located it on the demand side. At the same time, it differed sharply from standard economics in that it assigned to the downward redistribution of incomes a *productive function* as a mechanism of increasing and stabilising effective demand. In this sense, the Keynesian theory of full employment entailed the possibility of a *combination of egalitarianism and productivism*, which was why it was so universally embraced after the Second World War by trade unions and Social Democratic parties (Przeworski and Wallerstein, 1982; Vidich, 1982). The left-Keynesian principle that 'wealth is like manure: it is useful only if it is spread around' provided reformist labour movements in Western democracies with an intellectual and strategic compass to avoid the deadly trap of the 'equity-efficiency-dilemma' posed by classical, 'bourgeois' economics: the claim, that is, that equity detracts from efficiency; that there can be only as much equity as does not seriously obstruct efficiency, or else everybody including the presumptive beneficiaries loses; and that the extent to which political redistribution undermines efficiency is determined by the response of the supply-side, i.e. by markets and managements.

Today, the new pre-eminence of structural and supply-side problems has reopened the question of the relationship between equity and efficiency in reformist politics. The principal reason for the present weakness of trade unions and labour parties in the mixed economies of the West may well be their failure to find an *equivalent on the supply-side* for the Keynesian, demand sidebased reconciliation of equity and efficiency, or of *egalitarianism and productivism* - to establish, in other words, a similarly productive role for egalitarian redistribution in the creation of *effective supply* as was provided for in the Keynesian model of effective demand. The requirement for diversified quality production of a congenial ecology, redundant capacities and collective factor inputs, and the potential role of egalitarianism in their generation, may offer an opportunity for the Left to restore a productive function to redistributive politics and thereby recapture for itself an independent role in the management of advanced industrial economies.

A proper understanding of the dynamics of diversified quality production could lead the way towards *an alternative, non-classical supply-side response to the employment problem which would make productive use of institutional 'rigidities'*. An egalitarian supply-side approach to full employment would aim at enabling marginal workers to earn the high wages prescribed for them by rigid institutions, by helping them increase their productivity. Rather than matching the distribution of incomes to existing productivity differentials, which would result in a high level of inequality, a non-classical strategy would undertake to match the level and distributional profile of productivity to a politically determined, socially acceptable pattern of income differentials, with marginal productivity being adjusted to rigid wages instead of wages being adjusted to given productivities.

5. INSTITUTIONS AS CONSTRAINTS AND OPPORTUNITIES

To support a socially benevolent development of neo-industrial production, social and political institutions must simultaneously impose *constraints on* and provide *opportunities for* individual-rational actors. *Constraints* are necessary for the suspension of competition and the 'blocking of contracts' (Olson, 1983), so as to protect profit-seeking individuals from the temptations of hyper-rationality and prevent them from seeking short-term, quick-fix solutions - which might lead to a *Gresham's Law*-type erosion of ecological conditions, redundant capacities and collective production inputs and generating a downward spiral of collective irrationality driven by individually rational choices. Constraints are also required to impose limits on the hierarchical exercise of property rights so as to force managements, in Karl Deutsch's (1963) famous formula, to substitute intelligence for power. *Opportunities*, in turn, have to be offered for firms and managements in fact to be able to adjust to diversified quality demand; they include, among other things, facilitating support for the creation of the three functional conditions of congenial ecology, redundant capacity, and collective factor inputs. The difficulty is that the institutions that constitute an economy's social dimension must be so designed as to function as constraints and opportunities *simultaneously*; if they do just one and not the other, their capacity to drive diversified quality production is likely to be low.[14]

Institutionalised constraints and opportunities operate on a *chain of interdependent micro-level decisions* - on product ranges, production technology, work organisation, skill formation, wages, and wage differentials - that *link product markets to the social system of production*. In the world of standard economics, product markets are seen as *determining* - i.e., constituting overwhelming decisional rigidities for - the choice of product ranges. These, in turn, determine production technology, which then determines work organisation, which determines skill requirements, from which, finally, flow wage levels and wage structures. The result is believed to be a production pattern that makes for an optimally efficient allocation of resources, provided that management - which is supposed to 'read' and follow product markets better than any other actor - is powerful enough to organise the decision sequence hierarchically from the product market 'down' to the labour market and the social structures underlying it.

Standard economics recognise that in the real world, the decisional hierarchy that relates product markets to households as sellers of labour -

the *direction* of the *mutual conditioning* of decisions - is *contested* in that 'lower' levels will always try to impose their own preferences on 'higher' levels, through institutional rigidities that interfere with the free play of markets and hierarchies. In empirical studies of industrial production patterns, observations of a reversal of decisional hierarchies are frequent, with existing product ranges conditioning market choice, a given technology determining a firm's product range, an established work organisation affecting choice of technology, a present supply of skills shaping work organisation, and rigid wages and wage structures affecting the skill supply. Such *reverse conditioning* is regarded in standard economics as a source of inefficiency - the more so the closer one gets to the social system end of the chain. The study of diversified quality production, by contrast, suggests that successful product diversification at a high quality level is not likely to come about if the decision sequence runs unidirectionally from product markets downward, without encountering on the way *politically or culturally generated institutional rigidities, especially towards the social system end of the decision chain* - like egalitarian wage settlements, employment protection rules, co-determination rights, standardised training profiles, mandatory job enrichment requirements, and technology agreements. Institutions like these may, if they function well, *simultaneously force and facilitate* fortuitous micro-economic choices of wages, skill patterns, work organisation, technologies, product ranges and, especially, product markets that *fit a given, or politically preferred, social system of production* - rather than the latter having to be adjusted to the demands of presumably given markets and hierarchical decisions.

Not all institutional rigidities constraining markets and hierarchies are always and necessarily benevolent, and not all social systems of production can match the requirements of growing, turbulent and volatile markets for customised, non-price competitive goods. Not much is known on the generic properties of institutions that prevent firms from following their natural inclinations in times of economic stress - recovering profitability by cutting prices to become more competitive; cutting wages to cut prices; introducing labour-saving technology to cut employment; reorganising work so as to cut the autonomy of skilled workers, as well as their number; cutting training expenditures and procuring skills by 'poaching' from others through the external labour market; restoring managerial prerogative to cut decision-time and make possible all the other cuts - while at the same time enabling them to become profitable diversified quality producers.[15] Of particular interest in this respect is the contribution of trade unions, industrial relations, and collective bargaining. To the extent that it is necessary not just to offer firms and managements opportunities but also to impose constraints on them, some form of *institutionalised* conflict would appear to be an indispensable condition of supply-side restructuring towards advanced forms of demand. Understanding diversified quality production thus requires analysis of the complex, 'dialectical' *relationship between conflict and cooperation* among organised social classes in advanced political economies.

An example of how institutional constraints may create opportunities to move an economy into diversified quality production; and in particular of the potential role in this of institutionalised social conflict, is given by the *West German* case. On the face of it, West Germany appears to be an advanced case of what used to be called 'Euro-sclerosis'. Regulation of economic activities, by law and otherwise, is dense, and 'de-regulation', even after almost a decade of conservative government, is not much of an issue compared to the United States or Britain. Collective bargaining has remained centralised at the industrial level; the legal complexities of running enterprises under co-determination continue to puzzle managers and labour lawyers; involuntary dismissals of workers in large firms are still very difficult by comparison with other countries; the vocational training system with about 400 nationally standardised occupational profiles, clearly a bureaucratic nightmare by liberal standards, appears better established than ever; to enter a large number of markets, small and medium-sized firms have to get a license and join a quasi-public trade association with compulsory membership etc. But 'in spite of' these and other institutional 'rigidities', West Germany is, in terms of international competitiveness, one of the world's two or three most successful economies.

The explanation appears to be that, whereas West German institutional rigidities have largely foreclosed adjustment to price-competitive markets, they have at the same time and instead *forced, induced and enabled* managements to embark on more demanding high value-added, diversified quality production strategies (on the following cf. Streeck, 1987). While making structural adjustment and the maintenance of competitiveness more difficult, West German institutions have not made it impossible, and indeed they seem to have made *more difficult adjustment strategies more possible*. In particular, a range of *egalitarian-distributive constraints* seems to have operated as effective driving forces of a broad-based process of industrial upgrading. Among the most conspicuous examples of institutional rigidities in the West German political economy that oblige economically rational firms and managements to contribute to collective goods needed for diversified quality production, prevent them from consuming such goods without replacement, and make them invest in a congenial organisational ecology, in redundant capacities, and in non-appropriable production inputs, are:

1.   A system of 'rigid' *wage determination*, operated by strong and well-established trade unions and employers associations, that keeps wages higher, and variation between wages, lower, than in a free labour market. Unless employers are willing to move production elsewhere, this forces them to adapt their product range to non-price competitive markets capable of sustaining a high wage level. A high and even wage level also makes employers more willing to invest in training and retraining as a way of matching workers' productivity to the externally fixed, high costs of labour. Moreover, as wage differentials are relatively small, employers have an incentive not to concentrate their training investment on just a few élite workers. In addition, fixed high and even wages make it attractive for employers to organise work in a 'non-Bravermanian' way, so that the labour extracted and performed justifies its high price.[16]

2.   A policy of *employment protection* that compels employers to keep more employees on their payroll for a longer time than many might on their own be inclined to do. Large West German firms are subject to effective limitations on their ability to access the external labour market. High employment stability is imposed on firms through collective agreements, co-determination and legislation. To compensate for such external rigidities, firms have to increase their internal flexibility. By forcing firms to adjust through the internal labour market by redeployment, employment protection thus further encourages employer investment in training and retraining. Moreover, high employment security and the resulting identification of workers with the firm not only make for comparatively easy acceptance of technological change but also help create and support the cooperative attitudes among workers that are necessary for flexible organisational decentralisation of competence and responsibility. By foreclosing ready access to the external labour market, institutional rigidities thus *force as well as enable* firms to invest in long-term human resource development, thereby making it easier for them to compete in non-price-competitive markets.

3.   A set of binding rules that obliges employers to *consult* with their workforces and seek their consent above and beyond what many or most would on their own find expedient. Since West German co-determination is enshrined in law, firms' 'consensus spending' is relatively fixed and securely protected from cost-cutting temptations. One effect seems to be confidence among workers and their representatives in the persistence of

bilateralism regardless of whether the employer finds this to be in his immediate interest. Having an assured 'voice' in the management of the enterprise makes it possible for workforces to forego short-term advantages for larger, longer-term benefits, without having to fear that they may not be around to collect those when they materialise. This, in turn, enables managements to invest more in longer-term projects. Co-determination thus insulates both management and labour from opportunistic pressures. It is made meaningful by, and in turn supports, long-term stable employment and internal labour markets, not least by providing for an equitable institutional mechanism to administer redeployment. Co-determination also seems to affect product and market choices in that firms, if they cannot avoid paying for consensus, are likely to find it expedient to shift towards quality-competitive production for which social consensus at the workplace constitutes an important asset instead of an unnecessary cost burden.

4. A *training regime* that is capable of obliging employers to train more workers and afford them broader skills than required by immediate product or labour market pressures. The result is an excess pool of 'flexible', polyvalent workers and skills that constitutes an important advantage in periods of fast technological change. A wide distribution of high and broad excess skills also underwrites high wages and strong employment protection, as well as a relatively even wage structure. The West German training system with its nationally standardised and rigorously enforced curricula is governed in a 'corporatist' fashion, i.e. by employers, associations and trade unions together under a state umbrella. Firms' training activities are closely supervised by quasi-public Chambers with compulsory membership and far-reaching powers; in effect, these serve as conduits for pressures from the national level to increase and upgrade training activities. Training is also supported by co-determination drawing workplace trade unions into manpower management, works councillors regarding it as one of their main tasks to make firms train above and beyond short-term needs (to train, that is, as a matter of 'social obligation'). Being forced to invest in expensive skills, firms find themselves further induced to move into non-price competitive markets for high value-added products, use new technology in a way that makes the most of its potential for flexible retooling, adopt an organisation of work that allows workers to use discretion, and comply with a regime of employment protection that also protects their human resource investment.

5. A system of *rules regarding the organisation of work* , created by trade union or government intervention and obliging employers to design

jobs more broadly than many of them would feel necessary. Collective agreements, union-inspired government programmes ('Humanisation of Working Life') and co-determination in West Germany have in a number of ways restricted managerial prerogatives in the design of jobs and the organisation of the labour process. While the results are often less than satisfactory from the point of view of workers' representatives, together they amount to further pressure for the 'de-Taylorisation' of work through longer work cycles and job enrichment. Managements that have to live with unions pursuing higher 'quality of working life' as an independent objective may find themselves constrained to go for markets - of customised quality products - in which decentralised organisational competence is an asset. This holds in particular where workers have rights to co-determination and where therefore a stable working consensus with the workforce is a vital resource for management. Concessions on work organisation are made easier by the fact that de-Taylorisation not only facilitates flexible adjustment to changing technological and market conditions, but also enables employers actually to utilise the high and broad skills they are obliged to generate under the training system. In combination with high and even wages, high employment security, co-determination and training, the imposition on employers of non-Taylorist work rules thus impedes the use of new technology for 'rationalisation' purposes and encourages a 'modernisation' strategy of industrial adjustment that is highly conducive to diversified quality production.

West German institutional constraints and opportunities seem to form an interactive pattern of mutual reinforcement and causation. Based on studies of industrial adjustment in the automobile industry in the 1970s and 1980s, it has been suggested that this configuration be termed a 'virtuous circle of upmarket industrial restructuring' (Streeck, 1987). While its dynamics and origins still await systematic exploration, two claims can plausibly be made: (1) given the institutional constraints faced by West German firms in their social system of production, managements, short of migrating to Southern Europe or the Pacific Basin, had not much of an alternative to seeking out non-price-competitive market segments; and (2) given the available institutional opportunities, they may have been better able than their foreign competition to do so. Both observations together would explain why low volumeandhigh margin production has been found to be a characteristic not just of individual German firms but of entire industries or even the economy as a whole (Cox and Kriegbaum, 1980).

West Germany, or any country for that matter, cannot possibly be a 'model' on which other political economies could be built or rebuilt. But this does not mean that there are no lessons in the German case that could fruitfully be applied, *with different means adjusted to different circumstances*. The need to drive managements to greater efforts beyond what they would do if guided by 'the' product market alone, the indispensability of social obligations complementing economic interests as guides of economic action, the synergetic contribution of generalisation of advanced production patterns, and the central contribution of a particular kind of redistributive politics are examples of this. The question is not whether specific 'German' institutions are so specifically 'German' that they cannot therefore be transplanted to other 'cultures'. It is rather whether certain general principles that can be derived from the analysis of the institutional requirements of diversified quality production, and of the German 'virtuous circle' in particular, can be usefully applied to the design of post-Keynesian institutional infrastructure on the supply-side that can sustain socially benevolent industrial change.

6. CONCLUDING REMARKS

Further reflection on diversified quality production as an advanced production pattern would have to elaborate on subjects like the relative importance of *culture and politics* as sources of institutional differences between nations and regions, and the *possibilities and limits of institutional design* drawing on 'models' from other countries. Institutional analysis is, almost of necessity, comparative. Its practical application within a supply-oriented employment strategy therefore inevitably raises questions on the *transportability* of institutions and experiences from one 'cultural' context to another. The standard objection here is that what works in one 'culture' will not necessarily work in another, and that 'cultures' cannot be strategically changed. However, the difficulty of determining whether institutions are *culturally inert* or *politically malleable* is illustrated by the example of the Japanese industrial relations system with its 'three sacred treasures', the enterprise union, life-time employment, and seniority pay. While some accounts emphasise the deep roots of this pattern in Japanese culture, e.g. the structure of the family and the role of informal groups in Japanese society (Abegglen, 1958), others maintain that it was deliberately designed and forcibly imposed upon workers by employers in the 1950s after the 'Red Purge' of the Japanese labour movement (Koshiro, 1979). Similarly,

German co-determination has been described both as an innovative political construct and as an emanation of a presumed German 'culture' of consensus and incorporation.

Another of the many possible questions concerns the potential *deficiencies* and practical difficulties of an egalitarian supply-side industrial policy. For example, a clear disadvantage of an institutional design approach to supply-side economic policy, compared to neo-classical institutional minimalism, is that qualitative institutional intervention and innovation are simply *much more difficult* than de-regulation. Moreover, an economic strategy of institutional design, or *institutional gardening*, needs time for experimentation, elimination of unanticipated side-effects, and maturation. Fast results cannot, but may have to be promised. Given the short duration of political cycles, there should in fact be a strong temptation for policy-makers to have recourse to short-term solutions even if these, over time, erode crucial institutional conditions of long-term prosperity and stability.

In addition, a public policy that blocks contracts, apart from the risk of being held responsible for the less-than-full employment it tries to remedy, runs up against a voluntarist-libertarian mass consciousness, not least among the constituencies of left parties, for which the 'free choice' promised by neo-liberals has its strong attractions. Ideological resources to defend a non-liberal model of political economy are scarce at a time of proto-capitalist perestroika in what once used to be the heartland of socialism. The idea of prosperity coming in joint supply, of collective investment taking precedence over private investment, of institutional regulation superseding individual liberty, and of opportunities being accompanied by constraints, may sound too collectivistic for today's electorates - just as trying to protect collective investment from turning into collective consumption may be too *productivistic* to be acceptable.

It is also possible that a diversified quality supply-side strategy makes excessive and unrealistic demands on the *homogeneity* and *sovereignty* of socio-political systems. Blocking low-productivity and low-pay employment contracts may make sense only in a relatively homogeneous society without cultural divisions and mass immigration. Where cultural standards and expectations differ too much, preventing low-paying employment may result in societal dualism and a 'second economy' rather than equality. Moreover, if it is true, as Dore (1988) argues, that new technology gives greater weight to differences in natural ability as a basis for social stratification, the hope that marginal workers can be included into the core labour force through training and retraining may be in vain. Nor is it clear to what extent the generalisation of diversified quality production as a production pattern requires a viable, i.e. *sovereign*, national state - for redistribution between regional economies as well as to protect the social dimension of the supply-side from erosion in and by border-crossing markets for capital, labour and final products. The completion of the Single European Market in the coming years will offer an exciting opportunity to study these and other questions.[17]

NOTES

1 The paper tries to avoid a long and very likely bottomless definitional exercise as to what is and is not an 'institution'. In a perfectly acceptable sense, a market is an institution no less than, say, a Chamber of Commerce, and managerial chain of command is an institution in the same way as a trade union. For the purposes of this essay, however, we find it convenient to distinguish between what we call 'neoclassical', 'minimal', 'zero' or 'economic' institutions on the one hand and 'historical', 'political', 'cultural' or 'social' institutions on the other - sometimes, for simplification, reserving the concept of 'institution' exclusively for the latter. The generic difference between the two is that the first kind of institutions accommodate and facilitate rational-utilitarian *voluntarism*, whereas the second generate, impose and enforce social *obligations* that rational individuals would not voluntarily and contractually take upon themselves. In a strong Durkheimian sense, it is only institutions of the latter kind that make a society. Like Durkheim, we are in this essay less interested in categoric distinctions than in the notion that the relative significance of the two kinds of institutions may vary between societies, with institutionally 'thicker' societies subjecting the actions of rational individuals to a richer set of regulations and constraints.

2 In this respect the analysis of diversified quality production was informed by the study of *industrial interest politics*. Comparative research on the impact of trade unions and industrial relations on economic adjustment and competitive performace had revealed long and complex chains of causation and interdependence. Especially in a comparative perspective, the view that weak and accomodative trade unions, standing prescriptions, are necessarily conducive to economic performance had been found to be simplistic and misleading (e.g. Cameron, 1984; Castles, 1987; Crouch, 1985; Hotz, 1982; Streeck, 1987). While some economies seemed to thrive on institutional minimalism in general and the absence of organised industrial interests in particular, in others - and clearly not the least successful ones - strong and assertive trade unions performed a variety of, manifest and latent, positive functions. Indeed such functions were not limited to aggregate demand stabilisation through aggressive redistribution, rigid wage fixing or cooperative wage restraint in a Keynesian, demand-side oriented sense. Among the most important discoveries in the neo-corporatist debate of the 1970s and 1980s, sometimes introduced under misleading labels like 'microcorporatism' (Streeck, 1984 b), was the *supply-side dimension of neo-corporatist institutions*: their actual and potential role in the formation and functioning of competitive *production systems*. Such insights helped prepare the ground for a reorientation of the corporatist paradigm from the Keynesian concerns of the 1970s to the structural 'qualitative' concerns of the 1980s.

3 In the work of Arndt Sorge in particular (Sorge, 1985), the notion of *different and alternative production patterns* was derived from comparative studies of work organisation and, later, responses to technical change. Sorge's work, often co-authored with Marc Maurice and Malcom Warner, undertook to link distinctive national patterns of work organisation to different selections of product ranges and product markets, and to explain the resulting complex configurations with reference to different institutional endowments in the society-at-large. In this way, a society's specific 'culture', as crystallised in its institutional macro-structure, came to be conceived as a production factor in the widest sense, shaping both the process and the outcome of economic action. The objective was to account for the persistence of differences in work organisation and technology use in the face of 'identical' technology, and in patterns of industrial output in spite of 'identical' market pressures, by explaining them as *consequences of different institutional conditions generating alternative responses to similar technological and economic stimuli*.

4 It is at this point that the present paper's critique of rational choice as a sufficient basis for advanced industrial production patterns is particulaly pertinent. The paper's Durkheimian

concern with the regulatory, interventionist, and non-voluntary elements of social institutions corresponds to a strong emphasis on prisoners' dilemma-type co-ordination problems, and on the insuffiency and indeterminacy of rational individual calculations *vis-à-vis* complex, long-term decisions on the development of advanced productive capacities. Compared to this, much of the 'flexible specialisation' literature would appear to be written in a voluntaristic-liberal perspective, and would in that sense be much closer to standard economics.

5 Which means that the concept, while not accepting all implications of 'flexible specialisation', does cover and include the phenomena studied under this label. It therefore can fruitfully draw on the rich research tradition of the flexible specialisation school.

6 In other words, diversified quality production requires a specific pattern of *industrial organisation*; exhibits a particular *investment function*; and is characterised by a distinctive *production function*.

7 Indeed, the analysis of the 'social dimension' of diversified quality production could entirely be phrased in terms of the preconditions of an advanced form of productive flexibility, in particular in terms of the difference between *quantitative* (neoclassical) and *qualitative* flexibility, with the associated trade-off between different, corresponding forms of rigidity. More on this below, with reference to the constraints and opportunities for diversified quality production originating from the 'social system of production'.

8 The strong claim of this paper, and the theoretical core of its institutionalist argument, is that, to the extent that economic behaviour is - or better be - also social behaviour, rational individual calculations of costs and benefits have inherent *gaps* that make them less than instructive and that need to be filled, for action to be possible at all, by socially institutionalised *norms*. While in certain relatively simple or historically established production patterns this fact may for practical purposes be negligible - which is why it is neglected in standard economics - it is observable, for example, in the persistent differences in structure and practice between presumably equally rational organisations embedded in different institutional contexts. It is also visible in the considerable space economic exigencies regularly leave for cultural diffusion of organisational patterns and practices. *Instrumental rationality*, in other words, *is not enough to 'close' organisational structures*. This seems to hold in particular where 'the rational thing to do' would be the creation of an affluent supply of non-dedicated capacities and possibilities. While some organisations could be expected to understand the logic of redundant capacity building on their own, many others may not and may require institutional pressures to behave in line with their rational interests. Moreover, since each organisation's investment in a rich supply of redundant capacities is part of the other organisations' ecology of possibilities, the success of individual efforts at redundant capacity building depends on effective institutions providing for equifinal behaviour beyond the limits of individual rationality.

9 This distinction, of course, is at the heart of conventional 'human capital' theory.

10 This applies in particular in conditions when the kind of general skills that are needed cannot easily be generated outside the workplace in public schools (Streeck, 1989).

11 Strictly speaking, this is true only for 'modern' societies whose institutional substructure is not, or no longer, traditionally given, and therefore needs to be reconstructed through collective action and organisation. By and large, Japan represents the case of a society whose 'thick' institutions are of a traditonal kind. Sweden, by contrast, can be taken as an example of successful political reconstruction of social obligations in a modern society.

12 Productivist justifications of egalitarianism have a long history in European socialism, especially in Sweden. See Higgins (1985) on Ernst Wigforss.

13 Equity, in other words, performs a positive economic function in so far as it stands in the way of *excessive rationalisation* of social and organisational structures. Diversified quality production, we have argued, requires that production systems be not fully rationalised, in the sense of completely dedicated to specific instrumental purposes. To be able to withstand and contain economic rationalisation pressures, a society needs to institutionalise strong competing values that can successfully defy subsumption under the dictates of the 'economic principle'.

14 Institutions that are no more than *constraints* on firms, managements and workers will choke off economic growth and initiative; they are particularly likely to become strongholds of trade unions turned into rent-seeking 'distributional coalitions'. Institutions that merely offer *opportunities* will favour exploitation of the 'public' by the 'private' sector, for example by firms shopping around for subsidies.

15 The prime example of politically designed 'thick' institutions with negative - and, in fact, disastrous - economic consequences is, of course, the 'actually existing socialism' of the time until 1989. For traditional societies, compare India with Japan.

16 Thus, unlike in Keynesianism, the positive effect of high wages on diversified quality production takes place primarily through the supply-side - where they operate as a 'productivity whip' and, to the extent that they are sufficiency rigid, as a barrier to low-wage adjustment strategies. To what extent diversified quality production also requires the contribution of a high and stable wage to *effective demand* is more difficult to determine, given that markets for diversified quality production are typically worldwide and the overlap between producers and consumers is usually much smaller than in 'Fordist' mass production. In fact, large-scale adoption of diversified quality production in recent decades may well be interpreted, as it is in Piore and Sabel (1984), as a micro-level response to long-term declining institutional capacities - including those of trade unions - to make domestic demand stable and predictable. Product diversification and movement into quality markets are in this perspective insurance against permanently high local demand uncertainty and volatility - the assumption being that unsaturated demand for diversified quality production in non-local markets is, for whatever reason, large enough to be taken for granted. For a perceptive discussion of this topic that arrives at different conclusions, cf. Mahon (1987).

17 For initial reflections on the potential impact of the Single European Market on the German pattern of industrial relations, cf. Streeck (1990).

REFERENCES

Abegglen, J. C., *The Japanese Factory: Aspects of its Social Organisation*, Glencoe, Ill., The Free Press, 1958.

Boyer, R., 'The Eighties: The Search for Alternatives to Fordism - A Very Tentative Assessment', (*mimeo.*), 1987.

Brittan, S., 'Inflation and Democracy', in F. Hirsch and J. H. Goldthorpe (eds.), *The Political Economy of Inflation*, Cambridge, Mass., Harvard University Press, 1978, pp. 161-85.

Cameron, D. R., 'Social Democracy, Corporatism, Labour Quiescence and the Representation of Economic Interest in Advanced Capitalist Society', in J. H. Goldthorpe (ed.), *Order and Conflict in Contemporary Capitalism*, Oxford, Clarendon Press, 1984, pp. 143-78.

Castles, F. G., 'Neo-Corporatism and the 'Happiness Index', or What Trade Unions Get for Their Cooperation', *European Journal of Political Research 15*, 1987, pp. 381-93.

Child, J., 'Managerial Strategies, New Technology and the Labour Process', in R. E. Pahl (ed.), *On Work: Historical, Comparative and Theoretical Approaches*, Oxford, Basil Blackwell, 1988, pp. 229-57

Cox, J. and Kriegbaum, H., *Growth, Innovation and Employment: An Anglo-German Comparison*, London, Anglo-German Foundation for the Study of Industrial Society, 1980.

Crouch, C., 'Conditions for Trade Union Wage Restraint', in L. N. Lindberg and Ch. S. Maier (eds.), *The Politics of Inflation and Economic Stagnation*, Washington D.C., The Brookings Institution, 1985.

Demes, H. and Jürgens, U., 'Skill Formation in the Automobile Industry: A Comparison between West German, British, American and Japanese Enterprises', in T. Blumenthal (ed.), *Employer and Employee in Japan and Europe*, Beer Sheva, The Humphrey Institute for Social Ecology, 1989.

Deutsch, K., *The Nerves of Government: Models of Political Communication and Control*, New York, The Free Press, 1963.

Dore, R., 'Rigidities in the Labour Market: The Andrew Shonfield Lectures (II)', *Government and Opposition 23*, 1988, pp. 393-412.

Fox, A., *Beyond Contract: Work, Power and Trust Relations*, London, Faber and Faber, 1974.

Gustavsen, B., 'Evolving Patterns of Enterprise Organisation: The Move Towards Greater Flexibility', *International Labour Review 125*, 1986, pp. 367-82.

Heckscher, Ch. C., *The New Unionism: Employee Involvement in the Changing Corporation*, New York, N. Y., Basic Books, 1988.

Herrigel, G., 'Industrial Order in the Machine Tool Industry: A Comparison of the United States and Germany', in W. Streeck and J. R. Hollingsworth (eds.), *Comparing Capitalist Economies: Variations in the Governance of Sectors*, forthcoming.

Higgins, W., 'Ernst Wigforss: The Renewal of Social Democratic Theory and Practice', *Political Power and Social Theory 5*, 1985.

Hirschhorn, L., *Beyond Mechanisation: Work and Technology in a Post-Industrial Age*, Cambridge, Mass., The MIT Press, Part I, 'Machine Design', 1984, pp. 7-58.

Hotz, B., 'Productivity Differences and Industrial Relations Structures: Engineering Companies in the United Kingdom and the Federal Republic of Germany', *Labour and Society 7*, 1982, pp. 333-54.

Jaikumar, R., 'Postindustrial Manufacturing', *Harvard Business Review*, November-December 1986, pp. 69-76.

Kern, H. and Schumann, M., *Das Ende der Arbeitsteilung? Rationalisierung in der industriellen Produktion*, München, C. H. Beck, 1984.

Koshiro, 'Japan's Labor Unions: The Meeting of White and Blue Collar', in Japan Culture Institute, *Politics and Economics in Contemporary Japan*, Tokyo, Japan Culture Institute, 1979.

Lipietz, A., 'The Structuration of Space: The Problem of Land and Spatial Policy', in J. Carney, R. Hudson and J. Lewis (eds.), *Regions in Crisis*, London, Croom Helm, 1980.

Mahon, R., 'From Fordism to ?: New Technology, Labour Markets and Unions', *Economic and Industrial Democracy 8*, 1987, pp. 5-60.

Maier, H. E., 'Das Modell Baden-Württemberg. Ueber institutionelle Voraussetzungen differenzierter Qualitätsproduktion', *Discussion Paper FS I*, Wissenschaftszentrum Berlin für Sozialforschung, 1987.

Neuloh, O., *Der neue Betriebsstil*, Tübingen, J. C. B. Mohr, 1960.

Olson, M., 'Beyond Keynesianism and Monetarism', *Discussion Paper IIM/LMP 83-24*, Wissenschaftszentrum Berlin für Sozialforschung, 1983.

Ouchi, W. G., *Theory Z: How American Business can Meet the Japanese Challenge*, Reading, Mass., Addison-Wesley, 1981.

Peters, T. J. and Waterman, R. H., *In Search of Excellence: Lessons from America's Best-Run Companies*, New York, Harper and Row, 1982.

Piore, M. J. and Sabel, C. F., *The Second Industrial Divide: Possibilities for Prosperity*, New York, Basic Books, 1984.

Przeworski, A. and Wallerstein, M., 'Democratic Capitalism at the Crossroads', *Democracy*, July 1982, pp. 52-68

Sabel, C. F., 'Flexible Specialisation and the Re-emergence of Regional Economies', in P. Hirst and J. Zeitlin (eds.), *Reversing Industrial Decline? Industrial Structure and Policy in Britain and Her Competitors*, New York, St. Martin's Press, 1989, pp. 17-70.

Sabel, Ch. F., Herrigel, G. B., Deeg, R. and Kazis, R., 'Regional Prosperities Compared: Massachusetts and Baden-Württemberg in the 1980s', *Discussion Paper FS I*, Wissenschaftszentrum Berlin für Sozialforschung, 1987.

Sabel, Ch. and Kern, H., 'Trade Unions and Decentralised Production: A Sketch of Strategic Problems', (*mimeo.*), 1990.

Skidelsky, R., 'The Decline of Keynesian Politics' in C. Crouch (ed.), *State and Economy in Contemporary Capitalism*, London, Croom Helm, 1979, pp. 55-87.

Sorge, A., *Informationstechnik und Arbeit im sozialen Prozess: Arbeitsorganisation, Qualifikation und Produktivkraftentwicklung*, Frankfurt am Main, Campus, 1985.

Sorge, A. and Warner, M., *Comparative Factory Organisation: An Anglo-German Comparison of Manufacturing, Management and Manpower*, Aldershot, Gower, 1986.

Sorge, A. and Streeck, W., 'Industrial Relations and Technical Change: The Case for an Extended Perspective', in R. Hyman and W. Streeck (eds.), *New Technology and Industrial Relations*, Oxford, Basil Blackwell, 1988.

Streeck, W., (1984a), 'Co-Determination: The Fourth Decade', in B. Wilpert and A. Sorge (eds.), *International Perspectives on Organisational Democracy*, International Yearbook of Organisational Democracy, Vol. II, London, John Wiley & Sons, 1984, pp. 391-422.

Streeck, W., (1984b), 'Neo-Corporatist Industrial Relations and the Economic Crisis in West Germany', in John Goldthorpe (ed.), *Order and Conflict in Contemporary Capitalism: Studies in the Political Economy of West European Nations*, Oxford, Clarendon Press, 1984, pp. 291-314.

Streeck, W., 'Industrial Relations and Industrial Change: The Restructuring of the World Automobile Industry in the 1970s', *Economic and Industrial Democracy 8*, 1987, pp. 437-62.

Streeck, W., 'Skills and the Limits of Neo-Liberalism: The Enterprise of the Future as a Place of Learning', *Work, Employment and Society 3*, 1989, pp. 90-104.

Streeck, W., 'From National Corporatism to Transnational Pluralism: European Interest Politics and the Single Market', (*mimeo.*), 1990.

Vidich, A. J., 'The Moral, Economic and Political Status of Labour in American Society', *Social Research 49*, 1982, pp. 753-90.

Willman, P., *New Technology and Industrial Relations: A Review of the Literature*, Department of Employment Research Papers, London, HMSO, 1986.

3.   Against De-Industrialisation: A Strategy for Old Industrial Areas

Gernot Grabher

1.   THE WEALTH OF NATIONS - THE POVERTY OF REGIONS: DE-INDUSTRIALISATION AS A REGIONAL PHENOMENON

Shifts in the spatial organisation of the economy have been observed in several advanced industrialised countries. The discussion of such shifts started in the United States when the decline of the 'rust belt' was contrasted with the boom of the 'sun belt'. Analogous to the sun belt - rust belt polarity in the United States, regional variations in economic prosperity have been described in France with the model called 'La France a deux vitesses', and in both Britain and West Germany the discussion of the north-south divide indicates a growing awareness of shifts in the regional economic structure. (Only the German football association (Deutscher Fußballbund) seems to have perceived such a shift in time as it divided the second division into north and south: the polarity between industrialised agglomerations and rural areas - between centre and periphery - was superimposed by growing inequalities between north and south during the 1970s.)

However preliminary and simplified the models of recent changes in regional variations of prosperity may be, they have one particular point in common: the dramatic decline of the so-called old industrial areas. Decay of the economic base, high unemployment and migration are the most obvious signs of crisis in these areas, areas that had been considered as centres of economic dynamics up to the early 1970s. The decline of old industrial areas set all the analysts right who - pointing to the relative high growth rates of the advanced industrialised countries - had considered de-industrialisation as an economic myth. At the regional level de-industrialisation is - in its double literal sense - a hard fact.

The causes for the crisis of old industrial areas are discussed in the first part of this contribution in light of the specific problems confronting the Ruhr area (section 2). The explanation focuses not only on the dominance of a few traditional industries but also on the specific inter-industry and inter-firm linkages in old industrial areas: a production pattern of rigid and hierarchical relations between large dominant firms and small suppliers within the coal, iron, and steel complex. An analysis of the reorganisation of the coal, iron, and steel complex in the Ruhr area (section 3) will result in an outline of a highly adaptable production pattern embedded in regional networks (section 4). Arguments against the spreading cultural fatalism in regional policies conclude the paper (section 5): regional policy is not at the mercy of history and a specific regional culture predestinated to certain regional networks.

2. CRISIS OF OLD INDUSTRIAL AREAS OR CRISIS OF OLD INDUSTRIES?

The crisis of old industrial areas became visible through spectacular plant closures and mass dismissals at the end of the 1970s; the decline, however, had already begun in the 1960s. First, the time of post-war reconstruction with its enormous demand for basic materials and capital goods came to an end. Second, the income elasticity of demand for iron and steel - the main products of old industrial areas - dropped from 1.8 in 1950 to 0.9 in 1964 (cf. Schlieper, 1986, p. 178). In other words, in the mid-1960s just half the amount of iron and steel was required to produce an additional unit of gross domestic product as one and a half decades earlier. Third, the old industrial areas had to face increasing competition, especially from newly-industrialising countries enjoying comparative advantages in producing homogeneous mass goods. Together these developments resulted in severe production cutbacks and mass dismissals in old industrial areas. In concrete terms: between 1977 and 1986 in the Ruhr area the iron and steel industry reduced the number of working places by 23.2 per cent: about 53 000 workers lost their employment. In September 1988 the unemployment rate amounted to 15.1 per cent compared to 8.1 per cent in West Germany and 9.0 per cent in North Rhine-Westphalia.

The decline of old industrial areas however, cannot simply be traced back to the dominance of a few industries that faced dramatic decreases in demand. A purely structural approach is inadequate for at least two reasons. First, on a theoretical level a structural approach does not answer the question of why regional redeployment of the productive resources that were set free by the fall in demand did not occur. Second, as empirical analysis has pointed out, it is not just a few traditional industries that are affected by crisis. Even high-tech industries and the service sector are growing at below-average rates in such areas (cf. Junkernheinrich, 1989, p. 31). While the production of so-called high-technology products (according to the OECD categorisation) in West Germany grew by 39 per cent between 1977 and 1983, the Ruhr area attained production growth of just 25 per cent. The machine-building and steel construction industry of the Ruhr area fell far behind the development of these industries at the national level (see Figure 3.1).

An essential reason for the comparatively poor performance of these industries in the Ruhr area is the dominant production pattern there which consists of specific linkages between the dominant large firms and the regional small firm sector. The dominant large firms were established in locations which allowed a profitable exploitation of natural resources - coal and iron ore - but which frequently lacked even the rudiments of a pre-industrial handicraft infrastructure (cf. Herrigel, 1989). The missing infrastructure forced industrial enterprises to provide to a large extent their own supplies and services: cathedrals in the desert (cf. Lipietz 1980, p. 86) evolved. The regionally dominant large firms were - except for raw materials - largely self-sufficient with respect to both the building and maintenance of their production facilities and the marketing and distribution of their products.[1]

Figure 3.1 Development of the Engineering and Steel Construction Industries 1970-1985 (Index of Production Output)

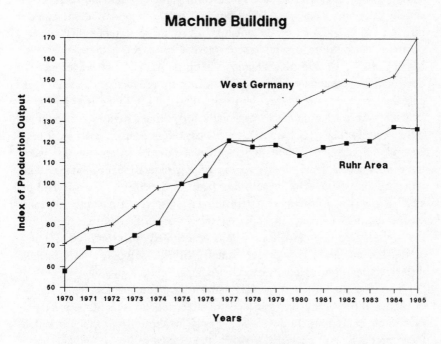

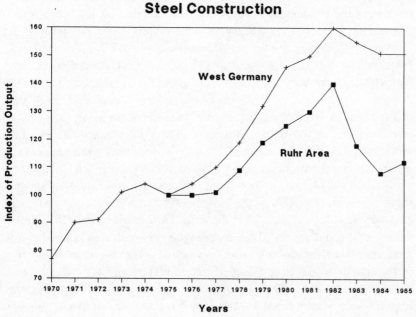

There was little change in the parallel existence of self-sufficient, vertically-integrated large firms during subsequent phases of development - for two reasons. First, the regionally dominant large firms sought to secure their monopsony position on the regional labour market through wage and real estate policies which made it more difficult for potential competitors on the labour market to establish themselves (cf. Massey 1984, p. 198; Kunzmann, 1986, p. 411). High wages in the dominant large companies were in part offset by productivity increases, in part they were passed on through prices. Particularly in the iron and steel industry where state demand - especially for military hardware - could be influenced by the 'steel barons', it was possible to pass on costs to prices. Second, on account of their high degree of internalisation, the dominant large companies deprived the region of agglomeration economies, thus reducing the potential for establishing firms in the region. The survival of small firms in the process of establishing themselves, frequently depends on the regional market. The missing supply opportunities resulting from the high degree of internalisation thus constituted an impediment for the establishment and growth of small firms, stopping the further differentiation of a regional sectoral structure.

The long shadows cast by the dominant large companies - particularly in periods of strong growth and relative labour scarcity - provided favourable conditions for development only for those firms which oriented their products and services towards the needs of the dominant large companies.[2] The sometimes feudal dependency relationships between the dominant large companies and the regional supplier industries resulted in serious shortcomings in the so-called decision-making entrepreneurial functions on the part of the suppliers. Production according to the blueprints of large enterprises made it possible for the suppliers largely to dispense with their own R & D. Good personal connections with the management of large client firms took the place of the small firm's own marketing and channels of distribution. These intense and hierarchical relationships within the regional coal, iron and steel complex proved economically rational under conditions of stable demand and long-term predictability - i.e. under conditions of low uncertainty. But as the stability and predictability of the environment came to a sudden end with the sharp downturn in demand in the early 1970s the small supplier firms lacked key resources to adapt to changing demand conditions and to reorientate towards new markets. Regional development was 'locked in' by the rigidity of the old production pattern created and controlled by the large dominant firms. The organisational 'lock-in' and rigidity of inter-firm linkages were caused by the long-term stability of the economic environment. As long as the dominant large firms produced mainly for the domestic market, the stability of the economic environment was anything but an exogeneous factor. 'Steel barons' were in a strong position to influence state demand for iron and steel - especially for military hardware and infrastructure. Because of the power of the large dominant firms, there was no need for the regional economy to learn to adapt. With the internationalisation of markets, however, the large dominant firms lost this power, and the regional economy failed to adapt. Intervention was no longer able to solve problems that called for innovation.

3. FROM MASS PRODUCTION TOWARDS DIVERSIFIED QUALITY PRODUCTION: THE JOINT CONQUEST OF PLANT ENGINEERING AND ENVIRONMENTAL TECHNOLOGY BY SMALL AND LARGE FIRMS

A process of reorganising the regional economy did not set in until the crisis resulted in dramatic decline. In the early 1970s - particularly on account of the long-term continuity in demand trends - the slumps in demand for iron and steel were at first interpreted as breaks in a growth path that was stable in the long run. The idea of a business 'cycle' was rediscovered (cf. Pichierri, 1986, p. 10). When however the interpretive pattern of short cyclical fluctuations on a stable long-term growth path became increasingly inconsistent with real demand trends, the dominant large companies began to reduce their steel divisions in favour of new fields of production with a significantly higher value-added component (Table 3.1). The strategic reorientation of former steel enterprises towards new markets can be seen from the changes in revenue shares accounted for by their processing divisions. Thus Thyssen alone - the largest of the former steel companies - increased the revenue share of its processing division between 1970 and 1986 from 4.2 per cent to 23.7 per cent. During the same period, the steel division was reduced from 60.3 per cent to 35.9 per cent.

At the centre of the strategic reorientation, although of course the situation varied between individual companies, are plant engineering, environmental technology, mechanical engineering, and electronics. Plant engineering especially has been traditionally part of the production range of large steel enterprises, though initially - within maintenance and repair departments - it was limited to serving the internal needs of the enterprise. With the cutting down of steel capacity to a level which no longer allowed the full utilisation of these maintenance and repair departments, the companies began marketing their plant engineering know-how externally (cf. Geer, 1985, p. 86). This led to organisational differentiation and decentralisation which was oriented towards product markets rather than towards internal production processes.

Table 3.1   Shares of Central Divisions in Total Sales of the five Most Important Steel Enterprises in West Germany (in %)

		1970	1980	1986
THYSSEN (1)	steel	60.3	37.8	35.9
	non-steel	39.7	62.2	64.1
	of which: processing	4.2	22.5	23.7
KRUPP (2)	steel	31.9	36.3	27.6
	non-steel	68.1	63.7	72.2
	of which: processing	34.0	36.5	47.0
MANNESMANN (3)	steel	43.9	30.4	25.1
	non-steel	56.1	69.6	74.9
	of which: processing	23.8	43.9	53.8
KLÖCKNER	steel	60.7	60.8	49.5
	non-steel	39.3	39.2	50.5
	of which: processing	28.3	38.8	49.5
HOESCH (4)	steel		40.5	40.9
	non-steel		59.5	59.1
	of which: processing		33.3	38.4

(1) Up to 30 September 1975 THYSSEN-Gruppe, thereafter THYSSEN-Welt.
(2) Steel, including about 50 per cent high-grade steel.
(3) Only pipes to be subsumed under steel.
     1970: domestic corporation, from 1975: global corporation.
(4) Until 1981 joined with Estel.

Source: Calculations according to business reports.

The large steel companies entered the field of environmental technology following two different approaches. In the first approach, the plant engineering divisions were confronted with the requirements of customers that had to adhere to new environmental regulations. In this sense the supply of environmental technology was not so much the result of an explicit marketing decision but an adaptation to changing demand conditions. Only at a later stage was this adaptation transformed into an explicit widening of the product range and opening up of a new market.[3] In many cases (e.g. Krupp Industrietechnik) this approach resulted not in an organisational differentiation in the manner of a separate unit environmental 'technology' but was developed as a 'cross sectional technology' within the existing organisational framework.

As the demand potential for environmental technology became clear - and therein lies the logic of the second approach - other large Ruhr firms entered this market on the base of explicit marketing strategies. These strategies aimed from the beginning at winning a completely new clientele and were realised primarily by acquiring licences and small specialised firms. Consequently these strategies led - as in the case of Klöckner Oecotec - to separate organisational units or subsidiaries. Both approaches to the development of environmental technology resulted in similar supply profiles. The large firms see their specific strength in offering integrated system solutions, from the conception of plants and equipments to their maintenance and servicing, rather than - and this is the decisive difference to the old structure of the coal, iron, and steel companies - themselves producing all components. Since plant engineering is customised individual production, it would not be rational from the point of view of the large enterprise to maintain resources for solving clients' specific problems. Rather, they attempt to deal with their clients' strongly varying demands such as in the areas of control systems as well as complex plant components by cooperating with specialised firms. The strategic know-how of plant engineers, as a Krupp manager has put it, consists precisely in knowing the right project partner for each problem.

Table 3.2   Structure of Orders in Plant Engineering (shares in total volume of orders)

(1)	30 per cent	plant infrastructure
(2)	20 per cent	steel engineering and machine components of low complexity
(3)	20 per cent	mechanical engineering of high complexity
(4)	30 per cent	control systems and system know-how

Source: Expert interview Krupp, May 1988.

The general contractor - and here lies the specific strength of large firms - is responsible for the financial expenditures connected with the planning and management of large projects, which would pose an insuperable barrier to market entry for small firms. Moreover, small firms usually are not able to provide co-specialised assets (cf. Teece, 1986) permitting the customer to utilise large plants to full advantage. Above all these 'co-specialised assets' include training of the plant operators, maintenance services and spare part guarantees. The specific strengths of small firms consist in adding to the planning and realisation of large plants their highly-specialised competence, particularly in the context of order components (3) and (4) (see Table 3.2). This applies especially with respect to microelectronic control elements and systems, an area in which the large companies of the coal, iron and steel complex have only limited experience.

More than 220 environmental technology firms in North Rhine-Westphalia, the federal state to which the Ruhr area belongs to, offer specialised inputs as components and accessory parts (Figure 3.2, page 71).[4] A considerable share of suppliers and cooperating firms of the large general contractors consist of young small firms that have gained increasing importance during recent years: about half of the firms that entered the market of environmental technology after 1981 are newly-founded firms (cf. IFO, 1988, p. 5).

To sum up, the Ruhr area is provided with an industrial potential of cooperating large and small firms capable of sustaining an innovative push through environmental technology: the outlines of a regional environmental technology complex become visible (Hamm and Schneider 1987/88, p. 176). In much the same vein, an analysis of the metal industry in the Ruhr area concludes:

The most conspicuous strong points of the region are the sectors of environmental technology and plant engineering. At the same time, they come closest to representing a production type of the future which brings together components of different sectors and contributions from various areas of technology in an interdisciplinary fashion and further develops them into tailor-made applied solutions (GEWOS/GfAH/WSI 1988, p. 151f.).

Figure 3.2 Profile of Suppliers of Environmental Technology in North Rhine-Westphalia

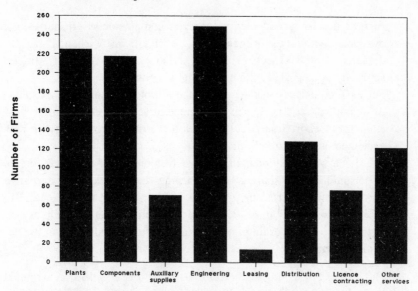

Source: IFO, 1988, p. 3.

4. FROM RIGID HIERARCHIES TOWARDS NETWORKS: THE ECONOMIC RATIONALITY OF REDUNDANT CAPACITIES

The reorientation of the Ruhr industry towards environmental technology for which evidence was provided in section 3 must not be allowed to obscure a crucial fact: the opening up of a new market *per se* is not a sufficient prerequisite for an enduring regional revitalisation. If this reorientation takes place within the old production pattern of rigid hierarchical inter-firm linkages, the next regional crisis will appear at the latest at the first fall in demand for environmental technology. In other words, whether the strategic reorientation towards environmental technology will lay the foundation for a renewal of the Ruhr area depends crucially on the ability of the regional economy - and regional policy - to replace the old hierarchical and rigid inter-firm linkages by flexible and innovation supporting cooperation networks.

Networks can be demarcated from the rigid and hierarchical inter-firm relations of the coal, iron and steel complex by the criterion of flexibility and redundancy. Redundancy in inter-firm relations has several advantages under conditions of a highly uncertain economic environment:

-   First, redundancy will secure access to complementary resources not available within the organisation, even if an exchange partner defaults. With respect to supply relations, the risks of 'single-sourcing' strategies are pointed out in this context.
-   Second, redundancy has the advantage of not threatening the existence of individual exchange partners if cooperative relations are interrupted even for a short time. In this way the costs of searching for new exchange partners are eliminated.
-   Third, network relations, in contrast to hierarchical relations, create opportunities for sharing the learning experiences of exchange partners resulting from their exchange relations with third parties.[5] In this context Sabel *et al.* speak of 'learning systems' such as are characteristic - according to their analysis - of industry in Baden-Württemberg:

    The premise that all economic exchanges must also be occasions for reciprocal learning implies that the parties anticipate problems, and that the problems will be solved jointly. This is the definition of a high-trust relation, and in the current economic environment it minimises transaction costs by freeing the parties from the impossible task of precisely specifying their respective rights and responsibilities through elaborate contracts (as in markets) or bureaucratic rules (as in hierarchy) (Sabel *et al.*, 1987, p. 48).

-   Finally, fourth - a general aspect suggested by Granovetter (1973) - loose and redundant relationship patterns are more capable of innovation and adaptation than very close relationships:[6]

    The strength of weak ties ... (An innovation) can reach a larger number of people, and traverse greater social distance ... when passed through weak ties rather than strong (Granovetter, 1973, p. 1366).

Neither markets nor hierarchies seem appropriate mechanisms to provide redundancy which makes for the flexibility of networks:

Redundant capacities are difficult to build in markets and through, or against, hierarchies, even if investing in them would open up superior market opportunities (Streeck, Chapter 2, above).

Therefore, investment functions require collective-political modification for diversified quality production to turn into a synergetic production pattern. To the extent that individual interests are not sufficiently instructive for investment in redundant capacities, following such interests may be the same as violating them - by letting present, short-term, defensive opportunism deprive actors of their capacity for future, long-term, offensive opportunism.

In this sense a strategy to develop networks with redundant capacities in old industrial areas cannot simply be reduced to a substitution of markets for the rigid hierarchies of the past. Pure market considerations would most probably result in low investment in redundant capacities because of the difficulty of calculating their future return: the 'economistic temptation'. In the absence of conclusive market signals as to where redundant capacities are best developed, their generation and allocation calls for regional policy redefining incentives and disincentives of regional actors or the making of a context, in which the desired social outcome of individual action - networks with redundant capacities - is achieved by individuals in their pursuit of personal interests and social values (cf. Matzner, Chapter 11, below).

5. AGAINST 'CULTURAL FATALISM' IN REGIONAL POLICIES: MAKING A CONTEXT FOR REGIONAL NETWORKS

For regional policy the creation and support of cooperation networks mean a serious challenge. However, it is not just the crisis of a production pattern based on rigid inter-firm linkages and mass production which manifests itself in the crisis of old industrial areas. The basic principles of mass production are reflected, too, in the organisation of the regional political system: rigid division of labour, extreme centralisation, and a predilection for routine solutions. In old industrial areas, not just the regional industry became highly dependent upon the dominant coal, iron and steel complex but also the regional political system adjusted its capacity for perceiving and solving problems to the needs of the dominant complex (cf. Romo *et al.*, 1989). Consequently, regional policy focused above all on financial subsidies for the dominant industrial complex. A policy following this logic would simply mean subsidising the large dominant firms in establishing an environmental technology complex. Obviously such an approach could support a *product* change of the regional industry but not the development of a highly adaptable *production pattern* embedded in regional networks. The ambitious aim of supporting networks calls for a combination of a centralised policy stimulating demand for environmental technology and a decentralised project oriented approach of supply-side policies.

Public programmes triggering investments in environmental technology in old industrial areas serve a double purpose. They not only back up the regional reorientation towards a market with considerable growth potential, but also contribute to the improvement of the environmental and living conditions in old industrial areas.[7] These improvements in turn have positive impacts on the economic attractiveness of old industrial areas. A first powerful investment surge was sparked in the Ruhr by extensive furnace and air quality regulations ('Großfeuerungsanlagenverordnung und Technische Anleitung Luft'); the investment set off by the step-by-step realisation of new water and soil protecting regulations are estimated to amount to more than 100 billion DM up to the beginning of the 1990s.

A particularly large investment potential is to be found in North Rhine-Westphalia, where the share of investment in environmental protection comes up to 9.7 per cent of total industry investments as compared to 6.3 per cent in West Germany as a whole. In total, industry and territorial authorities in North Rhine-Westphalia invested 3.9 billion DM in environmental protection in 1985, as much as the federal states of Bavaria and Baden-Württemberg together. Public programmes creating additional demand for environmental technologies provide a favourable macro-economic background for the development of networks through a decentralised project-oriented regional policy.

The contribution of a decentralised approach of regional policy to the development of networks in an old industrial area has been demonstrated in Lower Austria. There, federally appointed regional agents promoted the development of cooperation networks in two ways (cf. Grabher, 1988, pp. 197-201). First, the regional agents uncovered complementarities and, thereby, potential for cooperation in the regional industrial base. Lack of awareness of complementarities, namely resources and abilities of other regional firms, was a serious obstacle to cooperation, especially in the regional small firm sector, working in the shadow of the large dominant firms. Whereas the exchange of information traditionally was restricted to communication between the large dominant firms and their small suppliers, the regional agents set off an intense exchange of information within the small firm sector.

Second, the regional agents also initiated and stabilised cooperation. The essential contribution of the regional agents consisted in offering advice with technical as well as commercial and legal aspects and in the mediation of conflicts. The co-ordination and mediation through the regional agents was crucial until the mutual adjustments of the cooperating partners (of resources, products, or strategies) ensured stability due to the high costs of breaking off the cooperation. Stability of cooperation means above all substituting 'voice for exit' as mediation mechanism (cf. Johanson and Mattson, 1987, p. 39). Mutual orientation evolves through interaction in the context of mutual adaptation, a mutual orientation which is manifested in a common language regarding technical matters and contracting rules. A most important aspect of the mutual orientation is mutual knowledge, knowledge which the parties assume each has about the other and upon which they draw in communicating with each other. Mutual knowledge implies limits to opportunistic behaviour and thereby reduces transaction costs (cf. Lundvall, 1988, p. 353).

The cooperation networks in Lower Austria initiated by regional agents opened up access to research, engineering, and marketing capacities for small firms. Because of their prior dependence on large dominant firms these small firms were previously unable to provide these capacities for themselves. The lesson to be learned from the Austrian experience is that regional policy is not at the mercy of history and a specific regional culture predestinated to regional networks.[8] Even in old industrial areas, networks can be initiated and supported through a decentralised regional policy if - and these are basic requirements - regional policy shifts from programme-orientation to project-orientation and from financial transfers to real transfers. The most intelligent programmes and most generous subsidies produce no effect if research, engineering and marketing capacities are missing to turn these inputs into successful products. The participation of the Ruhr industry in public programmes stimulating innovation has, compared with other federal states, traditionally been below average (Müller, 1989, p. 192).

The initial conditions for a shift towards a decentralised project-oriented approach have been publicly initiated in the Ruhr area with the future-oriented initiative for the coal, iron, and steel region (*Zukunftsinitiative Montanregion*). This initiative leaves the accomplishment of its aims - support of innovation and training, modernisation of infrastructure, and the improvement of environmental conditions - to the local level. First successes of this approach, as modest they may appear *vis-à-vis* the gigantic dimensions of the old dominant firms, raise hopes that a further decision of the German football association (Deutscher Fußballbund) may find its equivalent in the regional development of West Germany: the decision to separate the second division into north and south was reversed at the beginning of the 1980s.

NOTES

1 Similarly, as an analysis of a traditional industrial region in Austria has indicated, the supply share (share of raw materials, auxiliary, and operating supplies in sales revenues) was below the national average in 15 out of 25 industrial sectors (Grabher, 1988, p. 185).
2 The close interdependence between industries characteristic for the Ruhr District, which is what constitutes the 'coal, iron, and steel complex', has also been borne out in more recent analyses (cf. Brazcyk and Niebur, 1986, p. 67; Schlieper, 1986, p. 205).
3 The increasing consideration of environmental technology by plant engineering firms has also to be seen in the light of recent shifts in clientele structure. With the decrease in demand from Third World countries, customers from highly-industrialised countries that pay greater attention to environmental problems, have gained in relative importance.
4 In all, the environmental technology sector of North Rhine-Westphalia accounts for more than 600 firms. Production is concentrated - with about 40 per cent of all suppliers - in air cleaning, some 30 per cent in sewage, and about 20 per cent of all suppliers in waste and recycling technology, including energy technology (cf. GEWOS/GfAH/WSI, 1988, p. 122).
5 Axelsson (1987) points to a cumulative dynamic resulting from the opportunity to share in the learning experiences of third parties. Membership in a network which is regarded as successful increases one's own attractiveness as a cooperation partner for network non-members.
6 Granovetter (1973), however, does not explicate this with reference to relationships between industrial enterprises, but with reference to the different abilities of various ethnic groups in the United States to adapt to changing environmental conditions. He shows that ethnic groups with very intensive internal relations are extremely limited in their ability to perceive changes in their environment and to respond adequately. By contrast, groups with weaker internal ties which leave some room for bridging relationships that transcend their own narrowly circumscribed group and create opportunities for new contacts, possess a significantly greater capacity for innovation and adaptation.
7 The connection between living conditions and economic attractiveness is explained by Massey (1983, p. 86): 'The non-generation of any real 'middle-class' strata ... has produced a lack of their associated 'culture and society'. This combines with another inheritance of the old industries - the despoilation of the natural and built environment - to reinforce the difficulties of attracting the upper echelon of technical and managerial staff in the new industries.'
8 Analyses of successful regional economies - above all the success stories of Baden-Württemberg and Emilia Romagna - regularly end up with the fatalistic conclusion that their extraordinary performance is the outcome of a specific culture, mentality, or hereditary cleverness. The undeniable importance of cultural factors should not result in a neglect of policies shaping the economic development of these regions, for example the technology policy of Steinbeis in Baden-Württemberg (cf. Maier, 1987).

REFERENCES

Axelsson, B., 'Supplier Management and Technological Development', in H. Hakansson (ed.), *Industrial Technological Development. A Network Approach*, London/Sidney, Croom Helm, 1987.

Brazcyk, H.-J. and Niebur, J. (1986), *Innovationsdefizit und Nord-Süd-Gefälle*, Frankfurt/New York, Campus, 1986.

Geer, T., 'Internationaler Wettbewerb und regionale Entwicklung: preisunempfindliche Branchen', in *Nordrhein-Westfalen in der Krise - Krise in Nordrhein-Westfalen?*, Berlin, Duncker & Humblot, 1985.

GEWOS, GfAH, WSI, *Strukturwandel und Beschäftigungsperspektiven der Metallindustrie an der Ruhr, Final report*, Hamburg, 1988.

Grabher, G., *De-Industrialisierung oder Neo-Industrialisierung? Innovationsprozesse und Innovationspolitik in traditionellen Industrieregionen*, Berlin, Edition Sigma, 1988.

Granovetter, M., 'The Strength of Weak Ties', in *The American Journal of Sociology*, Vol. 78, No. 6, 1973, pp. 1360-80.

Hamm, R. and Schneider, H.K., 'Wirtschaftliche Erneuerung im Ruhrgebiet. Ein Beitrag zur Diskussion der Umstrukturierung altindustrieller Ballungsräume', in *List-Forum*, Vol. 94, No. 3, 1987/88, pp. 169-85.

Herrigel, G.B., 'Industrial Order and the Politics of Industrial Change: Mechanical Engineering in the Federal Republic of Germany' in P. Katzenstein (ed.), *Toward a Third Republic? Industry, Politics and Change in West Germany*, Cornell, Cornell University Press, 1989.

IFO-Institut für Wirtschaftsforschung, *Das Angebot der nordrhein-westfälischen Wirtschaft auf dem Umweltschutzmarkt*, Project report, Munich, 1988.

Johanson, J. and Mattson, L.G., 'Interorganizational Relations in Industrial Systems: A Network Approach Compared with the Transaction-Cost Approach', in *International Studies of Management & Organization*, Vol. 17, No. 1, 1987, pp. 34-48.

Junkernheinrich, M., 'Ökonomische Erneuerung alter Industrieregionen: das Beispiel Ruhrgebiet', in *Wirtschaftsdienst*, Vol. 69, No. 1, 1989, pp. 28-35.

Kunzmann, K.R., 'Structural Problems of an Old Industrial Area: the Case of the Ruhr District', in W. H. Goldberg (ed.), *Ailing Steel. The Transoceanic Quarrel*, Aldershot, Gower, 1986.

Lipietz, A., 'The Structuration of Space, the Problem of Land and Spatial Policy', in J. Carney, R. Hudson and J. Lewis (eds.), *Regions in Crisis*, London, Croom Helm, 1980.

Lund, R. and Rasmussen, J., 'New Technology and Social Networks at the Local and Regional Level', in R. Hyman and W. Streeck (eds.), *New Technology and Industrial Relations*, Oxford, Basil Blackwell, 1988.

Lundvall, B.A., 'Innovation as an Interactive Process: From User-Producer Interaction to the National System of Innovation', in G. Dosi, C. Freeman, R. Nelson, G. Silverberg and L. Soete (eds.), *Technical Change and Economic Theory*, London, Pinter Publishers, 1988.

Maier, H.E., 'Das Modell Baden-Württemberg. Über institutionelle Voraussetzungen differenzierter Qualitätsproduktion. Eine Skizze', *Discussion Paper FS I 87-10a*, Wissenschaftszentrum Berlin für Sozialforschung, 1987.

Massey, D., 'Industrial Restructuring as Class Restructuring: Production Decentralization and Local Uniqueness', *Regional Studies*, Vol. 17, 1983, pp. 73-89.

Massey, D., *Spatial Divisions of Labour - Social Structures and the Geography of Production*, London, Macmillan, 1984.

Müller, G., 'Strukturwandel und Beschäftigungsperspektiven an der Ruhr', *WSI-Mitteilungen*, Vol. 4, 1989, pp. 188-97.

Pichierri, A., 'Diagnosis and Strategy in the Decline of the European Steel Industry', *Discussion Paper FS I 86-22*, Forschungsschwerpunkt Arbeitsmarkt und Beschäftigung, Wissenschaftszentrum Berlin für Sozialforschung, 1986.

Romo, F.P., Korman, H., Brantley, P. and Schwartz, M., 'The Rise and Fall of Regional Political Economies: A Theory of the Core', in J. Rothschild and M. Wallace (eds.), *Research in Politics and Society 3: Deindustrialization and the Economic Restructuring of American Business*, New York, JAI Press, 1989.

Sabel, C.F., Herrigel, G.B., Deeg, R. and Kazis, R., 'Regional Prosperities Compared: Massachusetts and Baden-Württemberg in the 1980's', *Discussion Paper FS I 87-10b*, Wissenschaftszentrum Berlin für Sozialforschung, 1987.

Schlieper, A., *150 Jahre Ruhrgebiet - ein Kapitel deutscher Wirtschaftsgeschichte*, Düsseldorf, Schwann, 1986.

Teece, D., 'Firm Boundaries, Technological Innovation, and Strategic Management', in L. G. Thomas (ed.), *The Economics of Strategic Planning*, Lexington, Lexington Books, 1986.

PART 2:

ON EFFECTIVE LABOUR MARKET AND SOCIAL POLICY

4. On the Institutional Conditions of Effective Labour Market Policies

Günther Schmid and Bernd Reissert

1. INTRODUCTION

In recent years the hopes of finding a cure for sustained high unemployment in Europe have shifted from global, fiscal demand and supply strategies to labour market institutions such as the system of regulation (for a critical review cf. Emerson, 1988) and industrial relations (e.g. Freeman, 1988; Soskice, 1990). Labour market policy has only been seen in a very restrictive way, either as an additional variable causing unemployment, especially through the alleged effects of high and/or long-term unemployment benefits (for a critical review cf. Burtless, 1987), or as a complementary element to global demand and supply strategies, in particular as an instrument to avoid inflationary bottlenecks due to skill scarcity or mismatch. It has been largely forgotten that labour market policy may itself be an important instrument in the fight against unemployment and that an effective labour market policy itself depends on favourable institutional conditions of which the established rules of financing are among the most important. This neglect is all the more strange if we consider the huge financial resources that are spent in many OECD countries for wage-replacement transfers to the unemployed ('passive' labour market policy) instead of for investment in human capital or in new jobs ('active' labour market policy).

In the following study we will argue that the institutionalised rules of financing 'active' and/or 'passive' labour market policy provide an important explanation for the misallocation of resources in many countries. In particular we will provide evidence for the thesis of *institutional incongruity of financing* of labour market policies in two respects.

Fiscal incongruity arises if state or parafiscal organisations responsible for formulating, implementing and financing active labour market policy cannot themselves collect most of the financial benefits of this policy. The general solution to this problem is to change either the political responsibilities or the fiscal flows.

Social incongruity arises if individuals, firms or collective interest organisations assume the financial burden of coping with structural change while the benefits of adjustment - due to external effects - accrue (to a substantial extent) to other individuals, firms or collective organisations. The general solution to this problem, again, is either to change the social responsibilities or to internalise the costs and benefits of readjustment.

After developing the analytical framework (section 2), the effects of different financing systems on expenditure on active labour market policy - as an essential element in fighting unemployment - are analysed (section 3). Financing systems, however, influence not only the level but also the structure of labour market policy. This in turn has implications for the allocative and distributive effects of labour market policy, as demonstrated by empirical evidence from an international comparison (section 4). Finally, suggestions are developed on how best to overcome 'institutional incongruity' and how to design financing institutions for an effective labour market policy (section 5). Our contribution aims to conceptualise the results of an international comparison of labour market policies in six countries (Austria, West Germany, France, Great Britain, Sweden and the United States). (For a detailed documentation of the study cf. Schmid, Reissert and Bruche, 1987 and 1991; for a short summary version cf. Schmid and Reissert, 1988).

2.   THE INSTITUTIONAL PREDETERMINATION OF PUBLIC CHOICE

The Filtering Function of Institutions

Institutions, in the wider sense of norms, habits, traditions, organisations, procedural and financing regulations, and the distribution of responsibilities and jurisdictions, greatly influence the choice of decisions to be made in a specific situation, who is to decide what, when, and with what resources, and how conflicts between participants are to be settled. Institutions legitimise both action and inaction! The absence of a full-employment policy therefore may well be an expression of an institutional framework that relieves functionally-competent organisations (or persons) from their responsibility in an orderly and thus legitimate fashion. The question which arises at this point is this: Which institutions ensure that responsibility for effective employment action is assigned in an adequate fashion with respect to its timing, relevance, and social implications?

Institutions function as filters for information and interests, as incentives for individual and collective decision-makers, or as norms for individual or collective behaviour, and thus immediately narrow the range of conceivable decisions and actions. They function selectively *vis-à-vis* possible alternatives for action by favouring some and impeding or altogether precluding others (cf. among others, Commons, 1959). Institutions thus have the character of 'preselections' or 'predecisions'. They are not politically neutral but rather reflect specific power relations; they are 'congealed' political will. As such, they can, in principle, be changed when a new political will is being formed. Once established, however, they take on a dynamic of their own and give rise to unplanned steering effects. On account of their 'invisible-hand' function and inertia they may clash with changing decision-making situations, new power relations, or political intentions. Institutions thus make 'public choice' not a purely rational undertaking but a decision process shaped largely by habits, beliefs, and (assumed) power relations.

This has to be borne in mind when considering financing institutions, the subject of the following discussion. Financing institutions embrace the 'established' regulatory and organisational arrangements which determine who is to suffer the consequences of unemployment or the costs of avoiding them; whether those affected by unemployment will receive any wage compensation at all, and if so the level and duration of benefits. They also determine whether, instead of financing unemployment ('passive labour market policy'), social resources will be used for preventive measures or the elimination of unemployment ('active labour market policy'). These institutional arrangements, in turn, have repercussions on the behaviour of labour market actors, affecting the search behaviour of the unemployed, the mobility behaviour of the employed, firms' hiring practices, wage negotiations between unions and employers, and finally the labour market policy behaviour of governments and bureaucracies at different levels.

Our attention will be focused on the latter. Persistent high unemployment in West Germany, for instance, which has existed for over 15 years, can certainly not be explained solely with reference to the financing system of labour market policy. However, as will be shown, the growing discontinuation of wage compensation payments for many of the unemployed in West Germany, the relatively modest level of measures to fight unemployment through active labour market policy, the procyclical instead of countercyclical responses of labour market policy, and the concentration of employment promotion measures on already favoured regions and groups rather than on those most severely affected are directly related to the structure of this financing system. Compared to other countries, however, some advantages of the German financing system may also be pointed out. In other countries, such as the United States, the discontinuation of unemployment benefits has run an even harder course; the social security of the unemployed who do remain eligible for wage compensation payments is much better in West Germany than in some other countries, such as Britain; and active labour market policy, particularly further training for the adaptation of qualifications and short-time working for bridging cyclical fluctuations, contribute more to preventing and reducing unemployment in West Germany than they do, for example, in Austria.

The specific characteristics on which the advantages and disadvantages of financing systems are based are the subject of the following analysis. How has public labour market policy developed under conditions of different financing systems, and to what extent have financing systems led to different forms of unemployment insurance and active labour market policy? In order to answer this question, an international comparison appears to be useful since the question of whether financing institutions do make a difference can be best answered empirically by observing different, actually existing, financing systems.

Possible Policy Reactions to Fiscal Strain

Before turning to the facts, however, we will provide a short sketch of the range of possible policy reactions to arise in unemployment, and will ask why we would, for theoretical reasons, expect different reactions by policy makers (PM) to an increase in fiscal strain (FS) due to rising unemployment (U) (for an extensive discussion see Schmid, Reissert and Bruche, 1987, pp. 92-115). Figure 4.1 represents a simplified view of our basic hypothesis.

Figure 4.1 Possible Policy Reactions to Fiscal Strain

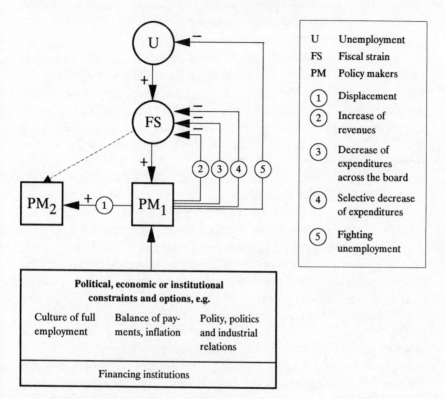

When unemployment soars, policy makers are faced with increasing fiscal strain. Five options can be distinguished by which this strain can be reduced.

1. Displacement, i.e. shifting the fiscal strain to another policy maker (PM_2), e.g. shifting the fiscal burden to the pension system by expanding early retirement regulations for the elderly unemployed.

2. Increasing revenues by raising tax rates or payroll taxes or other specific contributions (e.g. to the unemployment insurance fund) or by borrowing.

3. Decreasing expenditure across the board, e.g. by lowering unemployment benefits for all entitled persons.

4. Selectively decreasing expenditure, e.g. by sharpening the entitlement conditions for receiving unemployment benefits, for instance by extending the waiting period or by reducing the length of jobless pay.

5. Fighting unemployment, e.g. by measures of active labour market policy such as retraining, further training, temporary public job creation, public support for working-time reduction.

Which of the options or which policy mix political decision-makers choose, depends on many factors of which the institutionalised system of financing is only one. The probability of choosing option 5, for example, depends greatly on the culturally-determined priority of the full-employment goal relative to other (conflicting) goals such as price stability. This explains, for instance, to some extent the difference between Swedish and West German labour market policies. The probability of choosing option 1, to mention another example, depends much on the political constitution, i.e. on the vertical and horizontal decision structure. In a centralised and a highly-integrated system of social security - such as the British system - there is much less room for displacement than in a federal system with a relatively fragmented system of social security - such as the West German system. Whereas West German policy-makers at national level have (in principle) the option of shifting part of the 'fiscal costs' of unemployment to the municipalities (which are responsible for social security to jobless people who are not entitled to unemployment benefit or assistance or whose unemployment benefits are too small) or on to the pension system, their British counterparts do not have this option. This explains to some extent the differences in labour market and early retirement policy between Britain and West Germany as we will see later. Whereas West Germany has used the option of early retirement for relieving the labour market to a considerable extent, Britain has not (cf. Casey and Bruche, 1983).

Financing institutions, this is our hypothesis, play an important role when policy makers choose between options 3 and 4 and between options 2/3/4 and 5. The decisive characteristics of financing systems in this respect are the source of financing (taxes versus contributions) and the degree of institutional fragmentation (integrated versus fragmented budgets). The argument can be summarised in the following hypotheses:

(1) Policy makers will choose strategy 3 instead of 4 if unemployment benefits or measures of active labour market policy are financed out of the general state budget, i.e. primarily by taxes. If, on the other hand, labour market policy is financed from contributions, policy makers will opt for strategy 4 instead of 3. This is because contributory systems are based on the principle of equivalence; in other words, contributions establish some kind of property rights which general taxes do not, at least not explicitly. In the case of contribution-based systems policy makers are bound to

consider quasi-property rights (i.e. benefit levels) and to select persons with the weakest 'property rights' for benefit entitlement restrictions if they have to or wish to cut expenditure.

(2) Policy makers will choose strategy 5 instead of strategies 2/3/4 if (a) they are assumed to carry political responsibility for unemployment, and (b) the fiscal returns of active labour market policy (i.e., a reduction of the 'fiscal costs' of unemployment) flow essentially into their own budget - thus relieving fiscal strain. The latter condition may not be fulfilled in the case of vertically or horizontally fragmented budgets in which the fiscal returns may flow to a substantial extent to the budgets of other policy makers. The fiscal incentive to choose a full employment strategy is thus weakened in these cases.

(3) Policy makers will stick to options 2/3 or 4 if they are unable (or unwilling) to build a coalition with the trade unions regarding option 5. Trade unions will not enter such a coalition if their members have to take over the main fiscal burden of such a policy (which may be the case in contribution-financed systems) whereas the benefits will be far more widespread. Such a coalition is all the more unlikely if trade union members are covered by relatively generous unemployment benefit systems whose fiscal costs are borne by the general taxpayer.

(4) The institutionally predetermined choice of policy alternatives will have consequences for the functioning of the labour market and the distribution of employment opportunities that may well run counter to the (official) intention of policy makers. In particular, redistributive policy intentions are supported by tax-based but not by contribution-based financing systems of labour market policy.

These four propositions will now be differentiated and explained at length in the following sections which also provide empirical illustrations from our international comparison in their support.

3. EFFECTS OF FINANCING SYSTEMS ON EXPENDITURE ON ACTIVE LABOUR MARKET POLICY

Sources for Financing Active Labour Market Policy

What factors characterise the type of system used to finance labour market policy in a given country? One of the most essential features, on which we will focus in the following, is the source of financing. Other important characteristics include budgeting rules (who participates in preparing the labour market budget?), rules for balancing the budget (procedures for dealing with deficits or surpluses), and the relationship of various functional budgets with each other as well as to the state budget as a whole (integrated vs. fragmented, centralised vs. decentralised budgets).

Table 4.1 provides an overview of financing sources for specific functions of labour market policy. A rough distinction is made between financing from 'contributions' (C) and 'taxes' (T). Financing sources are classified as contributions if they consist of unemployment insurance contributions or other deductions for specific purposes (e.g. levies for winter or bankruptcy allowances). Labour market policy financed by the general state budget is classified as tax-financed since taxes constitute the principal financial source of the state budget. With respect to taxes, the principle of nonappropriation of public funds for specific purposes applies, i.e. tax revenues as a rule are not tied to specific purposes. Earmarked contributions, on the other hand, generally establish a claim for benefits if certain conditions are fulfilled (insurance principle). This distinction is of great significance for the way in which a financing system responds when it comes under financial pressure.

Table 4.1 Financing Sources of Labour Market Policy 1973-85[a]

Country	1 Wage Compensation Payments		2 Employment Agencies		3 Further Training, Rehabilitation		4 Job Creation Measures		5 Seasonal and Countercyclical Measures		6 Youth Integration Assistance		7 Sum	
	C	T	C	T	C	T	C	T	C	T	C	T	C	T
Austria	XXX		XXX	X	XXX	X	XXX		XX	X	-	-	11	3
W.Germany	XXX	X	XXX		XXX		XXX	X	XXX		-	-	15	2
France	XX [b]	XX		XXX	XXX	X	XXX		XXX		X	XXX	9	9
Britain	XX	XX		XXX	XX	XXX	X	XXX		XXX		XXX	2	17
Sweden	XX		X	XXX	XX	XXX		XXX	XX	XX	XX	XX	10	14
USA	XXX	X	XXX			XXX		XXX	-	-		XXX	6	10

C = contributions and levies
T = taxes or state budget
XXX = two-thirds and above
XX = between one-third and two-thirds
X = less than one-third
- = programme does not exist or is of marginal significance

Notes to Columns:
(1) Includes unemployment benefits and assistance, early retirement without rehiring.
(3) Only adult training and occupational rehabilitation.
(4) Temporary public job creation measures.
(5) Short-time working benefits, seasonal temporary assistance for the construction industry etc.
(6) Special youth integration assistance (mostly under 20 years of age).
(7) Sum of weights (X), not allowing for the relative importance of programmes.
a Average for period: in part, rough estimates.
b Unemployment insurance contributions are an integral component of general social insurance contributions.

Austria and West Germany operate essentially contribution-based systems, while Britain represents virtually the ideal type of a tax system; Sweden and the United States, while predominantly tax systems, nevertheless contain significant contribution elements, while France may be characterised as a mixed system. Taking into account only active labour market policies, the differences become even more pronounced. Britain and the United States (the latter with the exception of the relatively insignificant employment agencies) become pure tax systems while West Germany represents an almost completely contribution-based system.

Volume of Expenditure on Active Labour Market Policy

How much have the countries included in our analysis spent on active (as opposed to passive) labour market policy, and can any relationships be identified between expenditure levels and financing systems? Table 4.2 shows average expenditure in terms of gross domestic product, expenditure levels in recession years, and the average rate of unemployment during the observation period.

Sweden has by far the highest level of expenditure, Austria the lowest; the other four countries form an intermediate group with approximately the same volume of expenditure. The average share of expenditure on active labour market policy amounts to about 2 per cent of GDP in Sweden (during the investigation period); in Austria by contrast it is only 0.2 per cent, while in the other countries it ranges between 0.5 and 1 per cent.

These different expenditure levels are primarily a result of the different roles assigned to active labour market policy in individual countries in the context of their economic and employment policies. In Sweden, active labour market policy constitutes an essential element of employment policy whereas in Austria employment policy is based on different elements (particularly fiscal and incomes policies). However, independent effects of different financing systems can also be identified. Thus Swedish labour market policy could not have fulfilled its assigned employment policy function if it had been primarily financed by contributions rather than the state budget. Contribution systems always presuppose an (individual or group-specific) relationship between contributions and benefits ('equivalence') which is no longer given once they are put in the service of general employment policy objectives (rather than being aimed at specific contributors). Austrian labour market policy - which has a contribution-based financing system that in the longer term does not permit the accumulation of deficits or surpluses and is thus equivalent to a levy system - could not have been utilised for an extended and countercyclical employment policy since any increases in expenditure would have triggered higher contribution rates. However, it is the same financing system, which in the event of a fund surplus allows only contribution cuts or increased benefits (rather than the accumulation of reserves), that has facilitated (on a modest scale) the establishment of active labour market policy in Austria: in the early 1970s surpluses in the unemployment insurance fund in that country were used for initiating active measures - a process with parallels in the West German contribution-based system.

Table 4.2 Expenditure Levels of Active Labour Market Policy and Unemployment Rates

Country	Expenditures on Active Labour Market Policy as a Percentage of Gross Domestic Product			Average Unemployment Rate
	1973-1985	1975	1982	1973-1985
Austria	0.19	0.20	0.19	2.4
West Germany	0.68	0.77	0.82	4.5
France	0.95	0.73	1.16	6.1
Britain	0.58[a]	0.30	0.64	7.6
Sweden	1.95	2.34[c]	1.85[c]	2.4
USA	0.49[b]	0.46	0.31	7.1

a 1974-85
b 1973-83
c Data are for 1977 and 1981 when the Swedish economy reached its lowest points

Source: *Schmid, Reissert and Bruche, 1987, pp. 237, 264.*

Dynamics of Expenditure Trends

The effects of different financing systems on the dynamics of expenditure are even more pronounced than they are on the volume of expenditure. In Britain, Sweden and the United States, political priorities can be relatively easily translated into corresponding expenditure since active measures are financed almost exclusively out of the state budget. Expenditure trends therefore have corresponded to the very different political priorities in each country. In Britain, spending on active labour market policy (particularly aimed at unemployed youth) has been continuously expanded in line with political objectives; in Sweden, it has been adjusted countercyclically in accordance with its employment policy function; in the United States, following the political priorities of the administration and Congress, there was initially a significant expansion followed by a drastic - procyclical - reduction in the 1980s. In the United States, a flexible spending policy responding very quickly to changing political priorities has also been facilitated by the fact that most labour market policy programmes are of limited duration, are not tied to individual legal entitlements and are administered by local governments, individual states, and special local associations rather than by a separate organisation. Organisational rigidities and well-established vested interests, which in countries with separate labour administrations create stability and prevent rapid change, play only a minor role in the USA.

In those countries where the state budget is not the primary source of financing employment promotion measures, expenditure trends are clearly shaped by the way they are financed. In France, for example, the fragmentation of spending and financing responsibilities (which, among other things, spreads the burden through various deductions for special purposes) does not show labour market policy in its totality as a transparent expenditure bloc that could become the object of budgetary considerations; it thus favours continuous spending growth. In West Germany, the Federal Employment Institute is able, at least for an initial period, to deal with rising unemployment on account of its reserves with which it can finance both the growing demand for wage compensation payments and increased spending on active labour market policy. Extensive job losses, however, rapidly deplete the Federal Employment Institute's reserves; the federal government then has to make up the resulting deficit, subsequently adopting measures (cutbacks) to eliminate the deficit. These concentrate primarily on spending for active labour market policy, since this is considered the most readily disposable budget item. In the longer run, surpluses and reserves can be built up again which in turn benefit active spending programmes. The outcome of a decision-making framework influenced by financing in this way is a spending pattern in the area of active labour market policy that initially responds countercyclically to an increase in the unemployment rate, subsequently changes to a procyclical course, and finally may become expansionary again if the unemployment rate remains at a constant level.

Viewing expenditure trends on the premise that spending on active labour market policy should adjust itself to the labour market situation over time - i.e. by increasing spending when the situation on the labour market is unfavourable and decreasing it when it is positive - the following picture emerges. Active labour market policy systems financed by the general state budget facilitate a quickly adaptable countercyclical policy, provided the political will exists. If it does not exist, however, such systems permit spending variations that run entirely counter to a solution of the problem. One example of this is the drastic cuts in the labour market budget (for 'active' measures) in the United States in the late 1970s and early 1980s even though unemployment at that time was on the increase. Contribution-based systems - if, as in West Germany, they allow for surplus and deficit accumulation - have a built-in stabilising effect on the economy, which to some extent provides a good basis for a countercyclical spending policy. During severe and long-lasting recessions with their attendant financial problems, however, it is particularly in contribution-based systems combining active and passive policy elements that 'identifiable deficits' may occur, deficits which tend to be eliminated by cuts in active measures aggravating the unemployment problem.

'Activity Level' of Labour Market Policy

According to the official labour market policy objectives of most countries, active labour market policy is given priority over passive labour market policy. Measures and programmes of active labour market policy aimed at training, job creation and preservation are to take the place, as far as possible, of the 'passive' acceptance of unemployment and the 'mere' protection of the unemployed against the financial consequences of unemployment. This objective - as Table 4.3 indicates - has not been achieved in most of the countries examined. Only in Sweden is the 'activity level' of labour market policy, i.e. expenditures on active measures as a share of total labour market policy spending, considerably above 50 per cent. In almost all the countries analysed, it declined during the investigation period; only in Britain did it remain stable (though in part as a result of cuts in passive benefits).

In addition to other factors, differences in financing systems are also responsible for different activity levels of labour market policy in individual countries. To varying degrees, financing systems may facilitate the substitution of a 'passive' acceptance of unemployment by active labour market policy. Embarking on active labour market policy rather than accepting unemployment presupposes that labour market policy programmes can largely be financed through funds that otherwise would have to be used for maintaining the potential participants in such programmes while they remain unemployed. The extent to which this precondition is fulfilled differs widely between countries.

Table 4.3   Shares of Spending on Active Measures in Total Expenditure on Labour Market Policy

Country	Total Period 1973-1985	Recession Years 1975	1982	Coefficient of Variation
Austria	28.2	40.4	17.9	0.34
West Germany	43.0	44.3	34.1	0.21
France	45.5	52.5	35.2	0.24
Britain	30.7[a]	25.0	24.9	0.15
Sweden	78.2	85.5[c]	73.9[c]	0.08
USA	40.8[b]	27.4	26.4	0.31

a 1974-1985
b 1973-1983
c Data for 1977 and 1981 when the Swedish economy reached its lowest points.

Source: *Schmid, Reissert and Bruche, 1987, pp. 247, 250.*

In all countries the costs of labour market policy measures must be seen in the context of the roughly equal financial burden on public budgets that would otherwise arise as a result of the unemployment of programme participants (wage compensation and other social benefits, lost revenue from taxes and social insurance contributions). In other words, the 'net costs' (additional costs) of successful labour market programmes are substantially lower than their 'gross costs'. Yet the decreased burden on public budgets resulting from programmes that reduce unemployment does not in all countries accrue to those institutions charged with the responsibility of funding active programmes; frequently the benefits are reaped to a considerable extent by institutions that have no part in active labour market policy (cf. Tables 4.4 and 4.5).

The incentives and opportunities for the institutions responsible for labour market policy to apply a 'net-cost calculus' and substitute the 'passive' acceptance of unemployment by active labour market policy measures therefore differ widely from country to country. In Britain, on account of the far-reaching responsibility of the state budget for active and passive labour market policy and the centralisation of tax and social insurance systems, the diminished budget burden resulting from a reduction in unemployment for the most part accrues to the same institution that is responsible for active policy spending and the corresponding budget burden.

Table 4.4   *The Fiscal Costs of Unemployment in Six Countries: Size, Composition and Institutional Distribution. (Average costs for each unemployed per year in national currencies and percentages for individual revenue and expenditure items and institutions)*

	Austria (1983) AS	%	West Germany (1983) DM	%	France (1982) FF	%	Great Britain (1981/82) £	%	Sweden* (1982) SKR	%	USA* $	%
(1) Expenditures for												
(1,1) Unemployment compensation	65 342	47	11 400	48	22 803	48	1 481	33	33 718	38		
(1,2) Other social welfare benefits			600	3			128	3				
(2) Lost revenues from												
(2,1) Direct taxes	24 915	18	4 300	18	2 719	6	1 089	24				
(2,2) Indirect taxes	5 440	4	1 500	6	2 581	5	891	20	54 092	62		
(3) Lost contributions to												
(3,1) Pension systems	31 496	23	3 700	15			907	20				
(3,2) Unempl. insurance	5 684	4	1 300	5	19 382	41						
(3,3) Health insurance	5 103	4	1 200	5				-				
(4) Total	137 984	100	24 000	100	47 485	100	4 495	100	87 809	100		
(4,1) as % of the GDP per inhabitant	86		88		73	-	98		116			
(5) Institutional Distribution among the public budgets:												
(5,1) Central government		13		23		32		64	XXXXX		XXX	
(5,2) State governments		5		9		-		-	X		X	
(5,3) Local governments		4		5		-		3	XX		X	
(5,4) Unempl. insurance		57		43		27		-	3		XXX	
(5,5) Pension systems		17		15		41		33	XX		X	
(5,6) Health insurance		4		5		-		-				

* Comparable data on the costs of unemployment and their institutional distribution in the USA and Sweden are incomplete. The symbols for these countries in lines 5.1 to 5.6 are only rough indicators for the degree to which individual institutions are affected (each X representing roughly 10 per cent).

Source: Schmid, Reissert and Bruche, 1987, pp. 190-1.

Table 4.5 *Distribution of Burden on Public Budgets Due to Unemployment and of Spending Responsibility for Active Labour Market Policy on Individual Sponsoring Agencies*

Country	Budget Burden due to Unemployment (fiscal costs of unemployment)				Spending Responsibility for Active Labour Market Policy			
	Central State	Member States/ Municipalities	UI[a]	PI/HI[a]	Central State	Member States/ Municipalities	UI[a]	PI/HI[a]
Austria	X	X	XX	X		XXX	XXX	
West Germany	X	X	XX	X		XXX	XXX	
France	XX		X	XX	XXX			
Britain	XXX		XX		XXX			
Sweden[b]	XXX	X		X	XXX	X		
USA[b]	XX	X	XX	X	XXX		X	

XXX = two-thirds and above
XX = between one-third and two-thirds
X = less than one-third
a UI = unemployment insurance
   PI/HI = pension and health insurance
b Data on institutional distribution of the costs of unemployment for Sweden and the United States are based on rough estimates of Table 4.4.

Sources: Tables 4.1 and 4.4.

Much the same applies to Sweden. In other countries - particularly the United States and Austria - such an 'institutional congruity' of increases and potential decreases in budgetary strain does not exist, since active and passive labour market policies are either institutionally separated or to a large extent divorced from the tax and social insurance systems. These diverging conditions explain at least in part why the 'activity level' of labour market policy (which of course does not say anything about the quality of the measures adopted) is exceptionally high in Sweden, and why in Britain it has followed a more consistent course than in other countries. In countries with a low or negative incentive for substituting 'passive' by 'active' measures, variations in the 'activity level' are also significantly higher than in countries where such incentives do exist (cf. coefficients of variation in Table 4.3).

4. EFFECTS OF FINANCING SYSTEMS ON THE EFFICIENCY AND DISTRIBUTION OF LABOUR MARKET POLICY

Effects of Unemployment Insurance on Social Security and Distribution

At first sight an attempt to gain a comparative view of unemployment insurance benefits in individual countries, their 'generosity', and their distributive effects results in a confusing picture; eligibility criteria and the differentiation of benefits according to income groups, household types, and duration of unemployment differ to such an extent that no easily comparable structures emerge. Nevertheless, some patterns can be identified from existing studies. Sweden, West Germany, and France provide a relatively high level of wage compensation payments, whereas the corresponding levels in Britain and the United States are relatively low. The level of benefits thus does not necessarily depend on the financing system; largely contribution-based systems of unemployment benefits can be found in countries with both high and low wage compensation rates (West Germany and the United States, respectively), and the same is true for largely tax-financed systems (Sweden and Britain, respectively).

Differences in conditions concerning entitlement, on the other hand, *are* related to financing systems: contribution-based systems, predominantly characterised by the insurance principle, as a rule offer the longest protection while at the same time (increasingly) tie the benefit duration to preceding contribution periods. Largely tax-based systems, not based on the insurance principle, generally offer a shorter period of income protection while at the same time less closely tying benefit duration to the preceding length of employment. Instead they tend to differentiate benefits according to social criteria (cf. Britain).

Tax-based benefit systems of subsistence protection for the unemployed tend to have greater redistributive effects than contribution-based systems which are closely geared by the insurance principle. This becomes evident in both interpersonal and interregional comparisons: the redistributive effects of unemployment insurance with respect to regions tend to be greater in largely tax-based systems than in contribution-based systems. The extreme case is represented by the contribution-based unemployment insurance system in the United States which, on account of its highly decentralised nature has practically no regional equalisation effects. One reason for the greater redistributive capacity of tax-based systems is that they are under less of an obligation than contribution-based systems to gear their benefits towards acquired claims and instead are able to differentiate their benefits according to social criteria. In addition, tax financing tends to affect individual incomes and regions progressively, i.e. the wealthy contribute more to financing than the poor. Contribution financing, in contrast (particularly if income thresholds are low as in the United States), tend to be regressive, i.e. the poor pay proportionally more than the rich (cf. Disney, 1984).

Tax and contribution-based systems also respond differently to the financial strain resulting from high and long-term unemployment. In such a situation, financing systems without a close relationship between contributions and benefits tends to reduce benefits for all recipients, while not altogether excluding specific groups of the unemployed. This 'levelling effect' is very clearly illustrated in the case of Britain where the share of benefit recipients in the total number of unemployed has remained at a high and constant level while average benefits have drastically declined (cf. columns 3 and 4 of Table 4.6).

By contrast, countries strictly following insurance principles tend to restrict eligibility and increasingly to 'discontinue' benefits for certain individuals, a phenomenon which may be called the 'segmentation effect'. It can be observed in the United States and, to a lesser degree, in West Germany and France. Once again the reciprocity principle of contribution systems accounts for different responses. It provides a sort of 'property right' for insurance benefits, which makes general cuts difficult, but tends to exclude 'bad risks'.

Table 4.6   *Expenditure on Unemployment Benefits and its Main Determinants*

	1		2		3		4	
	Expenditure on unemployment benefits as % of GDP		Expenditure on unemployment benefits per unemployed (as % of wage income from dependent work per dependent worker)		Unemployment benefit recipients as % of the unemployed		Expenditure on unemployment benefits per benefit recipient (as % of wage income from dependent work per dependent worker)	
	1975	1982	1975	1982	1975	1982	1975	1982
Austria	0.25	0.61	21	26	73	75	29	34
West Germany	0.85	1.44	30	31	76	66	39	46
France	0.47	1.36	16	23	62	57	27	40
Britain	0.81	1.80	34	24	83	84	41	29
Sweden	0.24	0.70	22	32	63	77	34	42
USA	1.18	0.82	19	11	77	45	25	25

Notes to Columns:
(1) Data include unemployment benefits, unemployment assistance or supplementary benefit for the unemployed as well as pension and health insurance contributions which are paid for the unemployed, pro rated on their wage compensation benefits, out of unemployment insurance funds. The data exclude bankruptcy allowances, early retirement benefits and administrative costs.
(2) Calculated on an annual basis.
(3) Without unemployed persons in the process of applying for support payments.
(4) Calculated on an annual basis.

The table shows different expenditure trends and their determinants in individual countries (cf. text). However, it does not permit any conclusions with respect to different levels of 'generosity' of benefit systems in individual countries (i.e. with respect to different benefit levels in similar cases of unemployment) since the structure of unemployment (i.e. its composition by age groups, marital status, duration of unemployment) differs significantly from country to country.

Source: *Schmid, Reissert and Bruche, 1987, p. 168.*

Benefit systems not characterised by equivalence, on the other hand, are in principle open to all risk groups but are ill-protected against cuts in individual benefits. The Austrian contribution system at first glance appears to be an exception since the share of benefit recipients in the total number of unemployed has not declined. Austria's financing system, however, was not subject to any severe tests in the form of high unemployment during the observation period; if the thesis presented here is valid, a segmentation effect is to be expected in the coming years as a result of the recent significant increases in the number of unemployed.

Unemployment Insurance and Functioning of the Labour Market

There is considerable concern expressed in economic theory that a high level of wage compensation granted for a long period of time may adversely affect the adjustment function of the labour market. In this view increased benefit claims, the misuse or extensive use of benefits reduce necessary wage flexibility, increase the duration of unemployment, give individuals an incentive to register as unemployed even though they are not really available for the labour market, or even lead people to quit voluntarily (cf. Clark and Summers, 1982). On the demand side as well, according to this theory, unemployment insurance induces the adoption of production methods with higher lay-off risks and lowers employers' willingness to hire due to increased non-wage labour costs.

A survey of the empirical literature on the countries examined here shows that well-supported conclusions on the incentive effects of unemployment insurance are not yet available. While most existing studies agree that unemployment insurance tends to bring about a higher level of unemployment, they consider the total effect to be small even in a 'generous' system. In a comparative study Burtless summarises his conclusion as follows:

In this survey I find little to support the view that differences in jobless pay explain the differential trends in unemployment in Europe and the United States (Burtless, 1987, p. 152).

He even finds an argument that - ironically - making compensation more generous may increase unemployment when it is low but is not likely to add much to unemployment when it is high. In a tight labour market, where the number of vacancies is high relative to the number of unemployed, generous jobless benefits will to some extent induce the unemployed to search longer, which will cause the average duration of both unemployment and vacancies to rise and the unemployment rate to increase. But in a relatively slack labour market, where vacancies are not so plentiful, any job turned down by an unemployed person getting benefits will be snapped up by someone without such benefits. The composition of the unemployed will change - more of them will be drawing benefits - but neither the average duration nor the overall rate of unemployment will be substantially affected (Burtless, 1987, p. 150).

The modest negative incentive effects of unemployment insurance contrast with positive effects that are even more difficult to quantify, but which in the light of plausible theoretical considerations turn out to be no less significant. Effective social protection in the case of involuntary unemployment stabilises demand at the macro-economic level (not least because of the higher propensity to consume on the part of low income earners) and strengthens loyalty to fundamental social institutions at the macro-sociological level. At an 'intermediate system level' where the representatives of capital and labour meet, an effective unemployment insurance also encourages cooperation between interest groups, thus increasing particularly the willingness on the part of unions to participate in adapting to changing markets and technologies in an offensive rather than defensive fashion. At the micro level reliable and 'generous' social security benefits in case of unemployment also increase the willingness on the part of those in dependent employment for greater labour market mobility. This will be the case particularly if the preconditions for such mobility are accompanied by effective measures of active labour market policy. The opportunities provided by active labour market policy in turn will reduce the probability of the social security system being exploited. Given the prospect of acquiring insurance claims, unemployment insurance also enhances the desire for regular work ('eligibility effect') and thus may reduce moonlighting (cf. Hamermesh, 1979; Clark and Summers, 1982).

Distributive Effects of Active Labour Market Policy between Regions and Individuals

There are a number of theoretical reasons supporting the conjecture that tax-based systems of active labour market policy - as in the case of unemployment insurance - have different distributive effects than contribution-based systems. In particular, it is to be expected that tax-based systems are better able to concentrate their spending on problem regions and problem groups than contribution-based systems. The reason for this lies in the insurance element in contribution systems that tends to concentrate benefits on contribution payers and therefore on the core group of the labour market, thus conflicting with the aims of a more selective labour market policy.

Our empirical analyses for the most part confirm these expectations. The regional distribution of active labour market policy in tax-based systems largely responds to problem pressures, i.e. the shares of individual regions in labour market policy benefits and spending roughly correspond to their respective shares in total unemployment (e. g. in Britain). In the United States, problem regions even receive disproportionately high consideration. In West Germany's contribution-based system, on the other hand, the regions already favoured by the labour market situation benefit disproportionately from active labour market policy. The concentration of labour market policy measures on contribution payers and individuals eligible for unemployment benefits according to the equivalence principle is one reason why problem regions do not receive greater consideration.

Much the same results emerge when we turn to individual distribution effects. Tax-based systems of active labour market policy in Britain, Sweden, and the United States usually succeed in concentrating benefits on problem groups or at least in giving equal consideration to problem groups among those benefiting from the measures. In West Germany, by contrast, disadvantaged groups in the labour market tend to be under-represented in active labour market policy due to the equivalence principle.

5.   FIGHTING UNEMPLOYMENT BY REDUCING INSTITUTIONAL INCONGRUITIES

Our analysis has indicated that different political responses to mass unemployment can in part be explained with reference to different financing systems of labour market policy. Moreover, relationships between financing systems and the allocative and distributive effects of labour market policy have been identified. This result, however, should not be misunderstood as a scientifically established deterministic pattern. Financing rules and the organisational structures within which they are embedded do not have any direct effects. Rather, their effect is dependent upon objective and subjective configurations: technological, economic, and demographic initial conditions; the cognitive and normative orientations of individuals dealing with these institutions; experience passed on over generations and learning processes. The same formal structure may give rise to different effects under different configurations. Financing institutions are filters, and it is easier to predict what will not go through than what will actually come out at the end. Financing institutions thus share the ambivalent status of other institutions. They are necessary, but by no means sufficient conditions for the realisation of societal goals.

With these caveats in mind, the results of our international comparison may be used to explain failures or achievements of labour market policy in the context of specific institutional and political configurations. In the concluding section, we shall, for illustrative purposes, focus on the West German case and use our comparative results to look for clues as to how to solve the institutional incongruities that we consider partly responsible for the misallocation of resources and for the lukewarm employment policy in West Germany. We start with a summary of our diagnosis and then develop suggestions on how to fight unemployment by reducing institutional incongruities.

(1) *Institutional incongruity* in the West German financing system can be observed in two distinct, though related, aspects. On the one hand, the diminished budget burden resulting from a reduction in unemployment does not entirely accrue to those institutions that are responsible for active policy spending and the corresponding budget burden. This may be labelled the *fiscal incongruity* of the West German financing system. On the other hand, the largely contribution-based financing of active labour market policy does not correspond with the external effects going beyond the circle of contribution payers that a greater use of this policy would entail; this phenomenon may be called the *social incongruity* of the West German financing system of labour market policy. Both incongruities have repercussions in the political arena.

Among the countries included in our comparative study, the case of Sweden illustrates the institutional preconditions for an offensive use of active labour market policy. Swedish labour market policy could not have fulfilled its employment policy function had it been financed through contributions rather than the state budget. Contribution systems always presuppose an equivalent (individual or group-specific) relationship between contributions and benefits that is no longer given once the system is made to serve general employment policy objectives (not concentrated on contribution payers) - such as large-scale temporary public job programmes or job guarantees for teenagers and the long-term unemployed.

This is also confirmed by Austrian labour market policy. With its contribution-supported financing system, that permits neither long-term deficits nor surpluses and is in effect much like a levy system, labour market policy was not in a position to serve employment policy purposes since any spending growth would have led to contribution rate increases and thus met the resistance of contribution payers.

In West Germany, labour market policy is also financed in principle through contributions (to the Federal Employment Institute). However, this financing system is somewhat more flexible than Austria's. Surpluses, for example, may be used to build up reserves to be depleted again in harder times. The federal government is legally responsible for covering any deficits. It had been assumed that this situation would arise only under exceptional circumstances and on a modest scale, but since 1974 this assumption no longer corresponds to reality. The huge gaps in the Federal Employment Institute's budget during both recessions (1974/5, 1981/2) resulted in budget cuts at the expense of active labour market policy.

In an institutional framework, in which both types of expenditure - unemployment compensations as well as pay for jobs or training - are covered by the same fund, there will be an inherent tendency of crowding out in favour of unemployment compensation. As long as policy makers have to stick to this arrangement, the following measure would offer a solution. Since most programmes of active labour market policy are of the 'public good' type, i.e. they result in external effects that go far beyond the circle of contribution payers, partial funding by the central government budget - e.g. through regular federal subsidies to the Federal Employment Institute - could help to avoid the crowding out of active labour market policy by unemployment benefits that are deemed to be priority (for a somewhat different but comparable proposal cf. Mertens, 1981).

(2) By the same token, the vertical and horizontal fragmentation of financing institutions may impede or at least retard an offensive labour market policy, if spending responsibility and the financial repercussions of measures are disjointed. Active labour market policy, instead of accepting unemployment, presupposes that labour market programmes can largely be financed through funds that otherwise would have to be expended on unemployment benefits. In West Germany, however, this precondition is only partly fulfilled. Expenditures on active labour market policy measures are, to a large extent, outweighed by the fiscal costs of unemployment that would otherwise arise as a result of programme participants being unemployed (wage compensation and other social benefits, revenue losses on taxes and social insurance contributions) so that the net costs (additional costs) of successful labour market programmes are significantly lower than their gross costs. The reduced budget strain as a result of such programmes successfully lowering

unemployment, however, does not in all cases benefit those institutions responsible for active programme spending; frequently the benefit accrues in large part to institutions not involved in active labour market policy.

While in Sweden, for example, positive and negative budget effects largely occur in the same fiscal institutions, this does not apply in Austria and the United States. In West Germany an obvious incongruity between negative and positive budget effects can be seen with respect to temporary public job creation measures: programme expenditure by municipalities - which are the most important agencies for such measures and on whose initiative their success depends - are offset to only a relatively modest extent by positive budget effects; at the same time other institutions that do not shoulder any or hardly any share of the costs of such programmes realise a financial benefit (i.e., the federal government, the *Länder* (states), pension and health insurance funds). The incongruity between positive and negative financial effects, on the other hand, is less pronounced with respect to further training and retraining measures as well as short-time working. Both positive and negative budget effects for the most part arise for the same institutions (and in roughly the same proportion); only in the case of the Federal Employment Institute does the (significant) reduction in its budget burden not fully make up for its gross expenditure.

At this point we can again note some possible remedies for this kind of 'fiscal incongruity':

- A technical solution would be the establishment of an integrated labour market budget in which the costs and benefits of each programme are calculated at the end of a fiscal year; the programme budget would serve as a guideline for an *ex-post* horizontal and vertical fiscal equalisation between net payers and net recipients of financial programme effects. The basic problem with such a fiscalised 'programme tableau' is the difficulty of assessing the real employment impact of each programme which would be necessary to calculate the fiscal effects on the different state and parafiscal budgets of the programmes. These effects are often spread over longer time horizons than fiscal or calendar years; the longer the time horizon, however, the greater the uncertainty surrounding the allocation of specific effects to specific budgets.
- A variant to the above-mentioned proposal would be the establishment of 'joint employment ventures' at the local or regional level which are financed *ex ante* by the prospective shares of fiscal benefits from the

envisaged job promotion measures. Such 'joint ventures' are a worthwile area for experimentation. They are, however, only likely to function if a central institution (e.g. a State Government or the Federal Government or the Federal Bank for Reconstruction and Development (Kreditanstalt für Wiederaufbau)) provides a fall-back guarantee in case the expected employment effects and the consequent fiscal benefits are not realised.

(3) The scepticism concerning such solutions to the problem of fiscal incongruity leads us back to more general suggestions:

Part of the solution would be the already-mentioned regulation of federal subsidies to the Federal Employment Institute. This regulation could stipulate that a certain proportion, e.g. one third, of expenditures for job and/or training promotion be covered by the federal budget (i.e. by taxation or borrowing). The legitimation for a fixed proportion of financing from the central state budget can easily be developed for each of the main instruments of active labour market policy. To take recurrent labour market training as an example: if it is true that the diffusion and character of new technologies (in conjunction with the aging population and increasing international interdependency) require general rather than specific skills, then there is no reason why this type of generalised skill acquisition should not be financed in the same way as elementary, high school or public university training. In addition, as our analysis has shown, the direction of training measures toward the disadvantaged or most strongly affected groups and regions would be easier if the government (i.e. the central state budget) assumes a substantial share in financing since pure contribution systems are inherently ill-suited for redistributive policy functions.

- The change of fiscal regulation could also be concentrated on certain programmes of active labour market policy that are especially prone to external effects or redistributive aims, e.g. temporary public job-creation programmes. These programmes - which usually focus on the long-term unemployed whose benefit entitlements have been exhausted (or substantially diminished) and on regions with exceptionally high unemployment rates - could be financed exclusively out of the general state budget (like in Sweden). This suggestion gains credence under two further considerations:

(a) Temporary public job creation is especially suitable as an element of anticyclical employment policy. The effect of such a policy, again, is felt by the whole economy and not only by the dependent active labour force (which presently constitutes the contributors to the Federal Employment Institute).

(b) Trade unions are always extremely suspicious of the substitution effects which are often related to temporary public job creation measures. Such effects arise when municipalities or non-profit organisations shift regular employment (financed totally or substantially by taxes) to non-regular public job programmes (financed by contributions). Trade unions, therefore, have often resisted a further expansion of temporary public work (the poor conditions of employment often associated with these programmes being another reason for their sceptical attitude toward these measures). They would no longer be so concerned about such a substitution effect, if temporary public job programmes were financed out of the general state budget.

- A proposal that could be implemented quite easily would be an obligation on the part of the Federal Government to cover a financial share of the administrative costs of an active labour market policy. This proposal is of special value (a) for regional employment agencies faced with extremely high and rapidly rising unemployment as they have little scope to implement active labour market policy because their staff are occupied with the administration of unemployment benefit; and (b) in the case of special programmes launched by the government that require additional personnel resources in order to be implemented. Austria and Sweden are cases in which this institutional arrangement has already been realised.

(4) So far our suggestions for solving the problem of incongruity have only been concerned with the possibility of shifting or redistributing the financial flows to equalise the cost-benefit balance of fragmented budgets *ex post*. We have not yet considered the alternative of changing the political decision-making structure, i.e. the political responsibilities for full employment policy. Our comparative analysis of the decision-making processes in budgeting labour market policy has shown that the Swedish equivalent to the Federal Employment Institute (Bundesanstalt für Arbeit, BA) - Arbetsmarknadsstyrelsen (AMS) - has both *de jure* and *de facto* an important influence in the formulation process of the annual labour market budget. In contrast to this, real co-determination of the BA in the

budgeting process has declined since the mid-1970s, with the federal government gaining increased influence over the BA's budget (Bruche and Reissert, 1985, pp. 58-72). In particular, the BA cannot prevent the federal government from instrumentalising the BA's budget in order to consolidate its own budget (as happened in 1975, 1982 and 1989).

If, however, the full employment goal were more firmly institutionalised, then it would only be natural to think of an improved status of the BA in the decision-making process of the labour market budget. Such an upgrading would have the favourable side-effect of strengthening and reviving the tripartite structure of the BA's internal decision processes. The regulatory revision of the decision structure could range from minor changes to the creation of an autonomous status of the BA analogous to that of the Bundesbank; in the latter case, the BA would take over responsibility for full employment just as the Bundesbank is responsible for price stability.

For reasons of space we must refrain from discussing the conditions and consequences of such a fundamental change here. However, two suggestions concerning relatively minor changes seem appropriate at this stage:

-   The local (Arbeitsämter) and regional (Landesarbeitsämter) units of the BA should be *de facto* more closely involved in the formulation process of the annual labour market budget and should have regional budgets for active labour market policy over which they can decide discretionally.
-   The BA should have a right of veto if the federal government imposes tasks or new programmes whose financial implications evidently restrict the regular (legal) tasks of the BA. Such a veto might be subject to a qualified parliamentary majority, e.g. of two-thirds. A case for such a veto would have been the recent decision of the federal government that the Federal Employment Institute has to take over the costs of language training for refugees and immigrants of German origin (*Aussiedler*).

(5) We started our analysis by emphasising the preselection impacts and auto-dynamics of institutions. We have provided empirical evidence for this from different perspectives. A final piece of evidence may be mentioned in passing. Although the verbal and programmatic differences with respect to labour market policy between the major political parties in West Germany are significant, their actual practice has so far been similar. This discrepancy may be accounted for by the fact that politicians

(like the rest of us) are prisoners of institutions whose Janus-faced character is evident: on the one hand, institutions save us from imprudent experiments, insure the development of stable mutual expectations and of continuous and gradual learning processes; on the other hand, they disqualify - both in theory and in practice - alternative conceptions. What are the chances - to conclude with a thought experiment - of achieving a breakthrough for a real 'active' labour market policy analogous to (but not a copy of) the Swedish model?

The overwhelming view is that the institutional barriers mentioned above are not so high as to prevent a government and a parliamentary majority from making such a change if the necessary political will is there. That this road was not followed when, for example, the Social-Democratic-Liberal government was in power

was surely related to the fixation of all employment policy thinking on the instruments of economic and financial policy. Even labour market policy actors considered the 1967 Stability and Growth Act rather than the 1969 Employment Promotion Act to be the 'relevant' legislation in the fight against mass unemployment (cf. Kühl, 1982), and particularly those Social Democrats and union officials who were especially committed to employment policy saw labour market instruments at best as a measure of socio-political relief, but not as an instrument for fighting unemployment (Scharpf, 1987, p. 289).

What was missing therefore was the political will since the responsible politicians were not convinced that the model of active labour market policy was a necessary element of a full-employment programme.

Political will is thus certainly a crucial factor. But is it only persuasion that is needed to create the requisite political will? The present analysis suggests that the institutional barriers to a full-employment policy which is more strongly supported by active labour market policy are more serious than the arguments quoted above suggest. As long as an active labour market policy with independent employment policy functions is financed only through the contributions to the Federal Employment Institute (which, for example, does not include the self-employed and tenured civil servants), the necessary broad support from the unions and the work-force as a whole ('the insiders') can probably not be secured since they would be assuming the lion's share of the burden without being the sole beneficiaries. An offensive turn in active labour market policy, therefore, would require reforms in the direction we have suggested.

REFERENCES

Bruche, G. and Reissert, B., *Die Finanzierung der Arbeitsmarktpolitik*, Frankfurt/New York, Campus, 1985.

Burtless, G., 'Jobless Pay and High European Unemployment', in R.Z. Lawrence and Ch. L. Schultze (eds.), *Barriers to European Growth. A Transatlantic View*, Washington, The Brookings Institution, 1987, pp. 105-62.

Casey, B. and Bruche, G., *Work or Retirement? Labour Market and Social Policy Measures for Older Workers in France, Great Britain, the Netherlands, Sweden and the USA*, Aldershot, Gower, 1983.

Clark, K.B. and Summers, L.H., 'Unemployment Insurance and Labor Market Transitions', in M.N. Baily (ed.), *Workers, Jobs, and Inflation*, Washington, D.C., Brookings Institution, 1982, pp. 279-323.

Commons, J.R., *Institutional Economics. Its Place in Political Economy*, Madison, Wisc., University of Wisconsin Press (first ed. 1934), 1959.

Disney, R., 'The Regional Impact of Unemployment Insurance in the United Kingdom', *Oxford Bulletin of Economics and Statistics*, 46, 1984.

Emerson, M., 'Regulation or Deregulation of the Labour Market: Policy Regimes for the Recruitment and Dismissal of Employees in the Industrialized Countries', *European Economic Review*, 32, 4, 1988.

Freeman, R.B., 'Labor Market Institutions, Constraints, and Performances', *Working Paper No. 2560*, Cambridge, MA, National Bureau of Economic Research, 1988.

Hamermesh, D.S., 'Entitlement Effects, Unemployment Insurance and Employment Decisions', *Economic Inquiry*, 17, 1979.

Kühl, J., 'Das Arbeitsförderungsgesetz (AFG) von 1969. Grundzüge seiner arbeitsmarkt- und beschäftigungspolitischen Konzeption', *Mitteilungen aus der Arbeitsmarkt- und Berufsforschung*, 15, 3, 1982.

Mertens, D., 'Haushaltsprobleme und Arbeitsmarktpolitik', *Aus Politik und Zeitgeschichte*, No. 38, 1981.

Scharpf, F.W., *Sozialdemokratische Krisenpolitik in Europa*, Frankfurt/New York, Campus, 1987.

Scharpf, F.W., 'A Game-Theoretical Interpretation of Inflation and Unemployment in Western Europe', *Journal of Public Policy*, 7, 3, 1987.

Schmid, G. and Reissert, B., 'Do Institutions Make a Difference? Financing Systems of Labour Market Policy', *Journal of Public Policy*, 8, 2, 1988.

Schmid, G., Reissert, B. and Bruche, G., *Arbeitslosenversicherung und aktive Arbeitsmarktpolitik. Finanzierungssysteme im internationalen Vergleich*, Berlin, Edition Sigma, 1987.

Schmid, G., Reissert, B. and Bruche, G., *Unemployment Insurance and Active Labour Market Policy - An International Comparison of Financing Systems*, Dertroit, Wayne State University Press, 1991.

Soskice, D., 'Reinterpreting Corporatism and Explaining Unemployment. Coordinated and Non-Coordinated Market Economies', in R. Brunetta and C. della Ringa (eds.), *Markets, Institutions and Cooperation. Labour Relations and Economic Performance*, London, Macmillan, 1990.

5. Does (De-)Regulation Matter? Employment Protection in West Germany

Christoph F. Büchtemann

1. 'EURO-SCLEROSIS', EMPLOYMENT PROTECTION AND TEMPORARY WORK

In the current debate on labour market flexibility and 'institutional rigidities' a great deal of attention has been given to employment protection and job security regulations (OECD, 1986; OECD, 1989). Under the heading of 'Euro-sclerosis', legal employment protection regulations as well as collectively bargained job security provisions, introduced and expanded during the 1960s and early 1970s, have come to be widely regarded as rigidities hampering employment adjustment, increasing labour costs, and thus accounting, at least in part, for persistently high levels of unemployment in most Western European countries:

- by slowing down workforce reductions in times of declining labour demand, lay-off restraints such as legally imposed prenotification periods, redundancy procedures and collectively bargained severance payments have been assumed which reduce the willingness of firms to hire additional workers when the economy recovers, thus having a depressing effect on the overall level of employment over the cycle;
- moreover, by imposing restraints on individual dismissals employment protection regulations are said to induce firms to increase selectivity and to intensify worker-screening when filling vacancies, thus promoting tendencies towards a progressive segmentation between 'outsiders' and 'insiders' in the labour market as manifested in the relative increase in long-term unemployment in most Western European countries;

- finally, as a way to evade legal and collective bargained dismissal restraints, firms are assumed increasingly to resort to temporary work and subcontracting instead of hiring additional regular staff, thus promoting the growth of an 'unprotected sector', - a development that in the medium term may result in a 'two-tier society':

> one with rigid job security requirements covering high-paid, senior full-time workers in large firms, the other more flexible, with part-time, low-paid, insecure workers in small businesses (Hamermesh, 1988, p. 22).

Consequently a relaxation, if not partial abolition, of existing employment protection regulations has gained high priority on the agenda of a direct de-regulation of labour relations as a way to stimulate employment growth and to combat European unemployment. The attention these notions have received from both academics and policy makers in the current European debate on employment policy is, however, strongly contrasted by the relative absence of firm empirical evidence to support them. Most recent reviews, indeed, have concluded that 'the empirical evidence on the impact of job security policies is fragmentary at best' (OECD, 1986, p.92) and that at present it is therefore best to 'remain agnostic on this question' (Layard and Nickell, 1985; see also Franz, 1989).

Ironically, the current European debate on the allegedly detrimental effects of job security on job creation has been conducted with a strong reference to the 'American job miracle'. This is contrasted by the debate in the US, where policy advisers have recently emphasised the beneficial effects of employment protection on worker productivity and on adjustment to technological change, and, consequently, have advocated the introduction of basic job security provisions such as advance notification periods for plant closures (cf. Rosow and Zager, 1984). Recent developments in US legislation, court decisions and collective bargaining have in fact introduced significant deviations from the (still) prevailing doctrine of 'employment at will' (cf. Gould, 1987; Mendelsohn, 1989).

Despite this, since the beginning of the 1980s, many Western European governments (UK, Germany, France, Italy and Spain) have introduced legislative changes relaxing legal standards with regard to redundancy and dismissal protection and/or widened existing 'loopholes' within the established systems of employment protection, e.g. by facilitating the conclusion of fixed-term contracts or reducing legal restrictions on the use of temporary workers hired from agencies (cf. Emerson, 1988).

In 1985, the conservative government in West Germany passed the 'Employment Promotion Act 1985' (*Beschäftigungsförderungsgesetz 1985*), henceforth referred to as the EPA, which - apart from introducing new regulations in the area of part-time work and job sharing - has brought a relaxation of employment protection regulations for newly-established small enterprises by partly exempting such enterprises from the obligation to set up a 'social plan' in the case of major workforce reductions or production reorganisations and by changing the mode of calculation of the minimum number of employees required for the application of protection against dismissal under the 'Dismissal Protection Act' (*Kündigungsschutzgesetz*) of 1951. The EPA has prolonged the maximum period for the use of agency workers from three to six months, and has reduced legal restraints on the conclusion of fixed-term contracts. Of these innovations the relaxation of legal restraints on the conclusion of fixed-term contracts has certainly been both the most important and the most controversial. By this measure, which was initially designed to be in force for a limited period (1985-1990) only and which was recently prolonged for another six years until the end of 1995, the government hoped to exert a positive impact on the hiring decisions of firms in the face of persisting uncertainties about future labour demand. The facilitation of fixed-term contracts by the EPA can thus be regarded as a political compromise between the supporters of a more thorough 'de-regulation' of employment protection, on the one hand, and the opponents of 'de-regulation', headed by the unions, who are interested in maintaining a high degree of protection for their (employed) clientèle, on the other hand. In anticipation of the expiration of the new regulations on temporary work in early 1990, the West German government commissioned a comprehensive empirical evaluation study of the impact of the new temporary work legislation introduced by the EPA on the hiring decisions and manpower policies.[1]

2. THE REGULATORY CONTEXT: EMPLOYMENT PROTECTION AND LEGAL REGULATION OF TEMPORARY WORK IN WEST GERMANY

Both the legislative changes brought about by the EPA and their impact on the manpower policies of firms have to be seen in the wider context of the particular institutional framework of the West German labour market and the historically evolved system of legal and collective employment protection.

Employment Protection Regulations

From an international comparative perspective Germany must certainly be considered a country with an elaborate system of employment protection. In a recent survey conducted by the International Organisation of Employers Germany ranked in second place (after France) among those countries in which the legal obstacles to the termination of employment contracts are classified as 'fundamental' (cf. Emerson, 1988, p. 791).

Employment protection in Germany (see Figure 5.1) is regulated by legislation, court decisions, and collective agreements and covers the vast majority of the workforce. Apart from seniority-based advance notification periods laid down by the Civil Code (*Bürgerliches Gesetzbuch*) and extended by collective agreements, essentially *statutory* employment protection has been regulated through the West German 'Dismissal Protection Act' (*Kündigungsschutzgesetz*) of 1951 as amended in 1969, which covers all workers permanently employed for more than six months in establishments with at least six employees (excluding apprentices), i.e. roughly 80 per cent of the total dependent workforce. The core regulations of the Act require all dismissals to be justified by 'just cause'.[2] In the case of dismissals for economic reasons 'just cause' implies that redundancies cannot be prevented through work sharing (*Kurzarbeit*), retraining or reassignment of the workers affected. For collective redundancies the law further requires the redundant workers to be selected according to 'social criteria', such as seniority, personal economic situation, and individual reemployment prospects.

In addition to this legislation, West German labour courts have established relatively strict rules concerning individual dismissals for personal reasons, especially those on grounds of bad health and/or frequent absenteeism. As a rule, both law and court decisions require the employer to undertake all reasonable efforts to avoid job terminations. In case of unjustified dismissals or violations of procedural rules prescribed by the Act the worker may sue for reinstatement through the labour court. However, in most cases this results in monetary compensation rather than in actual reinstatement.

Figure 5.1 Range of Employment Protection Provisions in West Germany, 1987/1988

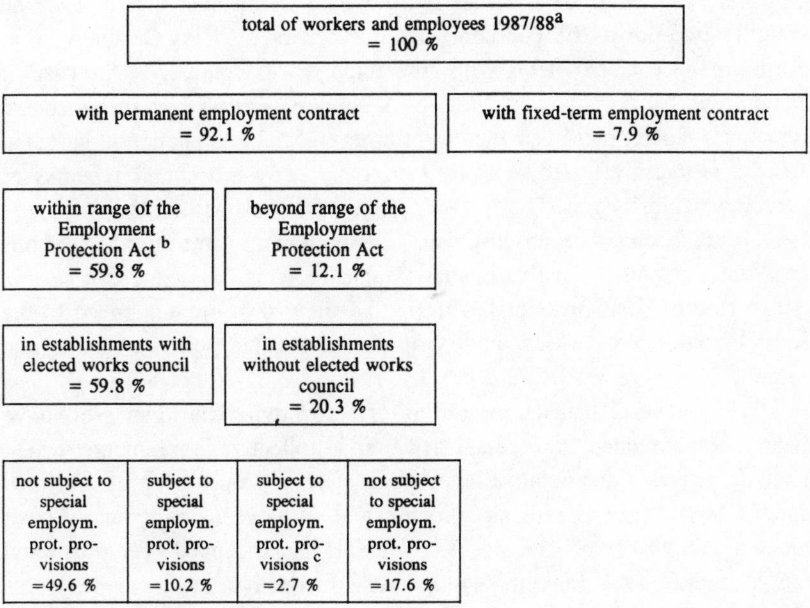

total of workers and employees 1987/88[a]
= 100 %

with permanent employment contract	with fixed-term employment contract
= 92.1 %	= 7.9 %

within range of the Employment Protection Act [b] = 59.8 %	beyond range of the Employment Protection Act = 12.1 %

in establishments with elected works council = 59.8 %	in establishments without elected works council = 20.3 %

not subject to special employm. prot. provisions =49.6 %	subject to special employm. prot. provisions =10.2 %	subject to special employm. prot. provisions [c] =2.7 %	not subject to special employm. prot. provisions =17.6 %

a   Excluding public servants, military personnel, and apprentices (n = 4.930).
b   Establishments employing at least six workers on a regular basis and with tenure exceeding six months.
c   45 years or older and at least 20 years of tenure with present employer or disabled under the Disabled Workers Act (*Schwerstbehindertengesetz*).

Source: *Representative telephone survey 1987/88.*

Employment protection in West Germany also has a strong *collective* component: Under the 'Works Council Act' (*Betriebsverfassungsgesetz*) as amended in 1972 all dismissals have to be approved by the works council. In case of disapproval, the employment relationship automatically continues until a labour court has decided whether or not the dismissal is justified. The range of this rule is illustrated by the fact that in 1987/88 roughly two-thirds (68 per cent) of all workers in West Germany were employed in establishments with an elected works council. In the case of major workforce reductions the works councils are further authorised to demand a 'social plan' designed to minimise social and economic hardship for the workers affected, e.g. by setting up early retirement schemes or granting seniority-graded severance payments, an institution which has been in the focus of recent criticism of employment protection regulations in West Germany. Finally, if unavoidable redundancies exceed a certain proportion of the firms' total workforce,[3] they must be announced to the local labour office, which may postpone them for a period of up to one month.

These general restrictions on lay-offs and individual dismissals have been complemented by special laws and collective agreements which exclude ordinary dismissals altogether for certain groups of workers. Such special laws apply to pregnant women and employees on parental leave, elected members of the works council, handicapped persons, and employees drafted for military service. Collective master agreements (*Manteltarifverträge*) in some industries also exclude ordinary dismissals for older workers after reaching a certain minimum tenure (of 15 or 20 years). Since the beginning of the 1980s such agreements have been in force in various industries representing 55 per cent to 60 per cent of all dependently employed workers (cf. Warnken and Ronning, 1990). In total it is estimated that in 1985 ordinary dismissal was excluded through collective agreements for more than 2.5 million workers (excluding public servants) or more than 13 per cent of the total dependent labour force in West Germany. In addition, West Germany's 1.6 million civil servants (some 7 per cent of the dependent labour force) enjoy guaranteed life-time employment. The number of workers enjoying absolute protection against ordinary dismissals thus amounts to 4.2 million or more than 20 per cent of the total dependent workforce.

The picture would, however, be incomplete without mentioning West Germany's relatively generous, insurance-based 'work-sharing scheme' (*Kurzarbeit*) which acts as an important public subsidy for the labour hoarding strategies of firms. The importance of the scheme is illustrated by the fact that even during the rather prosperous two-year period from

May 1985 to April 1987 more than 11 per cent of all firms in the private sector, representing roughly 20 per cent of all workers in private industry, temporarily introduced short-time work for economic reasons. Finally, it has to be taken into account that West Germany's various publicly-financed early retirement schemes have created selective 'outlets' offering a way of circumventing the relatively strict employment protection regulations applying to the majority of older workers; in West Germany roughly one-third of all persons entering retirement at the age of 55 or older in fact do so through special early retirement schemes ('59-rule' or *Vorruhestandsgesetz*).

Temporary Work Contracts Prior to and Since the EPA

The outline given above shows that both labour law and collective agreements have imposed substantial restrictions on the freedom of West German firms to dismiss workers for economic and non-economic reasons. From the point of view of radical supply-side economics it is logical to assume that temporary and fixed-term employment arrangements would be highly attractive to firms as a way of evading dismissal restraints which apply in the case of permanent work contracts (cf. Walter, 1988; Lazear, 1988).

This assumption seems to underlie not only the fears expressed by unions that the facilitation of temporary employment arrangements by the EPA would induce employers to resort to 'hire-and-fire' personnel strategies, it has also been the assumption underlying rulings on temporary work by the Federal Labour Court (*Bundesarbeitsgericht*), which - in the absence of any explicit legislative regulation of temporary work - has developed, since the early 1960s, a comprehensive set of norms and standards for the conclusion of fixed-term employment contracts with the aim of preventing an evasion of statutory employment protection regulations. Thus, court decisions have restricted the conclusion of fixed-term contracts for periods exceeding six months to a set of clearly defined 'legitimate' cases, such as seasonal work, replacement of temporarily absent permanent employees, temporary help in periods of peak demand, the carrying out of special tasks which are temporary in nature, and employment in the context of trainee programmes or public job-creation schemes. On the other hand, the Federal Labour Court has strictly ruled out economic uncertainty about future labour demand as a 'legitimate reason' for hiring workers on a temporary basis. In such cases, fixed-term contracts would be disallowed and treated as permanent contracts, i.e. involving all legal obligations concerning protection from unfair dismissal and redundancy.

These judicial restrictions on the conclusion of fixed-term contracts have been largely suspended by the EPA. By abolishing the requirement of a 'legitimate reason' for the conclusion of fixed-term contracts up to a maximum duration of 18 months, or 24 months in the case of new enterprises employing not more 20 workers, the government has explicitly legalised fixed-term contracts in case of uncertainty about future labour demand, hoping that firms would thereby be induced to substitute additionally hired workers for overtime hours of their core workforce. In fact, the abolition of the requirement of a 'legitimate reason' amounts to a *carte blanche* for all kinds of uses of fixed-term contracts, which would have been considered illegal prior to the EPA (e.g. the prolonged probation of new recruits beyond legal probationary periods).

Given the relative restrictiveness of both West German employment protection and the rules set up for temporary employment contracts by the Federal Labour Court prior to the EPA one might expect the EPA's new regulations to have had an enormous impact on the hiring and personnel practices of firms - a widely shared expectation which (ironically) fed both the hopes of its proponents and the fears of its critics.

3. EMPIRICAL RESULTS: IMPACT OF THE EMPLOYMENT PROMOTION ACT ON THE HIRING STRATEGIES OF FIRMS

Despite fears expressed by the unions that the EPA would cause an 'erosion' of the hitherto dominant standard employment relationship, the overwhelming majority (92 per cent) of the West German workforce is in fact still employed in more or less long-term, permanent jobs. In 1987/88 only a minority of less than 8 per cent (or 1 450 000)[4] of all workers were employed on a fixed-term basis. During recent years, however, fixed-term employment in West Germany and in most other Western European countries has shown a considerable increase in both absolute and relative terms. Between 1984 and 1988 the number of workers employed on fixed-term contracts had grown by more than 350 000 or 46 per cent, whereas the number of permanent employees had increased but at a much slower pace (+442 000 or 2.4 per cent). Indeed, more than 44 per cent of the overall increase in dependent employment over the period 1984-1988 took place in the form of temporary, i.e. fixed-term jobs. However, as shown in Table 5.1, this increase in fixed-term employment took place largely between 1984 and 1985, i.e. before the new regulations of the EPA came into force, indicating that the increase in temporary work has been strongly influenced by factors other than changes in the regulatory framework, such as cyclical variations in labour demand and medium-term *structural* changes of both labour supply and labour demand. The implications of this trend for labour market dynamics become apparent when the perspective is shifted from stocks to flows in the labour market. Under present labour market conditions, roughly 45 per cent of all newly-hired workers (36 per cent in private industry and more than 50 per cent in the public sector) in fact start their job with a fixed-term employment contract, similarly roughly one out of five job terminations is due to the expiration of a fixed-term employment contract.[5]

Table 5.1   Workers on Fixed-term Employment Contracts in West Germany, 1984-1988 (in 000 and %)

	1984 (EEC-LFSS)	1985 (MZ)	1986 (MZ)	1987 (MZ)	1988 (MZ)
Workforce[a] (in 000) total	19 375.1[b] = 100.0 %	19 577.6 = 100.0 %	19 979.8 = 100.0 %	19 948.7 = 100.0 %	20 389.9[c] = 100.0 %
of which:					
* on permanent working contract (incl. 80 000 agency workers)	18 461.8[b] 95.3 %	18 224.0 93.2 %	18 423.3 92.2 %	18 612.2 93.3 %	18 903.7[c] 92.7 %
* on fixed-term contract (incl. on public job creation programmes)	765.8[b] 4.0 %[d]	1 080.8 5.6 %[d]	1 230.2 6.3 %[d]	1 105.0 5.6 %[d]	1 119.2[c] 5.6 %[d]
* type of employment contract not specified	148.5 0.8 %	272.8 1.4 %	326.3 1.6 %	231.5 1.2 %	367.0 1.8 %

a Excl. public servants, apprentices, and persons on compulsory military/community service.
b Estimated.
c Preliminary data.
d Proportion of fixed-term workers in all workers with specification of type of employment.

Source: *Federal Statistical Office, EEC Labour Force Sample Survey, 1984; Mikrozensus (MZ), 1985, 1986, 1987, 1988; special tabulations at the author's request.*

The Use of Fixed-term Contracts by Firms

Despite the large proportion of fixed-term engagements among all new jobs, fixed-term employment is still largely concentrated within a small proportion of all firms in the private sector. In fact, two out of three (67 per cent) firms in the private sector were found to have made no use of fixed-term employment contracts in the first two years following the introduction of the new EPA regulations (although the majority of these firms - 80 per cent - had hired workers during the observation period). This group of non-user firms largely consisted of small and medium-sized enterprises (employing on average 23 workers) with a rather skilled workforce, low fluctuation of product demand and low worker turnover. The primary reason for not using temporary work contracts given by these firms was that they were 'exclusively interested in stable, long-term employment relationships'. While other reasons were hardly mentioned at all, this reason was given by 83 per cent of the non-users, representing roughly 50 per cent of all enterprises, and accounting for one-third of the total labour force in the private sector.

The remaining third of all enterprises in the private sector that did make use of fixed-term contracts has to be divided into two contrasting subgroups according to the intensity of their use of fixed-term contracts:

- more than half of these firms (or 19 per cent of all firms in the private sector) could be classified as selective or moderate users of fixed-term contracts, i.e. the large majority (74 per cent) of their new recruits were still hired on a permanent basis. This group of moderate users predominantly consists of medium-sized and larger enterprises in the manufacturing sector employing, on average, 121 workers and accounting for roughly 40 per cent of all new hires in private industry. These firms are characterised by relatively highly skilled workforces, which on average showed a clear expansionary trend over the period 1985-1987;
- the other half of the user-firms fall into the category of intensive users, hiring on average more than 74 per cent of their new recruits on·fixed-term contracts. This group, by contrast, largely consists of smaller enterprises (90 per cent do not employ more than 50 workers) and is subject to relatively strong fluctuations in demand due to irregular orders and high worker turnover, and is further characterised by both a relatively high share of wage costs in total production costs and a clearly negative employment performance between 1985 and 1987. Altogether these firms make up only 17 per

cent of all enterprises in the private sector, but account for not less than 32 per cent of all new hires and 70 per cent of all fixed-term contracts concluded in private industry since 1985.

Thus, fixed-term job arrangements can be shown to be highly concentrated within a small group of firms making more or less substantial use of them. Moreover, fixed-term contracts are not only concentrated within a small segment of firms in the private sector, but also within certain job categories. As might be expected from human capital theory (cf. Abraham, 1988), the majority of temporary jobs in the private sector require neither vocational skills nor any on-the-job training. In fact, more than 70 per cent of all personnel hired on fixed-term contracts are unskilled workers, who, under present labour market conditions, have a less than 50 per cent chance of being hired on a permanent basis. By contrast, skilled workers are still in most cases (80 per cent) hired on permanent contracts, reflecting the strong interest of firms to keep these workers for longer periods and to avoid voluntary notice being given.

Changes in the Recruitment Behaviour of Firms since 1985

With regard to the evaluation of the EPA, a strong focus of our research has been on the question of how and to what extent firms have modified their recruitment behaviour and use of fixed-term contracts since the EPA came into effect. The evidence shows that the majority (78 per cent) of user-firms have actually intensified their use of fixed-term hands (26 per cent) or used fixed-term contracts for the first time (52 per cent) since 1985: the larger part of the overall increase in fixed-term employment, however, falls upon those firms that had already used fixed-term contracts before 1985. Still, it would be erroneous to conclude that this change in recruitment behaviour was predominantly due to the new regulations introduced by the EPA. Rather, our evidence shows that the intensified or first use of fixed-term job arrangements by firms is due to a whole array of heterogeneous factors, such as cyclical demand for temporary help, new working time regimes, increased variation in business activity due to a reduction in product storage and an increase in production by order, of which the legal facilitation of fixed-term contracts through the EPA has played but a subordinate role, if at all.

The relevance of cyclical and structural rather than regulatory factors in accounting for the recent increase in temporary job arrangements is further reaffirmed by the type of fixed-term contracts concluded in the private sector. Of all fixed-term contracts concluded by firms, 93 per cent were found to conform to the rules and criteria set up for fixed-term contracts by the Federal Labour Court long before the EPA came into force. Most of the fixed-term contracts concluded were actually covered by one of the 'legitimate reasons' defined by the rulings of the labour courts (85 per cent) and/or did not exceed six months in duration (70 per cent) up to which there have never been any restrictions on the closing of fixed-term contracts. In total, only 7 per cent of all fixed-term hands (or less than 2 per cent of all new hires) in the private sector did not conform to these criteria and thus have to be considered as 'genuinely' de-regulated contracts closed under the new regulations of the EPA. These contracts were found to be concentrated within a small minority of not more than 4 per cent of all firms employing hardly 10 per cent of all workers in private industry. In contrast to the majority of firms using (traditional) fixed-term contracts, these firms consisted largely of medium-sized and larger enterprises in low-skilled, distributive and service industries such as retail, hotel, catering, transportation, cleaning, body care, and personal services other than health care and education, reporting a high degree of uncertainty about future labour demand. On average, more than 60 per cent of the new recruits of these firms were hired on fixed-term contracts.

The evidence presented so far suggests that the flexibility of firms' needs with respect to temporary job arrangements are met in most cases by the rules and regulations in force prior to the EPA. Only at first sight does this conclusion appear to be contradicted by the finding that a considerable number (26 per cent) of all fixed-term employment contracts in the private sector were formally closed with 'explicit reference' to the new regulations of the EPA. Even in those firms that hired personnel on a fixed-term basis with explicit reference to the EPA, however, 90 per cent of all fixed-term appointments were in fact covered by one of the traditionally accepted 'legitimate reasons' and/or did not exceed six months in duration, i.e. conformed with the more restrictive regulations in force prior to the EPA. The reason why firms nevertheless explicitly referred to the EPA when closing 'traditional' fixed-term contracts has to be seen primarily in the simplification of contractual procedures effected by the EPA (no requirement for a 'legitimate reason' to be mentioned in the contract) and the ensuing reduction in the judicial uncertainties (arbitration risks) of firms.

Firms' Motives for Using Fixed-term Employment Contracts

Firms were also asked to give information about their motives for using fixed-term contracts and the new regulations introduced by the EPA. The answers given show that the prime motive for firms making use of the EPA is the possibility of optimising 'on-the-job' screening of workers without facing dismissal restrictions in the case of inability or misconduct. This motive was classified as 'very important' by one-third of all firms making 'explicit' use of the new regulations. This finding supports the argument recently put forward by Flanagan (1988) that, in the presence of rigid employment protection regulations, the combination of uncertainties about future labour demand and uncertainties about the potential productivity of job applicants may in part explain both European employers' general hesitancy towards hiring additional staff and their intensified screening endeavours when hiring new workers. That employers have intensified their screening endeavours with respect to occupational skills as well as the social qualifications of job candidates was reaffirmed by the anwers given by the 1 968 placement officers surveyed in our study.

The motive of a more flexible adaptation of labour to variations in business activity due to the absence of employment protection was considered 'very important', but rated second by just a quarter of the firms that had made 'explicit' use of the new regulations (representing thus not more than 4.8 per cent of all enterprises in the private sector). The popular notion that many firms would use the new regulations in order to resort to a 'hire-and-fire' personnel strategy appears to have little basis in reality.[6] This conclusion is strongly supported by the finding that a substantial proportion (65 per cent) of all workers initially hired on the basis of the new regulations are subsequently taken over into permanent employment. Thus, it can be concluded that factors other than dismissal protection legislation alone appear to account for the prevalence of long-term employment relationships in West Germany and for the reasons why West German firms reject employment adjustment through high worker turnover.

Even less frequently, firms mentioned the motive of substituting additional hires from the external labour market for overtime work of the core workforce. This motive was classified as 'very important' by only 15 per cent of the user firms or 2.5 per cent of all firms in the private sector. The corridor within which firms are willing and able to substitute additional workers for hours seems to be rather narrow. This last finding has far-reaching implications with respect to the employment effects attributable to the EPA.

Employment Impact of the EPA

In order to assess the immediate employment impact of the new regulations under the EPA we focused on those 7 per cent of all fixed-term contracts in the private sector that would not have been legal under the previous rulings of the Federal Labour Court ('genuine EPA contracts'). Of these (roughly 110 000 fixed-term contracts concluded in private industry each year) only a small proportion not exceeding one in five (21.7 per cent or an estimated 25 000 p.a.) were classified by the firms as 'additional' hands that most probably would not have resulted but for the new regulations of the EPA. Additional fixed-term hires as a result of the EPA thus account for not more than 1.5 per cent of all fixed-term contracts closed by private enterprises, or at best 0.5 per cent of all new hires in the private sector. In line with our other findings, the facilitation of fixed-term contracts has apparently had hardly any positive effect on employers' willingness to take on additional staff. Of the remaining 80 per cent (or roughly 85 000 p.a.) of all fixed-term contracts closed under the new regulations of the EPA, most (75 000), indeed, have to be considered as 'substitution effects', i.e. in these cases the workers hired on a fixed-term basis most probably would otherwise have been given a permanent contract from the beginning. Direct substitution effects of the new regulations thus were found to be three times the volume of direct (gross) employment effects in the sense of additional hirings which (according to the firms) would not have resulted without the EPA. Of course, compared to the hopes and fears expressed in the public debate on the EPA, both effects have to be considered rather marginal due to the fact that the actual use of the new possibilities provided by the EPA has been restricted to a small number of cases (2 per cent of all new hires) and a small minority (4 per cent) of all firms in the private sector.

While a small number of additionally hired hands can be attributed to the EPA, the modest (gross) employment effects resulting from them tend to be largely offset by an increased speed of workforce adjustment in periods of slack demand, arising from the EPA's substitution effects. In the case of fixed-term contracts, firms were found to adjust employment more rapidly to declining demand than they do (or would do) with permanent employment contracts to which dismissal protection regulations apply. This is clearly illustrated by the results of our representative company survey: whereas, on average, two-thirds of all workers hired on the basis of the EPA were subsequently taken over into permanent employment by their firms, this share amounted to not more than 20 per cent in firms with a declining workforce over the observation period. This finding was reaffirmed not only by our in-depth interviews with personnel managers in 30 manufacturing firms but also by the results of our representative panel survey of newly-hired workers: all other things being equal, fixed-term employment arrangements, in fact, were found to imply significantly higher (involuntary) dismissal rates than were observed for workers hired on the basis of a permanent work contract. In total - taking both their positive and their negative employment impacts into consideration - the net employment impact of the new EPA regulations has to be regarded as negligible even under the overall favourable economic conditions prevailing since 1985. However, whether medium or long term, and especially in the case of a major economic downturn this (at best) marginal positive (net) employment effect may well be reversed due to the observed substitution effects and the enhanced risks of job-loss arising from them for the workers affected. Our findings thus support the conclusion drawn by other recent studies, such as the one by Bentolila and Bertola (1988, p. 22), that

a mere reduction in firing costs does not increase a firm's marginal propensity to hire while it strongly raises their willingness to fire.

Similar conclusions were drawn by Elbaum *et al.* (1986) for France, by Burgess (1988) for the UK, by Bayar (1987) for Belgium, and by Björklund and Holmlund (1987) for Sweden.

4. EMPLOYMENT PROMOTION THROUGH LESS EMPLOYMENT PROTECTION?

The empirical evidence reported so far has shown that the widely accepted assumption that a reduction in employment protection through the legal facilitation of temporary employment contracts is likely to result in more employment is ill-founded, at least with regard to West Germany. Moreover, the expectation that the 'liberation' of firms from strict employment protection regulations through the opportunity created by the EPA would have a strong genuine impact on their hiring decisions appears to be unjustified. Evidently, most (West German) firms do not share the notion put forward by radical supply-side economists that an increase in external labour turnover is likely to increase adjustment efficiency. Similarly, our findings are also apt to challenge the EPA's underlying 'diagnosis' that employment protection regulations, by restricting lay-offs and individual dismissals, have a strong deterrent impact upon firms' manpower strategies and hiring decisions of firms.

The question remains: What kind of positive lesson can be learned from the experiment of the West German 'Employment Promotion Act' with respect to the impact of (de-)regulation on the functioning of labour markets and on job creation. A preliminary answer can be given by taking a closer look at the reasons underlying the evident failure of the EPA to modify the employment decisions of firms as intended by the government. These reasons can be analysed at two levels: (a) from a theoretical institutionalist perspective, and (b) from the empirical micro-perspective on the employment and labour market behaviour of firms.

Why the EPA Failed: An Institutionalist Macro-perspective

A general conclusion to be drawn from the evidence summarised above is that focusing merely on single institutions such as employment protection, while neglecting the historically evolved institutional and economic context in which particular institutions and regulations are embedded is likely to result in misleading conclusions about the functioning of 'real' labour markets.

There is no need to emphasise that from an international comparative perspective West Germany certainly has a highly-regulated system of labour relations whose foundations were laid before the second World War and that the system was restored, complemented, and expanded during the 1950s, 1960s and early 1970s. This was a period of extensive economic growth accompanied by an enormous steady increase of both labour supply and labour demand during the 1950s and a succeeding period of nearly uninterrupted full employment and rapid industrial concentration from the beginning of the 1960s until the early 1970s. The basic institutional 'pillars' of this system are:

1. the *dual system of collective representation* with its two complementary components of (a) centralised wage bargaining at sectoral level covering all workers employed by the industry, and (b) decentralised co-determination on recruitment, dismissals, internal mobility, and work organisation at plant and enterprise level through elected works councils;
2. the *dual training system* (apprenticeship) involving alternating periods of 'on-the-job' training and attendance at vocational schools, the standards and curricula of which are regulated and continuously updated

by both the state and the social partners, and which has provided a large proportion of the workforce with broad general as well as specific professional skills; and finally

3. *an elaborate system of federal labour law and social security legislation* which - apart from setting the regulatory framework for collective bargaining and workplace representation - also guarantees a relatively high level of job protection and income security to the vast majority of the dependently employed workforce.

Together with the traditionally strong export orientation of West German industry this triangular institutional framework of the West German labour market largely explains the particular *mode of adjustment* frequently referred to as the 'West German model'. Centralised wage bargaining at industry level, which allows only limited inter-industry wage dispersion, in combination with a federally regulated, insurance-based social security system, has contributed to make West Germany a high-wage economy ranking near the top of Western industrialised countries in terms of labour costs. Moreover, the combination of a strong trend towards large-scale mass production and persistent labour shortages during the 1960s and early 1970s with the expansion of a seniority-based system of legal and collectively bargained safeguards against redundancy and unfair dismissal, and the strengthening of firm-level co-determination rights of the works councils in the late 1960s and the early 1970s has favoured the development and spread of internal labour markets (cf. Lutz, 1987, pp. 185 ff.) which manifest themselves in the prevalence of long-term job attachments and comparatively low, labour-turnover rates.

Within this particular framework of high labour costs, low wage dispersion and internal labour markets, West German enterprises in the export-oriented manufacturing sectors have been forced to maintain competitiveness through productivity increases, by improving product quality, as well as continuous product innovation (see Streeck's contribution to this volume, Chapter 2, above). It goes without saying that this has had various spill-over effects on other sectors of the economy. This adjustment strategy has so far proved successful, not least because West German enterprises have been able to rely on a relatively well-trained labour force as well as ample skilled reserves provided through both the dual training system and the expansion of the educational system as a whole. It has further been supported by the considerable expansion of vocational training and retraining measures within the system of 'active labour market policy' and the provision of relatively generous early retirement schemes which have facilitated necessary external, workforce adjustments within socially acceptable limits.

It is against the background of this historically evolved and institutionally stabilised context and the particular *logic* of adjustment it has produced that the Employment Promotion Act and its evident failure to modify the manpower strategies of firms has to be seen. From this perspective the EPA, with its underlying 'philosophy' of employment promotion through facilitating external labour market adjustments, is seen as a measure running more or less counter to the predominant *logic* of *internal* adjustment characterising large parts of the West German economy. Put in the more general terms of systems theory: minor external impulses alien to its own functional *logic* tend to be either *ignored* or *absorbed* by the economic system. In terms of our empirical evidence this can be illustrated as follows:

- The majority of firms in the private sector were found to make no use of fixed-term contracts at all, contending that they were '*exclusively interested in long-term employment relationships*'; these firms evidently have *ignored* the 'message' of the EPA.
- Of the remaining firms the large majority made use of fixed-term contracts either for more or less 'traditional' reasons such as temporary help, replacement of temporarily absent employees etc., or in order to optimise 'on-the-job' screening of candidates for integration into the core workforce, the latter being expressed by the high proportion of fixed-term workers taken over into permanent employment by these firms at the end of their term.[7] These firms, too, have in most cases ignored the impulse intended by the EPA.
- Only a very small minority of all firms in the private sector have actually made use of the new possibilities introduced by the EPA; in most cases, though, without at the same time modifying their hiring decisions (i.e. hiring more workers). Judging from the information we have on their characteristics, these firms can be assumed to have adhered to an external rather than internal mode of workforce adjustment long before the EPA came into effect. The majority of these firms have merely absorbed the impulse given by the EPA without hiring additional staff as intended by the legislator.

The EPA thus seems to provide a lucid example of policy failure due to what Teubner (1987, pp. 19-20) has termed an unsuccessful 'structural coupling' of policy, law, and the sphere of economic action.

Why the EPA Failed: The Micro-perspective of the Firm

In the preceding paragraphs the failure of the EPA to achieve its designated goal has been explained by the assumption that its rationale - facilitation of external manpower adjustment - runs more or less counter to the historically evolved *logic* of *internal* adjustment characteristic of large parts of the West German economy. This theoretically derived interpretation is strongly supported by a confrontation of the EPA's underlying 'philosophy' about the labour market behaviour of firms with empirical evidence collected at firm level.

First, our evidence gives support to the EPA's underlying notion of a widespread and increased reluctance of employers to take on additional staff. Thus, the overwhelming majority (74 per cent) of all placement officers in the public employment agencies asserted that firms had become altogether more hesitant towards increasing their workforces over the recent past years (1983-1988). This view was reaffirmed by our interviews with personnel managers in private companies: three out of five managers interviewed declared that as a rule hiring additional staff is not taken into consideration by their firms before all other measures of coping with the workload (overtime work, temporary help, contracting out, etc.) have been exhausted (50 per cent) or that their firms were presently exercising a total hiring stop due to (current or expected) excess capacities (10 per cent).

At the same time, however, our empirical findings raise serious doubts as to whether this widespread reluctance to hire can be attributed to 'deterrent' effects of existing employment security provisions and dismissal restraints. In fact, the vast majority (77 per cent) of personnel managers indicated that during the period studied they had been able to carry through (almost) all intended dismissals without incurring major legal difficulties or dismissal costs. Accordingly, only a small minority (27 per cent) of personnel managers, most of whom, as would be expected, reported major ongoing workforce reductions in their companies, attributed some kind of impact on the hiring decisions of their firms with regard to employment protection regulations. The impact mentioned, however, referred in most cases to the *quality* of recruits, i.e. a more careful productivity-oriented selection and screening of job candidates, rather than to the overall *quantity* of new hands. The general finding that firms do not perceive employment protection regulations as serious obstacles to necessary job terminations was found to be all the more true with respect to the *short-term* employment relationships not exceeding 18 months as referred to by the new regulations of the EPA.

According to 88 per cent of the managers interviewed the termination of such short-term jobs does not cause any legal or financial problems for firms at all. This explains why the evasion of legal dismissal restraints was hardly ever mentioned as a motive for firms' making use of the new regulations of the EPA.

Moreover, our micro-evidence also raises serious doubts as to the legislator's assumption that fixed-term hires can be substituted for (overtime) hours of the stable employed workforce. In fact, two out of three of the personnel managers reported significant amounts of overtime work in their firms. However, apart from the cost and flexibility advantages associated with overtime, as compared to hiring more workers, the large majority of personnel managers in these firms did not see any possibility of substituting additional workers for overtime hours of their workforce, the main obstacles to a reduction of overtime being limitations of space and capital equipment, problems in finding skilled workers from the external labour market, prolonged periods of 'on-the-job' training for newly-hired workers, and a high degree of irregularity of excess workloads over time as well as across different work areas within the firm. As the bulk of overtime hours falls upon the skilled sections of the workforce, additional hirings on fixed-term contracts could hardly function as a viable alternative to overtime work. Apart from the considerable reluctance of skilled workers to accept fixed-term contracts, firms, especially when hiring skilled labour, tend to be more or less exclusively interested in long-term (i.e. open-ended, permanent) job attachments, reflecting the high costs usually involved in finding and training such labour.[8] Consequently, firms reducing or planning to reduce overtime work were found in most cases to do so by rationalisation and productivity increases rather than by hiring additional staff from the external labour market. This explains both why the motive of a reduction of overtime work has not played an important role in accounting for firms making use of temporary job arrangements, and why the facilitation of fixed-term contracts through the EPA has created hardly any increase in labour demand.

There are also good reasons for disputing the assumption underlying the EPA that the use of fixed-term contracts, aside from satisfying the flexibility needs of firms in more or less traditional cases of temporary labour demand, is apt to increase the ability of firms to cope with economic uncertainty, i.e. uncertainty about future labour demand. By definition, fixed-term employment contracts require their duration or date of termination to be fixed in advance. In the case of premature terminations prior to the fixed date of expiration, West German law requires regular notice to be given by the employer involving all legal procedures and obligations applying in the case of permanent work contracts; when fixed-term contracts expire, their renewal for reasons of economic uncertainty is prohibited under the EPA. Therefore, from the firm's point of view it is rational to fix the duration of fixed-term contracts only up to that date, up to which labour demand can be anticipated at the time the contract is closed. Usually, this limit is defined by the time range of orders on hand, which in West German manufacturing amounted to not more than an average of 2.8 months during the period 1985-1988, i.e. well below the time threshold of six months beyond which the closing of fixed-term contracts has been facilitated by the EPA. This largely explains the fact that most (70 per cent) fixed-term contracts closed in the private sector do not in fact exceed six months in duration and thus fall out of the potential range of the new regulations introduced by the EPA.

Finally, it should not go unmentioned that even in those few exceptional cases in which firms acted according to the expectations and assumptions of the legislator (i.e. took on additional workers on the basis of the EPA), most personnel managers interviewed were not capable of clearly separating the various factors influencing the hiring decisions of their firms and thus of distinctly assessing the genuine impact of the new regulations introduced by the EPA. In other words, in as far as firms have actually modified their hiring decisions and recruitment practices following the enactment of the EPA, this is more likely to reflect an overall constellation of various factors, such as the positive economic climate prevailing since 1985, increased labour demand due to reductions in weekly working time, and medium-term structural changes in the employment practices of firms, rather than the impact of the new regulations alone.

Employment Protection Reconsidered: Reviewing the Evidence

Contrary to widespread notions in the recent debate on 'labour market flexibility' and to premature conclusions drawn from looking merely at the highly elaborate West German system of employment protection regulations from a neoclassical perspective, the empirical evidence presented above tends to refute the view that employment security provisions have played a major part in accounting for firms generally hesitating to take on additional labour and thus have contributed to persistent high unemployment in West Germany. On the contrary, our evidence obtained at firm level has shown that existing legal and collectively bargained lay-off and dismissal restraints are not perceived as obstacles to necessary job terminations by the overwhelming majority of firms in the private sector. This finding, which also casts doubts on the view that employment security, by preventing lay-offs and slowing down workforce reductions, is likely to have a positive impact on the overall level of employment, is in line with earlier research on the impact of employment security provisions (cf. Falke *et al.*, 1981; Maurau and Oudinet, 1988; Blanchard *et al.*, 1987).

Our own data further show that - just like fixed-term job arrangements - lay-offs and dismissals are also highly concentrated among a small minority of firms adhering to an intensive 'hire and fire' strategy. During the two-year period May 1985 to April 1987 almost 70 per cent of all lay-offs and dismissals by employers were actually accounted for by not more than 13 per cent of all firms in the private sector. During the same two-year period these 'hire-and-fire' firms on average laid-off or dismissed almost half (46 per cent) of all their workers employed at the beginning of the observation period, an *annual* involuntary separation rate of almost 25 per cent.[9] This group of firms consists mostly of small establishments (employing on average not more than 22 workers at the time of the survey) with a strong concentration in the construction and low-skill service industries (these two industries alone accounting for almost 50 per cent of the firms belonging to this category), a high proportion of unskilled and semi-skilled workers among their workforces (close to 50 per cent of all workers employed by these firms falling into these skilled categories), a relatively high share of labour costs in total turnover (labour costs exceeding 50 per cent of total turnover in more than a quarter of these firms), and strong fluctuations in demand (73 per cent of them reporting regularly recurring variations in capacity utilisation). It is interesting to note that it is by no means exclusively contracting firms with declining workforces that adhere to a pattern of adjustment involving massive lay-offs and dismissals: more than half (55 per cent) of these '*firing*' firms, in fact, show stable (18 per cent) or even increasing (37 per cent) workforces over the two-year observation period. Last but not least, firms adhering to an intensive 'firing' policy more frequently (59 per cent) report difficulties in filling vacancies than is true for the remaining firms in the private sector (30.6 per cent), indicating that even in these cases massive external labour turnover does not necessarily imply adjustment efficiency.[10] Regardless of economic efficiency considerations, the mere existence of a small group of firms adhering to an intensive 'hire and fire' strategy once again raises doubt as to whether existing employment protection and job security regulations have actually acted as a significant genuine restraint on the freedom of firms to dismiss and lay-off workers.

With respect to employment protection these findings tend to suggest that it is industry and firm-specific manpower policy options rather than the (universal) effect of legal job security regulations that account for the observed high degree of overall employment stability in West Germany. This conclusion is in line with previous studies that have shown that labour hoarding in the West German manufacturing sector during economic downturns was motivated primarily by the (economic) interest of firms to maintain their qualified workforce and to avoid the high costs of recruitment and training in the following upswing, rather than by the existence of legal and collectively bargained lay-off restraints (cf. Nerb *et al.*, 1977).

In combination with the results of our own research reported above, this evidence, indeed, can be summarised in terms of a partial congruence of lay-off and dismissal restraints imposed by legal regulations and collective agreements on the one hand, and economic interests of the overwhelming majority of firms in avoiding lay-offs and restricting dismissals to certain categories of workers, on the other hand. Such an interpretation also justifies serious doubts as to whether employment protection regulations act as a genuine deterrent with respect to the hiring behaviour of firms. Company surveys have indeed shown that it is primarily a lack of demand which has kept West German manufacturing firms from taking on more workers during the last economic upswing, whereas 'insufficient flexibility in hiring and firing' appears to play at best a subordinate role in the hiring decisions of firms (cf. Nerb, 1986; König and Zimmermann, 1985).

5. CONCLUSION

Reviewing the evidence, *de-regulation* of labour relations through facilitating temporary job arrangements and thereby the suspension of employment protection for newly-hired workers does not appear to be a successful policy agenda for stimulating employment growth in economies, such as that of West Germany. Of course, the question remains whether the evident failure of the EPA to modify essential parameters of the hiring and employment decisions of firms might be attributable to the insufficiency of the impulse or incentive provided by the EPA to hire additional workers, i.e. that a *stronger* dose of 'de-regulation' in the area of employment protection guarantees and job security standards would have induced more firms to give up their hesitancy to hire additional staff and thus would have stimulated employment growth (cf. Nerb, 1986). This assumption would, however, seem doubtful in the light of the findings reported above: most firms do not regard employment protection regulations as impediments to necessary workforce adjustments. Indeed, recent studies have shown that those industries with a relatively high degree of employment protection through collective bargaining agreements have fared more positively, not only in terms of employment performance but also in terms of innovative activities, than industries with a comparatively low level of institutional job security (cf. Warnken and Ronning, 1990).

NOTES

1 The study, which was completed in May 1989, is based on (a) a representative mail survey of 2,392 firms in the private sector, (b) a representative (telephone) panel survey of 4,930 employed workers and 1,539 unemployed job seekers, (c) a mail-survey of 1,968 placement officers of the Federal Employment Agency, and (d) 30 in-depth case studies in 30 selected enterprises of the metal processing and engineering industries. Empirical data were collected for the whole period from the enactment of the EPA in May 1985 to November 1988. For a detailed description of design and results of the study see the final report (Büchtemann and Höland, 1989).

2 Legitimate reasons for ordinary dismissals according to the Act are misconduct (unsatisfactory performance, unjustified absence from work, violation of safety regulations, etc.), lack of personal capability or bad health involving high absenteeism, and economic necessity (due to lack of demand or technological reorganisation); personal misconduct may also justify an 'extraordinary' dismissal of the worker in which case legal pre-notification periods do not apply.

3 More than five workers in companies with 21 to 59 employees, 10 per cent or at least 25 workers in companies with 60–499 employees, and at least 30 employees within companies with 500 or more employees ('Work Promotion Act'/*Arbeitsförderungsgesetz* of 1969).

4 Due to an under-representation of workers with marginal workforce attachment in the official population surveys (*Mikrozensus*) of the Federal Statistical Office (*Statistisches Bundesamt*) the numbers shown for 1988 in Table 5.1 are significantly lower than those found in our survey.

5 The difference in the proportion of fixed-term 'entries' and 'exits' is due to the fact that a considerable proportion (32 per cent) of workers initially hired on fixed-term contracts are subsequently taken over into permanent employment.

6 For a similar conclusion with respect to the prolongation of the initial waiting period for protection against unfair dismissal in the United Kingdom cf. Evans *et al.*, 1985, p. 62.

7 Workers hired on a fixed-term contract by firms which had classified the motive of prolonged probation of newly-hired workers as 'very important' in their decision to use the new EPA regulations were found to be subsequently taken over into permanent employment significantly more frequently than fixed-term workers in firms considering the 'screening' motive as secondary or unimportant.

8 Earlier studies have found firms to refrain from hiring skilled workers unless full utilisation is foreseeable for a period of at least 6 to 24 months, cf. Nerb *et al.*, 1977, pp. 303-4.

9 For the remaining 87 per cent of all firms in the private sector this annual separation rate amounted to not more than 0.8 per cent p.a.

10 It should not go unmentioned that an intensive use of lay-offs and dismissals seems to be inversely correlated with the use of fixed-term job arrangements. This once more casts doubt on the common expectation that fixed-term contracts would be welcomed by firms as an efficient means to evade the 'rigidities' allegedly inherent in permanent employment contracts.

REFERENCES

Abraham, K.G., 'Flexible Staffing Arrangements and Employers' Short-term Adjustment Strategies', in R.A. Hart (ed.), *Employment, Unemployment and Labour Utilization*, London, Unwin & Hyman, 1988, pp. 288-322.

Bayar, A., 'Labour Market Flexibility: An Approach Based on a Macrosectoral Model for Belgium', *Labour and Society*, Vol. 12, No. 1, 1987, pp. 37-53.

Bentolila, S. and Bertola, G., 'Firing Costs and Labor Demand: How Bad is Eurosclerosis?', (*mimeo.*), December 1988.

Björklund, A. and Holmlund, B., 'Worker Displacement in Sweden, Facts and Policies', (*mimeo.*), paper presented at the December 1987 American Economic Association Meetings, Stockholm 1987.

Blanchard, O. *et al.*, 'Employment and Growth in Europe: A Two-Handed Approach', in O. Blanchard *et al.* (eds.), *Restoring Europe's Prosperity: Macroeconomic Papers from the Center for European Policy Studies*, Cambridge/Mass., MIT-Press, 1987, pp. 95-123.

Büchtemann, C.F. and Höland, A., 'Befristete Arbeitsverträge nach dem Beschäftigungsfoerderungsgesetz 1985 (BeschFG 1985). Ergebnisse einer empirischen Untersuchung i.A. des Bundesministers fuer Arbeit und Sozialordnung (BMA)', Reihe *Forschungsberichte*, ed. Federal Ministry of Labour, Bonn, 1989.

Burgess, S.M., 'Employment Adjustment in UK Manufacturing', *The Economic Journal*, Vol. 98, 1988, pp. 81-103.

Elbaum, M. *et al.*, 'La suppression de l'autorisation administrative de licenciement: Des emplois ou des chomeurs', Paris (*mimeo.*), 1986.

Emerson, M., 'Regulation or Deregulation of the Labour Market: Policy Regimes for the Recruitment and Dismissal of Employees in the Industrial Countries', *European Economic Review*, No. 32, 1988, pp. 775-817.

Evans, S. *et al.*, 'Unfair Dismissal Law and Employment Practice in the 1980s', *Department of Employment Research Paper* 53-1985, London, 1985.

Falke, J. *et al.*, 'Kündigungspraxis und Kündigungsschutz in der Bundesrepublik Deutschland, *"Forschungsberichte"*', ed. Federal Ministry of Labour, Vol. 47, Bonn, 1981.

Flanagan, R.J., 'Unemployment as a Hiring Problem, *OECD Economic Studies*, No. 11, autumn 1988, pp. 124-54.

Franz, W., 'Beschäftigungsprobleme aufgrund von Inflexibilitäten auf Arbeitsmärkten?', in H. Scherf (ed.), *Beschäftigungsprobleme hochentwickelter Volkswirtschaften, Schriften des Vereins für Socialpolitik NF*, Bd. 178, Berlin, Duncker & Humblot, 1989, pp. 303-40.

Gould, W.B., 'Stemming the Wrongful Discharge Tide: A Case for Arbitration', *Employment Relations Law Journal*, Vol. 13, winter 1987, pp. 404-25.

Hamermesh, D.S., 'The Demand for Workers and Hours and the Effects of Job Security Policies: Theories and Evidence', in R.A. Hart (ed.), *Employment, Unemployment, and Labour Utilization*, London, Unwin & Hyman, 1988, pp. 9-32.

König, H. and Zimmermann, K.F., 'Determinants of Employment Policy of German Manufacturing Firms: A Survey-Based Evaluation', Institut für Volkswirtschaftslehre und Statistik der Universität Mannheim, Discussion, (*mimeo.*), 1985.

Layard, R. and Nickell, S., 'The Causes of British Unemployment, Centre for Labour Economics', *Discussion Paper* No. 204, London School of Economics, February 1985.

Lazear, E.P., 'Employment-at-Will, Job Security, and Work Incentives', in R.A. Hart (ed.), *Employment, Unemployment, and Labour Utilization*, London, Unwin & Hyman, 1988, pp. 39-61.

Lutz, B., *Arbeitsmarktstruktur und betriebliche Arbeitskräftestrategie. Eine theoretisch-historische Skizze zur Entstehung betriebszentrierter Arbeitsmarktsegmentation*, Frankfurt/M., Campus, 1987.

Maurau, G. and Oudinet, J., 'Précarité et Flexibilité: Un essai de comparaison des industries Européennes', *La note de l'IRES*, No. 18-4-1988, 1988, pp. 5-17.

Mendelsohn, S.R., 'Wrongful Termination Litigation in the US and its Effect on the Employment Relationship', OECD working party on industrial relations, Paris, (*mimeo.*), January 1989.

Nerb, G. *et al.*, 'Struktur, Entwicklung und Bestimmungsgrössen der Beschäftigung in Industrie und Bauwirtschaft auf mittlere Sicht', *Mitteilungen aus der Arbeitsmarkt- und Berufsforschung* (MittAB), No. 2, 1977, pp. 291-310.

Nerb, G., 'Employment Problems: Views of Businessmen and the Workforce - Results of an Employee and Employer Survey on Labour Market Issues in the Member States', *European Economy*, No. 27, March 1986, pp. 13-110.

OECD, *Flexibility in the Labour Market: The Current Debate. A Technical Report*, Paris, OECD, 1986.

OECD, *Economies in Transition: Structural Adjustment in OECD Countries*, Paris, OECD, 1989.

Rosow, J.M. and Zager, R., *Employment Security in a Free Society*, New York, Pergamon Press, 1984.

Teubner, G., 'Juridification: Concepts, Aspects, Limits, Solutions', in G. Teubner (ed.), *Juridification of Social Spheres: A Comparative Analysis in the Areas of Labour, Corporate, Antitrust and Social Welfare Law*, Berlin/New York, De Gruyter, 1987, pp. 3-48.

Walter, N., 'The Inflexibility of Labour Market Related Institutions - Some Observations for Germany', in G. Dlugos *et al.* (eds.), *Management under Differing Labour Market and Employment Systems*, Berlin/New York, De Gruyter, 1988, pp. 133-42.

Warnken, J. and Ronning, G., 'Technological Change and Employment Structures', in R. Schettkat and M. Wagner (eds.), *Technological Change and Employment: Innovation in the West German Economy*, Berlin/New York, De Gruyter, 1990.

6. Employment and Industrial Restructuring in the United States and West Germany

Eileen Appelbaum and Ronald Schettkat

1. INTRODUCTION

The success of the American economy in creating employment during the 1980s and the almost stagnant job growth in the West German economy and other European countries during the same time period have shaped much of the economic and political debate over the relationship between adjustment to structural change and employment growth. Between 1979 and 1987 the US added 14 467 000 jobs, an increase in employment of 15.2 per cent, while the West German economy added only 709 000 jobs, an increase of just 2.8 per cent. Slow employment growth has been attributed to 'rigidities' in the West German labour market related to statutory or contractual regulations that stabilise wages and make it more difficult to dismiss employees. In contrast to the flexibility found in the US labour market, these rigidities are believed to have impeded industrial restructuring and the shift to service employment in West Germany, and in this way has prevented employment growth. The discussion of full employment in West Germany has reflected this common view of the causes of slow employment growth, and measures to de-regulate the labour market in order to increase flexibility have figured prominently in the debate.

It is, however, an empirical question whether slow employment growth is the result of slower restructuring of the West German economy relative to the US. In contrast to the common view, the disaggregated data reported in this chapter show that industrial restructuring in West Germany during this decade has been even more dynamic than in the US.

The small net increase in employment results from very large employment declines in manufacturing and construction, and very large employment gains in service industries.

While service industries employ a much larger proportion of the labour force in the US than in West Germany, the trend toward increased employment in services has been quite vigorous in the German economy.

Industrial restructuring, as this chapter will show, has followed the same broad outline in both the US and West Germany. The increase in female employment and in part-time jobs which has been characteristic of the shift to services in the US has been present in the restructuring of the German ecomomy as well. Employment growth there, both in business and professional and in financial services, has been robust, though slower than in the US. This, however, may be explained by slow productivity growth in most US service industries.

2.   SURVEY OF INDUSTRIAL STRUCTURE AND EMPLOYMENT GROWTH

The US and West German economies differ substantially with respect to both industrial structure and employment growth. Despite steady gains in service sector output and employment in West Germany, the shift to a service economy is not as extensive as in the US. Employment in the West German service sector has grown by 1.7 per cent p.a. since 1979, and the real output of service industries by 2.4 per cent p.a. As a result, the employment share of the service sector increased to 53.9 per cent of the labour force by 1987. Despite these gains, however, the service sector in West Germany lags far behind the US, where service industries accounted for 71.6 per cent of employment in 1987. Even after the steep fall in employment in West German manufacturing and construction during this decade, the industrial sector continues to provide 40.7 per cent of all jobs, compared with only 24.8 per cent in the US (see Table 6.1).

The success of the US economy in generating new jobs is well known. Employment growth since 1979 has averaged a robust 1.8 per cent a year compared with only 0.3 per cent in West Germany. This has enabled the US to absorb successfully both a growing population and an increasing proportion of the female population into employment. Population growth in the US, while slower than in the preceding decades, averaged 1.0 per cent a year in the 1980s. In West Germany, population growth stagnated until the late 1980s when the borders were opened for Germans in East Germany, Poland, Romania and the Soviet Union.

Nearly two-thirds of American women are in the labour force, compared with only just over half of West German women. As a result, the employment ratio is higher in the US than in West Germany - 45.0 per cent compared with 43.1 per cent (see Table 6.1).

Table 6.1   Selected Labour Market and Economic Statistics, 1987

	West Germany	US
Civilian Employment		
Number (thousands)	26 350	109 854
Distributions (% of total)		
Agriculture	5.5	3.6
Industry	40.7	24.8
Services	53.9	71.6
Growth rate 79-87 (%)		
Total employment	0.3	1.8
Services	1.7	2.6
Population		
Number (thousands)	61 149	243 915
Growth rate 79-87 (%)	0.0	1.0
Unemployment Rate (%)		
Standardised definition	6.2	6.1
Employment Ratio	43.1	45.0
FEM LF Participation Rate, 1986 (%)	50.3	64.9
Growth Rate of Output		
GDP 79-85 (%)	1.3	1.7
Services 79-85 (%)	2.4	3.1
GDP Per Capita 79-86 (%)	1.5	1.4

Sources: OECD Economic Surveys 1988/89, Basic Statistics
OECD Economic Outlook (Dec. 1988)
OECD Labour Force Statistics, 1966-1986
OECD Historical Statistics, 1960-1986

Unpublished data from Bureau of Labor Statistics, Current Population Survey for US; from Statistisches Bundesamt, Mikrozensus for West Germany

Contrary to the generally accepted view, unemployment has behaved similarly in the two countries during this decade. Using the OECD's standardised definition of unemployment, unemployment rates in both countries peaked in 1983 - at 9.5 per cent of the labour force in the US and at 8.0 per cent in West Germany. The unemployment rate then fell steadily in both countries, leaving an almost identical 6.1 per cent of workers in the US and 6.2 per cent in West Germany still out of work in 1987 (OECD, 1988, Table R17). The perception that unemployment has been more intractable in West Germany than in the US arises from comparisons that use different definitions of the unemployment rate in each country. One important difference is that in West Germany the unemployment rate is measured as the ratio of unemployed workers to wage and salary workers, while in the US the ratio of unemployed workers to the entire civilian labour force is used. Taking the definitions actually used in each country, in the US the unemployment rate fell steadily from 9.7 per cent in 1982 to 6.2 per cent in 1987. In West Germany, it hovered at about 8.2 per cent from 1982 to 1985, then declined slightly to 7.9 per cent in 1987 (OECD, 1988, Table R18). These widely cited differences in the behaviour of unemployment may be more apparent than real, however.

Surprisingly, much faster employment growth in the US than in West Germany has not translated into a more rapid increase in per capita income. Output growth in the two economies has been far more similar than employment growth. The growth rate of real GDP between 1979 and 1985 averaged 1.7 per cent a year in the US and 1.3 per cent a year in West Germany, while service sector output grew in the two countries at average annual rates of 3.1 per cent and 2.4 per cent respectively. Gross domestic product per capita has grown at about the same rate, 1.5 per cent per year, in both countries since 1979 (see Table 6.1). The ability of the West German economy to achieve improvements in per capita income comparable to those in the US, despite much slower employment growth, is generally attributed to slower productivity growth in services in the US than in West Germany (Wegner, 1985; Thurow and Waldstein, 1989; Appelbaum and Schettkat, 1990).

3. THE CLASSIFICATION OF INDUSTRIES

The continuing shift to employment in service industries during the 1980s is evident in both economies. As can be seen from Table 6.2, the share of employment in the industrial sector declined by about 4 percentage points in each country while the share of employment in the service sector increased by 5.4 percentage points in West Germany and 4.6 percentage points in the US. In both countries, this increase in the share of service sector employment was split almost evenly between information and knowledge services and other services. Including agriculture and mining along with the industrial sector, employment in goods-producing industries in West Germany fell from 51.5 per cent of total employment on a labour force basis to 46.2 per cent. In the US, the decline was from 33.0 to 28.4 per cent.

This paper examines total civilian employment by industry in the US and West Germany in 1979 and 1987 using data from national household surveys of civilian employment conducted by each government. Data for the US are from the Current Population Survey (CPS) for March of both years; data for West Germany are from the Mikrozensus for May 1979 and March 1987. The CPS is a monthly survey of about 60 000 US households; the Mikrozensus is an annual survey of 1 per cent of the West German population. The years 1979 and 1987 were selected because both economies were relatively free of major distortions from the business cycle in these years.

In general, international comparisons of employment growth by industry and the resulting changes in industrial structure are complicated by national differences in the classification of industries. We have minimised these difficulties as far as possible by reclassifying detailed industries into the broader industry groupings shown in Table 6.2 on a consistent basis for both economies. (For details of the classification scheme used in this analysis cf. Appelbaum and Schettkat, 1990.) Despite our efforts to improve comparability between industries in the two economies, several classification problems remain. We briefly mention the most important of these:

Information and knowledge (I-K) manufacturing in the US includes: electronic and computing equipment; office and accounting machines; radio, TV and communications equipment; professional and photographic equipment; scientific and controlling instruments; and printing, publishing and allied industries. It is not possible to make these distinctions in West Germany for 1979. Except for printing and publishing, all of these industries are included in durable goods manufacturing in the German figures. Printing and publishing are usually classified as service industries in West Germany, rather than manufacturing industries as in the US. We have reclassified printing and publishing in the West German data, and count them as information and knowledge manufacturing. They are, however, the only industries classified as I-K manufacturing in the West German data. These differences in the classification of industries account for a larger share of employment in I-K manufacturing in the US than in West Germany - 3.2 per cent compared with 1.6 per cent in 1987 (see

Table 6.2). A better comparison of employment in the I-K manufacturing industries in the two countries can be made, for 1987 only, on the basis of the revised German industry classification system. On this basis, 2.7 per cent of employment in West Germany in 1987 was located in I-K manufacturing, much closer to the 3.2 per cent share in the US.

A second classification difference is that repair industries are included in services in the US and in manufacturing in West Germany. This accounts for the fact that guard, cleaning and repair services comprise 2.7 per cent of US employment in 1987 but only 0.5 per cent of West German employment. Correcting for this using the 1987 German classification scheme moves 330 000 workers from durable goods manufacturing to services in 1987 and increases the employment share of guard, cleaning and repair services in West Germany to 1.8 per cent.

Compared to the West German statistics, US figures distinguish more clearly between business and professional services on the one hand and personal and recreational services on the other. For example, legal services are included in business and professional services in the US, but cannot be separated out in the German data. Similarly, leasing services such as car rental and such membership organisations as employers' associations and unions are included in personal and recreational services in West Germany. In addition, some activities which are included in business services in the US are counted as wholesale trade, financial services, social welfare services, or transportation and public utilities in West Germany. These differences affect the distribution of employment among service industries, but not between the service and industrial sectors. Here, again, it is possible to make the industry classification systems more comparable in 1987, though some problems remain. On this basis, the employment shares of business and professional services for the US and West Germany are 5.7 per cent and 4.6 per cent respectively, rather than the 3.3 per cent reported for Germany in Table 6.2.

Finally, there are some classification differences in terms of which activities are considered to be construction and which are considered to be durable manufacturing.

Classification problems account for only a small part of the differences in industrial structure between the two economies, however. Adjusting for misclassification of industries on the basis of the 1987 industrial classification scheme reduces the employment share of the German industrial sector in 1987 from 40.7 to 38.6 per cent, compared with 24.8 per cent for the US and increases the employment share of the service sector in West Germany from 53.9 to 55.9 per cent, compared with 71.6 per cent in the US. Other classification problems undoubtedly remain, but it is unlikely that they account for more than a fraction of the remaining differences.

Our analysis of employment developments by sector follows the usual practice of aggregating industries into a primary sector (agriculture, fishing, forestry and mining), a secondary sector (industry, manufacturing and construction), and a tertiary sector (services). In addition, we find it useful to identify information and knowledge activities, and to make a distinction within the tertiary sector between information and knowledge services and other services (see Table 6.2 for details). This distinction was first proposed by Machlup (1962) and developed further by Porat (1977) and Albin and Appelbaum (1987, 1989). Extensive analyses of the importance of information activities in the West German economy can be found in Filip-Köhn, Neckermann and Stäglin (1984) and in Stäglin and Südfeld (1988). Other researchers, however, have proposed alternative distinctions in analysing the service sector. We report developments in service employment disaggregated into 14 service industries. These data are easily aggregated into a single tertiary sector or regrouped according to some other principle. In this way, no information is lost and comparison with other studies is facilitated.

4.   THE STRUCTURE OF THE US AND WEST GERMAN ECONOMIES

In general outline, industrial restructuring appears to be proceeding along the same lines in both the US and West Germany. The industry-specific growth rates for the two countries, displayed in Table 6.2, are highly correlated. The correlation coefficient between industry-specific growth rates is 0.78, indicating a general development pattern common to both countries: industries with high growth rates in one economy have experienced high growth rates in the other as well. Thus, factors common to both economies would seem to be the main driving force behind industrial restructuring. Nevertheless, there are important national differences in the details of the development process.

Employment Shares

The employment share of the goods-producing sectors - agriculture/mining and industry - is declining in both countries, but the sharpest decreases are currently occurring in West Germany. Employment in agriculture and mining has continued to grow slowly in the US, but declined at an annual rate of 2.2 per cent in West Germany.

Table 6.2   Share of Employment by Industry, 1979 and 1987 (labour force basis)

	West Germany shares 1979	shares 1987	growth (compound annual rate) 1979-1987	US shares 1979	shares 1987	growth (compound annual rate) 1979-1987
ALL INDUSTRIES						
Number (000)	25 641	26 350	709	95 387	109 854	14 467
Per cent	100.0	100.0	0.3	100.0	100.0	1.8
Agriculture/Mining (%)	6.7	5.5	-2.2	4.0	3.6	0.3
Industry (%)	44.8	40.7	-0.9	29.0	24.8	-0.1
Construction (%)	7.3	5.8	-2.6	6.1	6.2	2.2
Non-durable Manufacturing (%)	11.2	10.0	-1.0	7.2	6.0	-0.6
Durable Manufacturing (%)	24.9	23.3	-0.5	12.3	9.4	-1.5
Information and Knowledge Mfg (%)	1.4	1.6	2.0	3.4	3.2	1.1
ALL SERVICE INDUSTRIES						
Number (000)	12 446	14 197	1 751	63 907	78 595	14 688
Per cent	48.5	53.9	1.7	67.0	71.6	2.6
Information and Knowledge Services (%)	19.9	22.5	1.9	25.2	27.7	3.0
Education (%)	3.8	4.6	2.8	8.7	8.4	1.4
Communications (%)	2.5	2.6	0.8	2.1	2.1	1.7
Finance, Insurance, Real Estate (%)	3.6	4.4	2.6	6.0	6.7	3.3
Business and Professional (%)	2.2	3.3	5.3	3.9	5.7	6.9
Public Administration (%)	7.6	7.5	0.2	4.5	4.7	2.3
Other Services (%)	28.6	31.4	1.5	41.8	43.9	2.4
Health Services (%)	4.6	5.6	2.8	7.1	7.7	2.7
Social Welfare Services (%)	2.1	2.9	4.6	2.3	2.8	4.5
Personal and Recreation exc. HH (%)	1.5	1.6	1.7	2.8	3.0	2.6
Private Household (%)	0.3	0.3	-1.5	1.4	1.0	-1.9
Eating/Drinking Places, Hotels (%)	2.3	2.6	2.0	5.0	5.8	3.7
Retail Trade (%)	8.9	9.0	0.5	12.2	12.0	1.6
Wholesale Trade (%)	3.4	3.7	1.4	3.9	4.1	2.4
STET, Cleaning and Repairs (%)	0.4	0.5	2.8	2.2	2.7	4.5
Transportation/Public Utilities (%)	5.2	5.1	0.2	5.0	4.9	1.3

Source: Unpublished data from Bureau of Labor Statistics, Current Population Survey for US; from Statistisches Bundesamt, Mikrozensus for West Germany. Authors' calculations.

Employment in industry declined by 0.1 per cent p.a. in the US and more steeply (0.9 per cent) in West Germany (see Table 6.2). Manufacturing employment declined in both countries between 1979 and 1987, with Germany experiencing sharper declines in non-durable goods and the US in durable goods industries. Construction employment behaved very differently in the two countries, dropping sharply in West Germany by 2.6 per cent annually while growing strongly in the US at 2.2 per cent a year.

The employment shares of information and knowledge services in 1987 are roughly similar in both countries, 22.5 per cent in West Germany compared with 27.7 per cent in the US. Almost the entire difference is due to education, which comprises 4.6 per cent of employment in West Germany compared with 8.4 per cent in the US. In part, this reflects differences in the way in which young people are educated in each country. In West Germany, apprenticeship programmes administered by factories, banks and other business firms provide educational services found in vocational and technical schools or two-year community colleges in the US. In addition, access to a college education is more broadly available in the US, and about 25 per cent of the labour force has completed a four-year college or university programme.

The US also 'exports' educational services, educating a substantial number of foreign students. Interestingly, employment in education in West Germany has grown quite rapidly during this decade, expanding at an annual rate of 2.8 per cent, that is twice the 1.4 per cent annual rate in the US.

The shares of public sector employment in the two economies differ as well, with 7.6 per cent of the West German workforce employed in public administration compared to 4.7 per cent in the US. In part, this reflects the different organisation of health and pension insurance in the two economies. These risks are covered by the compulsory social insurance system in West Germany to a much larger extent than in the US, where private insurance companies play a more prominent role. If employment in 'social insurance' is moved out of public administration in West Germany and reclassified under finance, insurance and real estate, the share of public administration is reduced to 6.7 per cent and that of financial services is increased to 5.2 per cent. In addition, the US is one of the world's major financial centres, and this is reflected in both the larger size of and the more rapid employment growth in financial services in the US. US employment growth in the public sector, though slower than in the 1970s, continues to be quite strong. Employment in public administration grew at 2.3 per cent a year between 1979 and 1987 compared with a modest 0.2 per cent annual increase in West Germany. The slow growth of employment in public administration in West Germany runs counter to popular views of rapid growth in the public sector. Employment growth in West German business and professional services, however, has been quite strong since 1979, averaging 5.3 per cent a year compared with 6.9 per cent in the US.

The US and West Germany are rather similar in the overall employment shares of the information and knowledge services sector: the former being somewhat more and the latter somewhat less than a quarter of all employment respectively. In the other services sector, however, much sharper differences between the two economies are evident (see Table 6.2). Other services accounted for more than two-fifths (43.9 per cent) of employment in the US, but less than one-third (31.4 per cent) in West Germany in 1987. Two-thirds of this difference is due to differences in employment shares in retail trade (12.0 per cent of employment compared to 9.0 per cent), eating and drinking places and hotels (5.8 per cent versus 2.6 per cent), and recreational, personal and private household services (4.0 per cent to 1.9 per cent). Employment growth in these industries is also slower in West Germany (see Table 6.2). Explanations for these differences, to be taken up in subsequent sections, highlight differences in the two economies with respect to wage growth and the growth of personal income, wage differentials, productivity growth, and the employment of part-time workers.

Job Creation by Industry

Job growth in the US resulted from more even developments in the broad sectors of the economy than in West Germany, where restructuring was mainly the result of variations in positive growth rates. Nevertheless, we find that industries that accounted for substantial job creation in the US tended to play the same role in West Germany. The correlation coefficient on industry shares of new job creation between the two economies is 0.67.

Since employment growth in both economies occurred in the service sectors, it is easier to compare the contribution of the various service industries with the creation of new jobs by focusing on the share of each service industry in overall service sector employment growth (columns (3) and (4) in Table 6.3). Again, both similarities and surprises emerge.

Table 6.3   Share   of   New   Jobs*   by   Industry   and   Labour   Force
Characteristics, 1979-1987 (in per cent)

	West Germany	US	West Germany	US
ALL INDUSTRIES	100.0	100.0		
Agriculture/Mining	-39.5	0.7		
Industry	-107.5	-2.3		
Construction	-49.6	7.4		
Non-durable Goods Mfg	-31.0	-2.3		
Durable Goods Mfg	-35.4	-9.5		
I-K Mfg	8.6	2.1		
ALL SERVICES	247.0	101.5	100.0	100.0
I-K Services	116.5	44.2	47.2	43.6
Education	34.4	6.6	13.9	6.5
Communications	6.2	1.9	2.5	1.9
FIRE	30.2	11.6	12.2	11.4
Bus & Prof	41.9	18.2	17.0	17.9
Public Admin	3.8	5.9	1.5	5.9
Other Services	130.5	57.3	52.8	56.5
Health Serv	41.6	11.1	16.8	10.9
Social Welfare	32.4	6.3	13.1	6.2
Person & Rec	7.6	4.2	3.1	4.1
Private HH	-1.4	-1.3	-0.6	-1.3
Eat/Drink/Hotel	14.5	11.3	5.9	11.1
Retail Trade	13.4	10.6	5.4	10.5
Wholesale Trade	14.8	5.4	6.0	5.3
STET/Clean/Repairs	3.9	6.0	1.6	5.9
Transp./Pub. Utilities	3.5	3.7	1.4	3.7
Part-time		23.2		
Full-time		76.8		
<21 hrs.	44.4			
21-39 hrs.	684.8			
40+ hrs.	-602.8			
Self-employed	-27.2	6.6		
Employees		93.4		
Men	5.8	35.5		
Women	94.2	64.5		

*   calculated as: increase (decrease) in industry/total increase

The shares of new jobs in the I-K services sector and in the other services sector are quite similar in the US and West Germany. A slightly larger share of new jobs was created in I-K services in West Germany than in the US (47.2 per cent compared with 43.6 per cent), and a slightly smaller share in other services (52.8 per cent compared with 56.5 per cent). This overall similarity masks some unexpected differences, however, in the shares of new jobs created in education and in public administration. In West Germany, 13.9 per cent of new jobs created between 1979 and 1987 were in education. This is more than double the share of new jobs (6.5 per cent) in this area in the US. At the same time, the share of new jobs created in public administration in West Germany was only one-quarter the share in the US, 1.5 per cent compared with 5.9 per cent. The shares of new jobs created by the remaining I-K service industries - communications, finance, insurance and real estate, and business and professional services - are roughly the same in both economies.

In comparing job creation in the other services sector of the two economies we find, as expected, that about twice as many new jobs - as a proportion of the total - were created in the US in retail trade and in eating and drinking places and hotels as in West Germany. In the US, 10.5 per cent of new jobs were in retail trade and 11.1 per cent in eating and drinking places and hotels, compared with 5.4 per cent and 5.9 per cent respectively in West Germany (see Table 6.3). A less obvious finding is that job creation in health services and social welfare services was much greater in West Germany than in the US. Health services were responsible for 16.8 per cent of new jobs in West Germany and 10.9 per cent in the US; social welfare services for 13.1 per cent in West Germany and 6.2 per cent in the US. Turning, finally, to the labour force characteristics of the new jobs (see Table 6.3), we find that less than 7 per cent of new jobs in the US since 1979 have been filled by the self-employed, while self-employment actually decreased in West Germany during this period, mainly as a result of the decline in agriculture. The increase in female employment amounted to 94.2 per cent of net job creation in West Germany compared with 64.5 per cent in the US. Hours of work are declining in West Germany. The small net increase in employment is a result of a sharp decline in wage and salary jobs requiring 40 or more hours of work per week and a sharp increase in those requiring 39 or less. While it is not possible to distinguish clearly between part-time and full-time jobs, nearly all of the increase was in the category of 21-39 hours a week, in which workers are covered by the full range of social insurance. Casual part-time jobs - 20 hours or less - amounted to only 6 per cent of the increase in jobs with a working week of less than 40 hours. In the US, where most part-time employment is casual, part-time jobs amounted to almost one-quarter of net job creation. We turn now to a more detailed examination of these labour force characteristics.

5. LABOUR FORCE CHARACTERISTICS OF EMPLOYMENT GROWTH

Employment deveiopments need not affect all sectors of the labour force equally. Interest has centred on the extent to which the shift to a service economy has created employment opportunities for women, and on whether employment growth in service industries is associated with self-employment or part-time work. These issues will be examined in this section.

Self-Employment

Contrary to the prevailing view, a larger proportion of the labour force is self-employed in West Germany, where self-employment accounts for 11.7 per cent of all employment, than in the US where it accounts for 8.7 per cent (see Table 6.4). This is not merely the result of the relatively larger size of the agricultural sector in West Germany as self-employment accounts for a larger proportion of employment in the service sectors in West Germany as well. Overall 10.9 per cent of employment in service industries in 1987 was self-employment, with 6.9 per cent of those in I-K services and 13.7 per cent of those self-employed in other services.

In the US, the figures are 8.1 per cent in all service industries, 5.9 per cent in I-K services and 9.6 per cent in other services. In the very important category of business and professional services, 25.4 per cent of employment in West Germany and 17.8 in the US was self-employment; in financial services the proportions were approximately the same in both countries. Self-employment is also far more extensive in West Germany than in the US in hotels, restaurants and bars and in wholesale and retail trade. Nearly one-third of employment in eating and drinking places and hotels in West Germany (32.8 per cent) is self-employment, compared with only 5.5 per cent in the US. However, this result might be influenced by the different importance of unpaid family members caused by differences in business organisation: in the US, large chains dominate this sector whereas small companies are more common in West Germany. In retail trade, 16.6 per cent of employment in West Germany is self-employment compared with 9.5 per cent in the US; in wholesale trade the proportions are 12.6 per cent and 7.0 per cent respectively. In personal services, self-employment is somewhat higher in the US than in West Germany (30.9 per cent to 25.1 per cent).

Although self-employment remains higher in West Germany than in the US, it declined at an annual rate of 0.8 per cent in West Germany between 1979 and 1987 while increasing by 1.3 per cent p.a. in the US. The German decline in self-employment occurred almost entirely in agriculture and construction, two industries in which employment in general declined sharply. Self-employment in the information and knowledge services sector grew at an annual rate of 4.4 per cent in West Germany, about the same as in the US (4.3 per cent), with strong increases in both countries in business and professional services and financial services. In the other service sectors, it declined slightly by 0.1 per cent a year in West Germany, while growing at 1.2 in the US.

These data create a rather different impression of entrepreneurship in West Germany from the view commonly held. Importantly, in the technologically progressive service industries, self-employment is already higher in West Germany than in the US and, moreover, has grown as rapidly in West Germany as in the US since 1979 despite the replacement of regular employees by self-contract labour in some US firms. In industries dominated by small establishments - in restaurants, bars and hotels and in retail trade - West Germany has a higher proportion of self-employment, though the number has stagnated since 1979 while it has grown in the US. However, a recent study of the US (Christopherson, 1990) suggests that US service industries in both service sectors are now entering a period of consolidation and centralisation in which small firms are being displaced by large companies with small establishments.

Hours of Work

Hours of work underwent a major change in West Germany in the mid-1980s when shorter working hours were collectively negotiated. Full-time employment, which in the 1970s was defined as 40 or more hours of work per week, today refers to a working week of between 37 and 40 hours. As a result, employment in jobs requiring 40 or more hours of work per week has declined since 1979, with the sharpest declines in durable and I-K manufacturing industries.

Employment expanded very rapidly in jobs with a working week of between 21 and 39 hours, growing at a rate of 20.1 per cent a year, and increased at a more modest 2.5 per cent annual rate in jobs with a working week of 20 or fewer hours (see Table 6.3). By 1987, 57.6 per cent of employment consisted of wage and salary workers on weekly schedules of 40 hours or more, 24.0 per cent on schedules of 21 to 39 hours, and only 6.6 per cent on schedules of 20 hours or less (see Table 6.4).

Table 6.4 Labour Force Characteristics by Industry, 1987

	WEST GERMANY						US			
	Number Employed (000)	Per cent Self-Emp*	Employees Per cent <21 hrs	Per cent 21-39 hrs	Per cent 40+ hrs	Per cent Female	Number Employed (000)	Per cent Self-Emp*	Per cent <35 hrs	Per cent Female
All Industries	26 350	11.7	6.6	24.0	57.6	39.8	109 854	8.7	18.2	45.0
Agriculture/Mining	1 438	63.8	1.3	3.7	31.2	38.2	3 964	39.1	18.7	18.7
Industry	10 715	5.9	3.1	35.5	55.5	25.5	27 294	6.0	6.1	16.9
Construction	1 530	10.9	2.5	7.2	79.4	10.3	6 847	19.0	9.6	8.4
Non-durable G. Mfg.	2 639	6.3	3.8	15.2	74.6	40.5	6 552	1.2	4.9	40.8
Durable G. Mfg.	6 134	4.4	2.4	50.4	42.8	21.9	10 334	1.9	3.6	25.1
I-K Mfg.	412	7.3	10.2	49.5	33.0	40.3	3 561	2.0	8.8	40.7
All Services	14 197	10.9	9.9	17.3	61.9	50.8	78 595	8.1	22.4	52.8
I-K Services	5 927	6.9	10.2	13.7	69.2	45.1	30 395	5.9	16.5	54.5
Education	1 222	3.4	16.9	14.3	65.4	56.5	9 271	1.1	27.3	65.3
Communications	697	6.2	8.9	13.1	71.9	36.7	2 274	0.3	5.5	39.5
FIRE	1 149	8.9	7.6	18.0	65.6	47.1	7 386	7.4	12.4	59.7
Bus & Professnal	873	25.4	9.6	14.4	50.5	46.0	6 329	17.8	16.8	49.1
Public Admin	1 986	0.0	8.3	10.7	81.0	39.5	5 136	0.0	7.6	41.2
Other Services	8 270	13.7	9.6	19.9	56.7	54.8	48 200	9.6	26.1	51.6
Health Services	1 471	10.5	11.4	11.2	67.0	74.2	8 394	4.0	20.5	77.5
Social Welfare	764	0.9	14.4	16.4	68.3	62.3	3 073	7.6	31.6	69.1
Person & Recrn	427	25.1	9.6	12.6	52.7	72.6	3 311	30.9	31.8	60.3
Private HH	76	3.9	38.2	18.4	39.5	97.4	1 119	0.4	65.7	88.2
Eat/Drink/Hotel	688	32.8	6.8	7.3	53.1	58.7	6 403	5.5	39.9	56.8
Retail Trade	2 370	16.6	10.6	31.9	40.8	63.0	13 150	9.5	30.7	49.9
Wholesale Trade	985	12.6	6.0	30.3	51.2	36.3	4 485	7.0	8.7	28.8
STET/Clean/Repairs	140	10.0	34.3	20.0	35.7	65.7	2 928	26.2	20.2	23.0
Transp./Pub. Utilities	1 349	7.7	3.4	11.5	77.4	17.3	5 338	6.2	9.6	20.8

* Includes unpaid family workers

151

It is not possible, with these data, to determine the full-time or part-time status of workers on schedules of 21 to 39 hours per week. There is some evidence that the negotiated reduction in the working week has positively influenced full-time employment in industries with working time reductions (Stille and Zwiener, 1988; Schettkat, 1990), so that increases in these sectors in the 21-39 hour category are mainly increases in full-time work. However, the pattern of increases in employment in both the 40+ and the 21 to 39 hour working time categories in some industries (see Table 6.3) suggests that part-time work is probably an increasingly important phenomenon in these industries. The industries in which employment in both of these working time schedules increased are: finance, insurance and real estate; business and professional services; health services; social welfare services; personal and recreational services; and eating and drinking places and hotels.

Whether jobs in the 21 to 39 hour category are full time or part time, all of them are fully covered by the West German social insurance system and cannot be considered marginal employment. This is not the case, however, for many of the part-time jobs with very short hours found in the less than 21 hour category. Overall, employment in this category has grown by 2.5 per cent a year since 1979, and by 3.5 per cent in services. Not all of this is casual part-time work without the benefits of social insurance. In some industries the increase in employment in this category is due to employment contracts which are defined by half the working time of a full-time employee. A decline in the full-time working week to 37 to 40 hours will put such workers below 21 hours a week. Nevertheless, much of the job growth in this category is in short-hour jobs without the protections of the social insurance system (Büchtemann and Schupp, 1988). Despite growth in employment in this category, only a very small proportion of the West German labour force is employed in marginal part-time jobs. Just 6.6 per cent of wage and salary workers were on schedules of less than 21 hours in 1987.

In the US 18.2 per cent of employment in 1987 was in part-time jobs, defined as a working week of less than 35 hours. Part-time employment is concentrated in the other services sector, where it accounts for 26.1 per cent of all employment. Nearly one-third of employment in social welfare services, personal and recreation services, and retail trade is part-time; in eating and drinking places and hotels the proportion is 40 per cent (see Table 6.4). Part-time employment has increased since 1979 when 17.4 per cent of overall employment was in part-time jobs. Contrary to the usual view, however, this increase was not due to an increasing proportion of part-time jobs in service industries. In information and knowledge services, the proportion of part-time jobs actually decreased, from 17.1 per cent of employment in this sector in 1979 to 16.5 per cent in 1987; and in other services, the proportion remained virtually unchanged, 26.4 per cent in 1979 and 26.1 per cent in 1987. Full-time employment grew more rapidly than part-time in I-K services, and at about the same rate as part-time in other services. The increase in part-time work in the US has two distinct causes - the rapid employment growth in industries such as retail trade and restaurants and hotels, in which part-time employment is already concentrated; and the substitution of part-time for full-time workers in manufacturing. Full-time employment in durable and non-durable manufacturing decreased between 1979 and 1987, while part-time employment increased.

It is possible in the US to distinguish between voluntary part-time employment and the involuntary employment in part-time jobs of those who desire full-time jobs. Much of the increase in part-time employment since 1979 has been involuntary, and in 1987 about 5.5 million of the nearly 20 million workers holding part-time jobs did so involuntarily. Concern over part-time work in the US centres on the increase in involuntary part-time work and on the low wages and lack of health and pension insurance in many part-time jobs. About 42 per cent of the part-time workers in the US have no health insurance coverage and 70 per cent are not entitled to retirement benefits. Average hourly wages of part-time workers in 1987 were only $4.24 compared with $7.24 for full-time wage workers and $9.22 for all wage and salary workers (Appelbaum and Albin, 1989).

Part-time employment has increased since 1979, but it has not been a driving force in US employment growth. Overall employment decreased in the industrial sector of the economy (see Table 6.2) despite the substitution of part-time for full-time jobs in this sector and the growth of part-time work. The proportion of part-time jobs in information and knowledge service industries actually declined, and full-time employment grew more rapidly than part-time in both the I-K services and other services sectors.

Distribution of Employment by Gender

In both the US and West Germany, women comprise slightly more than half the labour force in service industries, 52.8 per cent of employment in services in the US and 50.8 per cent in West Germany (see Table 6.4). However, in West Germany women are seriously under-represented, in comparison with the US, in information and knowledge services, particularly in financial services and education. Women hold 54.4 per cent of the jobs in the I-K services sector in the US but only 45.1 per cent in West Germany. In financial services, women hold 59.7 per cent of jobs in the US compared with 47.1 per cent in West Germany; in education the figures are 65.3 per cent and 56.5 per cent, respectively. The situation is reversed in the other services sector, with women holding 54.8 per cent of jobs in this sector in West Germany and 51.6 per cent in the US. The sharpest differences are in retail trade and in personal and recreational services where, surprisingly, women hold a larger proportion of jobs in West Germany than in the US. Nearly two-thirds of the labour force in retail trade in West Germany is female compared with only one-half in the US - 63.0 per cent compared with 49.9 per cent. In personal and recreational services, 72.6 per cent of employment in West Germany is female compared with 60.3 per cent in the US. However, employment of women in retail trade and in personal and recreational services has grown far more rapidly in the US than in West Germany. In retail trade, the employment of women grew by 2.4 per cent p.a. in the US compared with 0.3 per cent in West Germany, and in personal and recreational services the growth rates were 2.9 and 1.2 per cent, respectively. Women also hold a larger proportion of jobs in industry in West Germany than in the US, due mainly to the smaller size of construction (in which women hold few jobs in either economy) in West Germany and not to any differences in the proportions of women employed in the various branches of manufacturing. Women are also more heavily employed in agriculture in West Germany than in the US.

The difference in employment opportunities in the two countries - women account for 39.8 per cent of total employment in West Germany and 45.0 per cent in the US - is the result of the under-representation of women in the West German I-K services sector and the smaller size and slower growth of employment in the other services sector. Nevertheless, the concentration of employment growth, since 1979, in both economies in the service sectors has expanded employment opportunities in both countries for both women and men.

On aggregate, the employment of men has hardly increased in West Germany since 1979; of the small net increase in jobs, 94.2 per cent was accounted for by the net increase in female employment (see Table 6.3) Aggregate figures on net changes are very misleading, however. Except for public administration and transportation and public utilities, where the employment of men has declined since 1979, the employment of men in service industries in West Germany has expanded quite strongly, often as much as, or even more than, the employment of women. Men have fared as well as, or better than, women in financial services, business and professional services, health services, social welfare services, personal and recreational services, restaurants and hotels, and retail trade. Employment of men in these industries grew at rates of between 1 per cent (retail trade) and 5.5 per cent (business and professional services, social welfare services) a year. These gains have been obscured in the aggregate data on male employment growth, which show no net increase in employment between 1979 and 1987, by declines in male employment in agriculture and mining, construction, and manufacturing. Again, these results - rapid declines in male employment in goods-producing industries and rapid expansion in some service industries since 1979 - suggest that labour market structures in West Germany did not prevent employment in declining industries in the goods-producing sectors from shrinking and employment in the expanding service sectors from growing.

The employment growth of women in West Germany was also quite strong in services, growing by 2.5 per cent annually in the I-K services sector and by a more modest 1.6 per cent in the other services sector. However, women's employment growth equalled or outpaced that of men only in education, communications, business and professional services, wholesale trade, and cleaning services. This is very different from the US, where the employment growth of women in service industries outpaced that of men in every industry except education, hotels and restaurants, and domestic servants. The employment growth of women in the I-K services sector in the US averaged 3.4 per cent a year compared with 2.5 per cent in West Germany. The differences are sharpest, however, in the other services sector, where the employment of women increased at 3.0 per cent p.a. in the US and by 1.6 per cent in West Germany.

6.   CONCLUDING SUMMARY

Our analysis shows that in general outline, industrial restructuring appears to be proceeding along the same lines in both the US and West Germany. Structural factors common to both economies seem to be the main driving force behind economic dynamics. Nevertheless, there are important national differences in the details of the development process.

The employment share of the goods-producing sectors - agriculture/mining and industry - is declining in both countries, but the sharpest decreases are currently occurring in West Germany. The shares of public sector employment in the two economies differ, with about 7.6

per cent of employment in West Germany in public administration compared to 4.7 per cent in the US. In part, this reflects the different organisation of health and pension insurance in the two economies. If employment in 'social insurance' is moved out of public administration in West Germany and reclassified in finance, insurance and real estate, the share of public administration is reduced to 6.7 per cent and that of financial services is increased to 5.2 per cent. In addition, the US is one of the world's major financial centres, and this is reflected in both the larger size of and more rapid employment growth in the US in financial services. US employment growth in the public sector, though slower than in the 1970s, continues to be quite strong. The slow growth of employment in public administration in West Germany runs counter to popular German views of the rapid growth of the public sector.

Between 1979 and 1987, total civilian employment increased by 15.2 per cent in the US and by 2.8 per cent in West Germany. These net changes in overall employment, however, are the result of divergent developments in different industries in which strong employment growth in some industries is cancelled out by sharp declines in others. The declining industries in the US shed a total of nearly 1.9 million jobs between 1979 and 1987. In an economy one quarter the size of the US economy, shrinking industries in West Germany lost more than 1.1 million jobs over the same time period. As a result, the small aggregate increase in employment in West Germany is comprised of a sharp decrease in goods-producing industries (equal to 1.5 times the increase in total employment) and an even sharper increase in service industries (equal to 2.5 times the increase in total employment). While aggregate employment increased by only 709 000 in West Germany, service industries added more than 1.8 million to the job total. Despite slow aggregate employment growth, structural change in West Germany was more pronounced than in the US.

As a result of the substantial economic restructuring of West Germany - and the offsetting employment declines in agriculture and mining, construction, and manufacturing - each of the two broad service sectors - information and knowledge services, other services - contributed more than 100 per cent to overall employment growth in West Germany (see Table 6.3). In other words, the broad service sectors grew, in employment terms, by more than the overall economy. The picture that emerges, of a very rapid and dynamic restructuring of the West German economy, is quite different from the usual view and raises serious questions about the hypothesis that labour market structures in West Germany are too rigid. (For additional evidence challenging this hypothesis, cf. Franz, 1987; Schettkat, 1990). We find no empirical support for the view that, compared with the US, the West German labour market is too rigid to allow for structural adjustments. Reasons for the slower employment growth in service industries in the West German economy must be sought, instead, in developments in demand conditions, in productivity growth, and in part-time work.

The increase in female employment and in part-time jobs which have been characteristic of the shift to services in the US have been present in the restructuring of the West German economy as well. Employment growth in West Germany, both in business and professional and in financial services has been robust, though slower than in the US. This, however, may be due to slow productivity growth in these service industries in the US.

The important difference between the US and West Germany, with respect to employment growth in services, is to be found in the area of consumer services purchased by households. We have argued elsewhere (cf. Appelbaum and Schettkat, 1990) that these differences are related to differences in demand conditions in the two countries and to differences in relative wages as well. The growth of consumption in the US, driven by the pseudo-Keynesian policies of the Reagan administration (which combined a military build-up with tax cuts for the wealthy to produce record federal budget deficits and a near tripling of the national debt), resulted in rates of employment growth in personal and recreation services, restaurants and hotels, and retail trade in the US far in excess of those in West Germany. Steady job growth at low wages has characterised these industries and contributed to a worsening of dualistic economic structures in the US.

REFERENCES

Albin, P. and Appelbaum, E., 'Productivity and Employment Implications of Computer Rationalization', paper presented at the American Economic Association Meetings, (*mimeo.*), Chicago, December 1987.

Appelbaum, E. and Albin, P., 'Employment, Occupational Structure, and Educational Attainment in the United States: 1973, 1979, and 1987', in OECD and CERI, Research Program on Technological Change and Human Resources, final draft, Washington, D.C., (*mimeo.*), 1989.

Appelbaum, E. and Schettkat, R., 'Employment and Industrial Restructuring: A Comparison of the US and West Germany', in E. Matzner (ed.), *No Way to Full Employment? Discussion Paper FS I 89-16*, Vol. I, Wissenschaftszentrum Berlin, 1990, Appendix, pp. 445-8.

Appelbaum, E. and Schettkat, R. (eds.), *The Impacts of Structural Change and Technological Progress on the Labour Market*, New York, Praeger, 1990.

Büchtemann, C. F. and Schupp, J., 'Socio-economic Aspects of Part-Time Employment in the Federal Republic of Germany', *Discussion Paper FS I 88-6*, Wissenschaftszentrum Berlin, 1988.

Christopherson, S., 'Emerging Patterns of Work in the US, OECD and CERI Research Program on Technological Change and Human Resources', in T. Noyelle, 1988.

Filip-Köhn, R., Neckermann, G. and Stäglin, R., *Information Activities: Updating and Improving the Data Base for the Federal Republic of Germany*, Berlin, DIW, 1984.

Franz, W., 'Beschäftigungsprobleme auf Grund von Inflexibilitäten auf Arbeitsmärkten?', *Discussion-Paper No. 340-87*, Universität Stuttgart, 1987.

Machlup, F., *The Production and Distribution of Knowledge in the United States*, Princeton, Princeton University Press, 1962.

Noyelle, T. (ed.), 'Service and the World Economy: Towards a new International Division of Labour', in P. Cooke and N. Thrift (eds.), *Captive Britain*, Cambridge University Press, 1988.

OECD, *Economic Outlook*, 44, December 1988.

Porat, M.U., *The Information Economy: Definition and Measurement*, US Department of Commerce, Office of Telecommunications, Washington, D.C., US Government Printing Office, 1977.

Schettkat, R., 'Adjustment Processes in the Economy: Labour Market Dynamics in the Federal Republic of Germany', in Appelbaum, E. and Schettkat, R., 1990.

Stäglin, R. and Südfeld, N., 'Der Informationssektor in der Abgrenzung nach informations- und kommunikationstechnischen Erzeugnissen', *Vierteljahreshefte zur Wirtschaftsforschung*, 4, 1988.

Stille, F. and Zwiener, R., 'Beschäftigungswirkungen der Arbeitszeitverkürzung von 1985 in der Metallindustrie', *DIW-Wochenbericht*, 20, 1988.

Thurow, L.C. and Waldstein, L., *Toward a High-Wage, High-Productivity Service Sector*, Washington DC, Economic Policy Institute, 1989.

Wegner, M., 'Die Schaffung von Arbeitsplätzen im Dienstleistungsbereich', *ifo-schnelldienst 6/85*, 1985, pp. 3-13.

PART 3:

ON EFFECTIVE DEMAND CONDITIONS

7. External Constraints on Fiscal Policy: An International Comparison

Hansjörg Herr

In West Germany, fiscal policy is largely discredited. In 1980-82, with a comparatively moderate budget deficit, leading German economists and a section of the public saw the danger of state bankruptcy or even currency reform. The result of this 'emotional' debate was a generally restrictive fiscal policy during the 1980s. In respect to fiscal policy West Germany seems to be a rather special case, having been much less inclined to use fiscal policy to stimulate the economy than other countries. The outcomes of expansionary fiscal policies have been quite varied in different countries and periods. They have been accompanied by both depreciations and appreciations, destabilising deficits of the current account and improvements in trade figures. It is the aim of this paper to explain these different outcomes of fiscal policy. The analysis will be developed within the monetary Keynesian paradigm which still possesses considerable explanatory power when confronted with the sometimes puzzling empirical findings. It should be noted that only short-term or medium-term effects of fiscal policy will be discussed. This seems sensible since even within Keynesian thinking the 'capital budget', which has the aim of stabilising long-term investment, should generally be balanced (cf. Kregel, 1985).

In section 1 the concept of the different quality of money is developed. The confidence effect of fiscal policy is analysed in section 2. Section 3 develops typical scenarios of fiscal policy. Four short case studies - Japan and West Germany after 1975, France after 1981 and the USA after 1982 - are presented in section 4. In the last section a few general remarks about the preconditions of successful expansionary fiscal policy are made.

1. THE QUALITY OF MONEY AND THE STATE OF CONFIDENCE

Since the 1970s, standard theory is puzzled by the behaviour of the exchange rate system. The simple purchasing-power-parity theory is indeed no longer a corner-stone of exchange rate economics. Even its extension to an interest-rate-parity theory and overshooting models is not a much better explanation of exchange rate movements. From a Keynesian point of view this failure is not surprising since the role of expectations and of money is not correctly perceived by standard theory. In the Keynesian paradigm expectations do not reflect the 'fundamentals' of a 'real' world - i.e. a 'world' without money. In a monetary production economy there is no place for the distinction between a world without money as the basis of the economy and a monetary sphere which can be considered as a veil. The completely different perception of the functioning of a market economy results in different theories about international processes.

In the Keynesian paradigm, economic agents and especially wealth holders are confronted with uncertainty in the tradition of Knight and Keynes that is not adequately taken into account by objective probability theories. Of course, any economic agent can form a subjective view of the probability of future events. But in a nonergodic world - a world with historical time - such views do not correspond to objective probabilities because, in the absence of ergodic processes, objective probabilities cannot be formed (cf. Davidson, 1988). This means that economics is always on the edge of science and on the edge of history (cf. Hicks, 1979). For wealth owners who have to act in an uncertain world this implies that they not only have to decide whether to hold their wealth in the form of money, bonds or real property: it is of vital importance for them to decide *in which currency wealth is to be held*.

Depreciating currencies generally imply the loss of individual wealth in comparison to appreciating currencies. Future exchange rate movements cannot be known with certainty in a nonergodic world. They can be compensated by interest rate differentials only to a limited extent. Wealth holders are forced to judge the property protection quality of a currency on a subjective and rather vague, fluctuating and uncertain basis. Under such circumstances the state of confidence becomes a very important element with which to judge the future quality of a currency. This is analogous to the state of confidence argument which was used by

Keynes (1936) to explain investment behaviour. The quality of a currency can be expressed as a non-pecuniary rate - again analogous to the Keynesian liquidity premium (cf. Keynes, 1936). Thus, portfolio equilibrium between countries implies different pecuniary rates of return to take into account the different qualities of currencies (cf. Riese, 1986). In this sense international capital movements can only partly be explained by interest rate differentials (or differentials in pecuniary rates in general); to a large extent they are due to the state of confidence in the different currencies.

It has been frequently pointed out that the horizon in exchange markets is extremely short and that short-term speculation now dominates the market (Schulmeister, 1987; Dornbusch and Frankel, 1988). There is little question about the destabilising impact of short-term speculation creating irrational bubbles and cumulative processes. The question is rather whether these short-term capital movements merely create volatility around exchange rates which are regulated by medium-term expectations or whether short-term speculation dominates exchange rate movements even in the medium term. According to the latter model, medium-term exchange rate movements are the result of a series of purely speculative sequences without any connection to economic 'fundamentals' of any kind. It leads to the vision of a 'casino capitalism' and denies the importance of medium-term considerations. In the average, wealth holders make approximate evaluations of countries within a medium-term horizon in order to judge the quality of a currency; the effect of short-term speculation is then to increase exchange rate volatility around a given medium-term level. In this case, large medium-term exchange rate movements must be the result of changes in a more fundamental evaluation of the quality of a currency.

In the estimation of wealth holders the central elements of the quality of a money are *stability and convertibility*. Expected stability in the sense of a stable exchange rate is needed as an unstable currency cannot fulfil the desired property protection functions of money. It should be clear that external stability is ultimately related to internal stability. This relation can be roughly defined as a stable price level in international comparison. In this sense external stability can be seen as a measure of internal stability. Stable exchange rates can be considered as one aspect of convertibility as only stable currencies can be transferred into other currencies without losses. Another element of convertibility is the extent and likelihood of capital controls, as countries with extensive capital controls are not likely to have a high quality in the eyes of wealth owners. Last but not least the quality of a currency depends on factors which are more or less exogenous for economic theory - from the political stability of the country, to the institutional bargaining patterns in the labour market and the degree of independence of the central bank. The state of confidence of a currency thus depends on the expected economic, institutional and political development of the money-issuing country.

2. THE CONFIDENCE EFFECTS OF FISCAL POLICY

As pointed out above, in the Keynesian paradigm expectations can only be explained historically. In spite of this partly exogenous character of expectations for economic theory, typical scenarios can be developed. If we leave purely political and institutional factors aside, the expected future course of economic policy must be seen as the element dominating the quality of a currency. This is where fiscal policy comes into play. Fiscal policy together with monetary and incomes policy largely determine the macro-economic performance of an economy. Incomes policy cannot be easily used as a macro-economic instrument as it is influenced by institutional factors which are difficult to change. This leaves fiscal and monetary policy as the main tools with which to regulate macro-economic performance.

Macro-economic policies thus more or less determine the stability and convertibility of currencies. If wealth owners believe that a country will always make external stability the first aim of economic policy and if the political and institutional circumstances make such a strategy likely, the quality of the currency will be high. Such positive stable expectations can be considered as *brand-name capital* (cf. Klein, 1974). Brand-name capital cannot be built up in a short time. It rather reflects the long-term experience of economic agents. This argumentation is in line with the theory of rational expectations which stresses the important point that economic agents take into account - however imperfectly - government action (cf. Hahn, 1982). The central flaw of the neoclassical theory of rational expectations is, however, that it neglects that rational expectations are compatible with any economic paradigm. Agents who believe in Keynesian theory can expect completely different results of government policies than agents who believe in neoclassical theory. This is not only a problem for theory, it is even more a problem for economic policy as expectations are, to a certain extent, self-fulfilling. Nevertheless, rational expectations remain a justified critique of hydraulic IS-LM-Keynesianism and its extension by Mundell (1968) and Fleming (1962) to international relations. It is true that this kind of Keynesianism fails to take into account endogenous preference shifts induced by economic policy.

During the 1930s the British Treasury criticised the Keynesian demand for an expansionary fiscal policy by pointing out the adverse confidence effects of credit-financed public demand. According to the Treasury, expansionary fiscal measures would destroy the state of confidence, would lead to decreasing profit expectations of entrepreneurs and would increase liquidity preference, resulting in higher interest rates. This argumentation implies a psychological crowding out as the fiscal expansion is neutralised by a deterioration of private demand due to the fall in the state of confidence. The argument was also extended to external considerations, the Treasury arguing that the attractiveness of London as a financial centre would be damaged. Together with the expected deterioration of the current account this would lead to balance of payments problems - at least under the weak position of the British economy following the return to the Gold Standard after the first World War. Keynes did not reject the possibility of psychological crowding out. In a situation of unemployment he judged it to be irrational but self-fulfilling. In his opinion the orthodox strategy of the Treasury reinforced the negative expectations which - at least in principle - could be overcome (cf. Middleton, 1985, p. 172).[1]

A collapse of the state of confidence following fiscal expansion is in no way certain or even the most likely result. In fact, an expansionary fiscal policy can stabilise the state of confidence and the quality of a currency if it is carried out in certain circumstances. First of all, a fiscal expansion does not necessarily lead to higher budget deficits while a fiscal contraction can fail to balance the budget. Expansionary fiscal policy can create more growth and employment and so increase the tax base. On the other hand, in a cyclical crisis a policy aimed at balancing the budget is counterproductive and unlikely to be successful. Even expected tax increases in the future will not depress a fiscal stimulus. If unemployment exists, income can be influenced by fiscal policy and rational agents expect the increase in income to be high enough to pay future increased taxes (cf. Tobin, 1980, pp. 61f.).

Within the Keynesian paradigm, fiscal policy is a necessary condition for controlling the endogenous instability of a fully developed market economy. Its anticyclical use improves the general performance of an economy and can be seen as a vital instrument to stabilise the state of confidence. The stabilising impact of fiscal policy has many elements. Among other things it improves the growth of the social product and stabilises profits, can control a cumulative profit and income deflation (cf.

Keynes, 1930) and leads to greater political stability. Taking these arguments together, rational economic agents can and often do judge fiscal expansion in a situation of unemployment as improving the state of confidence and consider the orthodox theory of a balanced budget as destabilising.

3. TYPICAL SCENARIOS OF FISCAL EXPANSION

At this stage the arguments presented may appear unsatisfactory as the negative Treasury view and the positive Keynesian view of expansionary fiscal policy are crudely contrasted. Both theoretical and empirical work suggests that the national and international *context* in which fiscal policy is put forward is of vital importance. In this way it is possible to develop typical scenarios of success and failure.

In the *internal context* the possibility of stimulating investment and controlling inflation are the most important points. Fiscal expansion leads to higher capacity utilisation of a given physical capital stock. But in a situation of mass unemployment the capital stock might be not large enough to employ all agents who would like to work for a given wage. Within a medium-term depression with net investment negative the capital stock will even decrease and intensify the disproportion between the workforce and the capital stock. In a situation of high capital utilisation government demand can lead to excess demand and rising prices without improving the employment situation. This means that while fiscal stimulus is always effective in a deep slump to increase the utilisation of capital in the medium-term it can only be successful if it stimulates investment demand. On the Keynesian view fiscal policy has to stabilise or improve the expected marginal efficiency of capital to be successful in the medium-term.[2]

If there exists a shortage of capital stock in comparison to the workforce, then during a phase of accumulation a certain amount of inflation is almost unavoidable - this at least is the position of Keynes (1930) and Schumpeter (1926). Thus, generally even a very successful fiscal policy will be accompanied by a modest inflation rate which must be tolerated by the central bank. Central bank policy which is fixed on an inflation rate of zero certainly 'belongs to the species of remedy which cures the disease by killing the patient' (Keynes, 1936, p. 323). However, even low inflation rates bear the seeds of a cumulative destabilising process, if higher prices lead to higher nominal wages and a wage-price spiral is triggered off. It should be noted that this can happen even in a situation of mass unemployment. To control such a process, labour market institutions and incomes policy are extremely important (cf. Scharpf, 1987; Soskice, 1988).[3]

In the *international context* it is changes in the current account and the exchange rate which are most important. With *fixed exchange rates* and without international cooperation, successful fiscal stimulus will run into the problem of current account deficits. Higher growth and eventually higher prices will lead to increasing imports and to a diffusion of the demand stimulus to other countries. Clearly it is much more difficult to pursue an isolated fiscal expansion than a coordinated world-wide expansion. Current account deficits must be financed by surplus on capital account. In the Mundell-Fleming world this task is easily achieved by higher national interest rates. One major shortcoming of this postulate is its complete disregard of different quality of monies. It can be extremely difficult for a country to achieve a positive cash flow on reasonable terms, indeed if the quality of the currency is sufficiently low the creation of capital imports may fail completely. Unfortunately a current account deficit is a negative factor for the state of confidence. This is not surprising as a deficit country has greater difficulty in controlling its cash flow than a surplus country - especially if it is already a debtor country - and is likely to depreciate or to take steps to control its capital exports (cf. Minsky, 1979). Often countries with current account deficits sooner or later suffer a confidence crisis which triggers off destabilising capital exports and forces them to follow restrictive economic policies. The first measure which can be taken to ward off a confidence crisis is to introduce a restrictive monetary policy. This signals wealth holders that the external stability of the currency is to be defended by an internal recession. If a country is forced to use higher interest rates to create capital imports, an asymmetric adjustment process is already at work. In Keynesian thinking it is nearly impossible to stimulate an economy with high interest rates as they depress investment: expansionary monetary policy can fail to stimulate the economy, but restrictive monetary policy never fails to create an economic crisis. Keynes judged 'easy money policy' as a precondition of economic expansion. Consequently he recommended capital controls to secure an internal expansion and never high interest rates (cf. Keynes, 1930).[4]

Given *flexible exchange rates*, an internal fiscal expansion can theoretically be accompanied by a moderate depreciation to keep the external balance in equilibrium. However, this attractive vision of an isolated fiscal expansion in one country entails several serious problems. First, the danger of cumulative rising prices is increased as every depreciation is followed by an internal price push that can trigger off a depreciation-wage-inflation spiral. Thus favourable institutional and political circumstances are required, providing for an effective incomes policy and the acceptance of higher employment against terms of trade losses. But this does not seem to be the most difficult problem. Much more serious is the danger that a depreciating currency might lose its quality and be exposed to destabilising capital exports. Capital flight can create such strong depreciations that the inflationary impact becomes intolerable and the state of confidence in the currency deteriorates even further. Such a process can only be stopped by high interest rates and an internal recession. The combination of expansionary fiscal policy and moderate depreciation to control the external balance implies an effective incomes policy and in certain circumstances a more or less effective control of international capital movements. Flexible exchange rates together with an unstable leading world currency - both characteristic of the world economy since the early 1970s - have resulted in an intensification of the competition between currencies. It has become a rational strategy for nations to save the national currency from destabilising capital movements by fighting for current account surpluses and avoiding deficits and depreciations as far as possible. Unfortunately such mercantilistic policies, if even pursued only in a few important countries, are sufficient to create the generally restrictive bias which has been characteristic of the world economy since the 1970s. In such an economic and political environment a strategy of fiscal expansion plus depreciation becomes considerably more difficult.

Under a system of flexible exchange rates - i.e. in the real world today - a number of typical scenarios of fiscal expansion can be drawn up. First, fiscal policy along with depreciation and without restrictive monetary policy is only successful if there is an effective incomes policy and a degree of regulation of capital movements. Of course, such a strategy is especially difficult where the current account is already in deficit. The 'classical' scenario of the failure of fiscal expansion can be described by the combination of a current account deficit, capital flight and a cumulative depreciation-inflation spiral. In such a scenario the situation becomes unsustainable within a short time and economic policy has to change course (cf. OECD, 1988). Second, current account deficits, depreciation and the fear of losing control over the external and internal value of the currency force countries to the combination of expansionary fiscal and restrictive monetary policy. Such a contradictory policy must be judged as part of an asymmetric adjustment process and is very costly in respect to the twin deficits of the budget and the current account. In the medium term such a strategy has difficulty in stimulating investment and easily becomes inflationary. Usually this scenario implies an overvaluation of the currency to control inflation. Third, countries with surpluses in the current account can be considered to have the greatest room for manoeuvre for fiscal expansion. They find it relatively easy to combine expansionary fiscal and monetary policy with a stable exchange rate. Surplus countries which use their room for manoeuvre to expand their economies contribute to international cooperation as restrictions for deficit countries are thereby reduced. Fourth, the combination of expansionary fiscal and monetary policy, stable exchange rates and a deficit on the current account is a very special case. It implies that there is a strong, usually not purely economic, factor which gives the currency a high state of confidence that can be exploited.

In summary, there are three types of successful fiscal expansion. All three types are characterised by the combination of expansionary fiscal and monetary policy. But the circumstances that allow such a policy are very different. A country can use its current account surplus as an unused store of 'expansionary policy potential' to stimulate its economy; a deficit country can use its high liquidity premium - its brand-name capital which can also be interpreted as an unused potential for an expansionary policy - to stimulate its economy; or a country can successfully follow fiscal expansion if it is able to manage a controlled depreciation without the instrument of high interest rates.

4. FOUR SHORT CASE STUDIES OF FISCAL POLICY[5]

The arguments presented above suggest that there is no deterministic causality between expansionary fiscal policy and success or failure. Of central importance is the economic, institutional and political context within which expansion occurs. This point will now be illustrated by discussing four short case studies of fiscal policy.

Japan after 1975: The Exploitation of the Surplus on Current Account

During the early 1970s Japanese economic performance was rather poor: the inflation rate and wage increases in Japan were among the highest in the OECD, the current account went into deficit after the first oil price shock, there was considerable strike activity, and the external value of the yen decreased after 1973. Within a few years Japan had managed to change the situation considerably, following massive fiscal expansion from 1975 to 1978. In 1975 nearly all Western countries applied expansionary fiscal stimuli but from 1976 on Japan acted completely against the international trend. The fiscal expansion was accompanied by a surplus on the current account, substantial real growth, low unemployment and even an appreciating yen. The basis of this success must be seen in specifically Japanese labour market institutions and the system of industrial relations. Japan was able to introduce an effective incomes policy which reduced nominal wage increases substantially and even allowed an absolute decrease in unit labour costs. In 1975 the major change came when the unions and the conservative government modified their strategies and adapted quickly to the changed economic and social environment, joining with business to win the so-called international 'economic war' (cf. Deutschmann, 1986). There was a kind of implicit social contract that offered the unions deficit-led economic stimulation - to a large extent in the form of social improvements - in return for lower wage increases. The cooperative 'regime' between the employers, unions and government could be seen not only at the national but also at branch and firm level (cf. Levine and Taira, 1985).

After 1975, internal and external conditions were favourable for Japan. This was mainly due to the weakness of the dollar as the leading world currency. The yen started to appreciate and Japan could easily combine fiscal expansion with expansionary monetary policy. The preference for the yen was a vital factor in reducing internal inflation and wage increases. The basis for the preference for the yen must be sought in the rapidly improving current account after 1973.

As a result of the extremely favourable development of unit labour costs Japan could combine nominal appreciations with real undervaluation - an ideal combination to produce a high quality of the national currency. In the international context the expansionary fiscal policy was one instrument applied to control the export surplus without severe appreciation. Until 1978 Japan tried to stimulate its growth rate to play its part in international cooperation and to fight against its 'appreciation crisis'. In 1979, however, Japan turned to a restrictive fiscal policy, a change motivated by the sharp turn of US policy towards stabilising the dollar in that year. Unlike West Germany, Japan did not act against an early recovery of the dollar. It rather followed a depreciation strategy to improve its international competitiveness; it also controlled the deficit on current account which occurred after 1979. As early as 1979 the yen depreciated against the dollar and other leading Western currencies and Japan only tried to control the depreciation at a certain point.

To summarise: after 1975 Japan consequently used its room for manoeuvre for fiscal expansion provided by the surplus on current account and the preference for the yen. It contributed to international cooperation and at the same time stabilised internal growth and employment. It achieved an ideal combination of incomes policy and expansionary fiscal and monetary policy. During the period analysed, the isolated fiscal expansion in Japan must be judged as a clear success.

West Germany after 1975: The Unused Chance to Reduce Unemployment

It is especially interesting to compare West German fiscal policy after 1975 with that in Japan because, during this period, Germany found itself in a similar situation. The D-Mark appreciated against major currencies and West Germany enjoyed substantial current account surpluses. In spite of this similarity and much higher unemployment rates than in Japan, West German policy-makers acted completely differently. After 1975 fiscal policy became extremely restrictive, being largely responsible for poor German growth in 1977/78. Even the Council of Economic Experts argued that the consolidation of the budget was too sharp in the light of the German growth performance (cf. Sachverständigenrat, 1978). The restrictive fiscal policy cannot be justified as having been necessary to fight inflation or discipline the unions, as the West German inflation rate was the lowest of the larger industrial Western countries and nominal wage increases had been even lower than in Japan.[6] It could be argued that West Germany was not able to follow fiscal expansion because of the lack of an effective incomes policy. Certainly the 'Concerted Action' which was introduced in Germany in 1967 was not a success, but after 1974 the German unions had been very disciplined in respect to wage increases and technological change: as far as labour market conditions were concerned an expansion would have been possible.

West Germany's restrictive fiscal policy and current account surpluses led to conflict with the United States. In the so-called 'Carter-Schmidt controversy' Carter pressed Schmidt to pursue fiscal expansion, arguing that surplus countries should - like Japan - act as locomotives for world growth. The background of this debate was the weak dollar, which in spite of disciplined US fiscal policy, again came under pressure in 1977-78. At various summit meetings Schmidt rejected the US demands until 1978; in Germany moderate fiscal expansion then started in 1979. Its lack of success was due to the fact that it was not supported by the central bank and only became effective after the international economic situation had completely changed.

From 1976 to 1978 the Bundesbank practised expansionary monetary policy and repeatedly accepted higher growth rates of monetary aggregates than planned. The expansionary monetary policy was motivated by the desire to control the appreciation of the D-Mark, but it was not able to achieve satisfactory economic growth. In late 1978 the US started to pursue restrictive monetary and fiscal policy to stabilise the weak dollar. The institutionally independent Bundesbank, unlike the Schmidt government, not only rejected cooperation it even prevented an early recovery of the dollar against the D-Mark. Any increase in US interest rates was followed by an increase in German rates. Paul Volcker who became president of the Fed in July 1979 tried once more to reach agreement with the Bundesbank over exchange-rate stabilisation and exchange market intervention in October 1979. The 'Hamburg meeting' was a failure and later in the year the Fed intensified its restrictive course (c.f. Emminger, 1986). The recovery of the dollar against the D-Mark did not commence until the election victory of President Reagan in November 1980. The very restrictive US monetary policy was in large part due - especially in 1979 - to the uncooperative policy of the Bundesbank, begging the question why the Bundesbank followed such an uncooperative course. In the light of higher growth of monetary aggregates than projected the Bundesbank argued that there was the danger of a new wave of inflation. The restrictive economic policy in the US, so the argument goes, provided the opportunity to return to the internally favoured policy of controlling the growth of the money supply. This policy also fitted into external considerations. The Bundesbank preferred a complete regeneration of the dollar as a stable world money and wanted to relieve the D-Mark of its role as an international reserve currency as it led to destabilising capital flows. Rather the Bundesbank wanted to play a restricted role as the 'stabilisation anchor' within European monetary relations. A half-hearted stabilisation of the dollar obviously was not enough for the Bundesbank to enable it to play a stable and only regionally hegemonic monetary role in Western Europe.

The radical turn in US policy changed the world economy completely and created a worldwide recession. The West German current account went into deficit from 1979 until 1981. This was due to the appreciation of the D-Mark in the previous years, the now isolated fiscal expansion of Germany and the second oil price shock. In Germany this situation was regarded as a disaster (cf. Fels and Fröhlich, 1987) and indeed the D-Mark started to weaken and was in danger of losing its leading role within the European Monetary System. The Bundesbank diagnosed a crisis of confidence in the D-Mark and intensified its restrictive monetary policy. It acted according to the strict rule, which has been followed since the 1950s, never to allow a depreciation of the D-Mark and to counter a deficit in the current account by creating an internal recession. For the Bundesbank a strategy of depreciation to control the deficit in the current account - as followed in Japan - was not acceptable. Besides the strong preference of the Bundesbank (and the West German population) for a stable price level and current account surpluses, this policy finds its explanation in the role West Germany plays within European monetary affairs as a second reserve currency. Obviously the international role and reputation of the D-Mark were more important to the political establishment in West Germany than higher employment. In such circumstances - deficit in the current account and restrictive monetary policy - there was no room for a successful fiscal policy. In 1982, after intense political and academic pressure, fiscal policy started to become restrictive and had a strong, procyclical, negative effect on growth and employment.

To summarise, from 1976 until 1978 Germany failed to take the opportunity of stimulating internal employment and so acting responsibly within the international context. A Keynesian expansionary fiscal and monetary policy would have been possible. There is not much point in speculating about the outcome of this different approach, but it seems certain that the United States would not have followed such a restrictive policy if Germany had been more cooperative. In Germany the co-ordination of different macro-economic policies has been extremely poor. Before 1978 monetary policy was expansionary and fiscal policy restrictive, while after 1978 it was the other way round. In comparison to Japan the German policy was badly timed, much less pragmatic and not without a trace of Prussian rigour.

France after 1981: The Failure of Fiscal Stimulation

The context - both national and international - within which French fiscal expansion took place was extremely unfavourable. In May 1981, when Mitterrand came into office, the world economy was on its way into a deep recession which was due in large measure to the worldwide restrictive economic policies led by the US. Of considerable importance was that Germany, the major trading partner of France, simultaneously pursued particularly restrictive policies in its fight against the current account deficit. Of the larger Western industrial countries France was the only one which followed an expansionary economic policy in 1981-82. At the same time the internal French situation was characterised by a deep crisis of confidence in the business community (cf. Sachs and Wyplosz, 1986). The negative 'Mitterrand effect' (Dornbusch, 1986) was the result of the uncertain economic and political future of France under the new socialist government. Announcements of nationalisation of industries, redistributive measures, etc. could not be without negative effects - possibly largely on irrational grounds - on the state of business confidence. Compared with successful fiscal cases the magnitude of the French fiscal expansion was moderate. The fiscal stimulus in 1981-82 did not do much more than compensate for the cyclical decrease in aggregate demand and the loss of export demand. The result was, however, a much smaller recession in France than in other Western countries.

French policy mainly failed because of external instability; a current account deficit, capital flight, depreciation and high inflation created a cumulative process which led to an unsustainable situation. When President Mitterrand, came to power the current account was already in deficit. High French growth and inflation rates compared with other industrialised countries led to a sharp deterioration in the current account. Of importance was also the poor competitiveness of French industry due to structural problems and the impossibility of pursuing a depreciation strategy to the extent necessary. The central point, however, was that France was not able to finance the deficit in the current account by private capital inflows. In 1981 private capital inflow was about zero and in 1982 it was only about half of the deficit. This meant that the reserves of the French central bank melted away swiftly. From 1982 on the government created official capital inflows by taking credits abroad to spare central bank reserves. But this was not enough to finance the deficits. Shortly after the election of President Mitterrand, French interest rates increased sharply to control capital flight. The effect was unsatisfactory and severe capital controls had to be introduced. These controls were more or less effective but they could not of course create the required private capital inflows. In 1981-82 the franc, in spite of considerable official intervention, was extremely weak. Several realignments within the European Monetary System were necessary and the franc depreciated against non-EMS-countries as well. The point was reached where further depreciations to improve French competitiveness and to balance the current account became impossible. The French inflation rate was one of the highest within the OECD and there was the danger of an accelerating depreciation-inflation spiral. The stabilisation of the exchange rate had to be used to control internal inflation. This is a clear sign that France -

unlike Japan - was not able to use an incomes policy to reduce inflation and that it was not able to combine international competitiveness with a stable exchange rate. After the election victory of President Mitterrand the policy rather was to increase wages by higher minimum wages and a general stimulation of consumption. To control wages or even to accept terms of trade losses by depreciations did not fit into the concept of the unions and the economic policy of the new government.

In 1982 the expansion policy was reduced and in 1983 a 'socialist' austerity programme was introduced. Finally, the external pressure in the exchange market, a fall in official reserves and an increasing public foreign debt 'persuaded' the French government to change course. The EMS in particular acted as a disciplinary factor. The French government was forced to choose between pursuing a course without Europe as backing or the integration of France into West European policy. In the end there was a clear decision for the EMS which was politically considered as a synonym for Europe.

In summary, the moderate French fiscal policy failed because of a negative confidence effect that led to low private investment, capital flight, depreciation, inflation, etc. This was certainly not due to the fiscal policy itself, but was rather the outcome of the unfavourable context in which it was put into effect. Remarkable - for example compared with British or Italian policy during the 1970s - was the swift and decisive response of the French government. The 'Keynesian phase' of socialist policy lasted less than two years.

The United States after 1982: the Exploitation of the Liquidity Premium of the Dollar

When President Reagan came into power in early 1981 he put forward the concept of supply-side economics. The tax cuts introduced shortly after the election created a severe budget deficit. In complete contrast to the expectations of the Reagan administration the budget could not be balanced during the following years - there was no Laffer-effect at work. In fact the reduction of the budget deficit failed because of a combination of tax cuts, high defence expenditure and the impossibility of sufficiently large offsetting cuts in civilian public expenditure. The only moderate deceleration of the increase of non-defence expenditure was largely due to the political conflict between the administration and Congress. The budget deficit obviously was the easiest way to 'solve' this conflict. But what is most interesting, in this context, is the fact that in 1982 the United States started a phase of largely unintended fiscal stimuli. In 1983 a period of high economic growth, sharp decline in unemployment and inflation started. At the same time the deficit in the current account reached new records without weakening the dollar - until 1985. It would be misleading to judge US economic policy as fitting the logic of the Mundell-Fleming model with the combination of restrictive monetary and expansionary fiscal policy. Of course, in 1979 US monetary policy became extremely restrictive and was the major reason for the deepest recession since the 1930s. But in 1982 monetary policy too turned expansionary. The reason for the sharp change can be found in the outbreak of the debt crisis in both the Third World and the US which forced the Fed to act as a lender of last resort internationally as well as nationally. The change in monetary policy, however, did not create a conflict for the Fed since, after three years of restrictive monetary policy, the property protection quality of the dollar had been regenerated. Only *after* monetary policy had turned expansionary did the strong US recovery start leading to high growth rates during the following years. Thus, the US expansion followed the traditional Keynesian logic of expansionary fiscal and accommodating monetary policy.

High US growth and the appreciation of the dollar explain the increasing current account deficit in a purely traditional manner. International wealth holders were not only prepared to finance a given deficit, obviously there was an *ex-ante* surplus demand for dollars which caused the dollar to appreciate. The high trade deficit certainly increased the leakage of public demand stimulation, but in spite of this it had a very favourable effect on the US economy. It was an ideal instrument to reduce inflation without the cost of creating a profit deflation and unemployment. The appreciation of the dollar largely reduced the sacrifices required to bring down the US inflation rate without the necessity of an effective incomes policy (cf. Sachs, 1985).

Early in 1985 the dollar boom ended and a sharp depreciation started which lasted until about 1988. The depreciation was welcomed by the administration (in fact in 1985 the leading Western central banks tried to induce a controlled depreciation of the dollar) since this was seen as a means to reduce the deficit in the current account without an internal crisis. The depreciation did not trigger off a new wave of inflation and in this sense was successful. In retrospect, appreciation and subsequent depreciation appear as a masterpiece of political economy, squeezing out inflation without the high costs that were paid for this purpose in Western Europe (cf. Dornbusch, 1987, p. 14).

For some time at least, US economic policy must be considered as a clear success. In the long run, however, instabilities will develop because of the transformation of the US from a creditor to a large debtor country and the difficulty of the latter in controlling its cash flow and producing permanent confidence in its currency. The problem is not a deficit in the current account as such - a hegemonic power with a strong reserve currency can afford a deficit in the current account - the problem is how to control it. The sharp fall of the dollar in spite of huge central bank intervention in 1985-87 and the stock exchange crash in 1987 may be indicators of the possible problems. It also should not be forgotten that the United States are indebted in its own currency and - like any debtor which is indebted in its own money - is tempted to reduce the debt by inflation. In spite of this the US has shown that isolated medium-term fiscal expansion in combination with huge current account deficits is possible. After 1982 there was certainly no negative confidence effect: on the contrary the fiscal expansion was associated by an improved state of confidence that showed itself in high investment in the US and a high demand for the dollar. There was a 'Reagan effect' and not a 'Mitterrand effect'. It could be argued that economic agents believed in 'Reaganomics' and in a balanced budget and current account in the medium term. This argument is only convincing for the early years since it soon became clear that the budget would not be balanced in the medium term. The positive state of confidence remained in spite of the expected future twin deficits in the budget and the current account.

Again, the period analysed shows the importance of the context in which fiscal policy is practised. In the case of the US, this cannot be reduced to the 'Reagan effect'. To understand the success of the US, the international role of the dollar has to be taken into account. Since the late 1960s the dollar has been acting as the (unstable) leading world currency and thus as a centre of instability. But as there is no real candidate that could take over the role of the dollar it is comparatively easy for the United States to regenerate the property protection quality of its currency. To put it slightly differently: it is easy for the US to present itself as the safe haven for international wealth since it still has sufficient economic, political, and military power to maintain its hegemonic position. After the election of Reagan it seems that economic agents expected a complete and permanent regeneration of the dollar as a stable world currency. In retrospect, the expectations of a stable dollar have proved false. The dollar boom until 1985 can be judged as an irrational bubble (cf. Bliss, 1985). However, the irrational element was not dominated by short-term speculation, but seems to have been due to false expectations of US economic policy. In 1985 it would have been relatively easy for the US to stabilise the dollar by a restrictive monetary policy and the creation of an internal recession. Instead the US lowered its interest rates and attempted to bring the dollar down - a consistent policy to prevent unemployment. The US did not follow the rule of stabilising the external value of the dollar - as did Great Britain as the emitter of the leading currency under the Gold Standard - and indeed it has been extremely difficult for wealth holders to determine 'the rules of the game' since the breakdown of the Bretton Woods system.

Because of the special role of the US and the dollar within the Western world it is clear that the 'masterpiece' of expansionary fiscal and monetary policy, increasing deficits in the current account and simultaneous appreciation of the currency cannot easily be copied. After 1982 the US used the brand-name capital - the high liquidity premium - of the dollar as world money to pursue its policy. Especially within a regime of flexible exchange rates, for most nations a positive current account is the main means of producing and preserving a high state of confidence of their currencies. The combination of a deficit in the current account and a high liquidity premium must be primarily seen as a privilege of the nation emitting the leading world currency.

5.   ROOM FOR MANOEUVRE FOR EXPANSIONARY FISCAL POLICY

The Keynesian paradigm and empirical investigations suggest that in spite of the integrated world market there is still room for successful fiscal expansion. Highly-integrated international capital markets sometimes act as a restriction on national economic (and thus, political) autonomy, but sometimes they create additional room for manoeuvre in the form of high preferences for certain currencies. Whether expansionary fiscal policy creates a negative confidence effect ('Treasury view') or a positive confidence effect ('Keynesian view') depends largely on political and institutional factors. While the system of flexible exchange rates intensifies the instability of the world market, it would be false to judge it as a general restriction on expansionary fiscal policies. It confronts governments and central banks with the additional sometimes positive and sometimes negative factor of the exchange rate which is central for trade flows and even more for movements in the price level.

Integrated international capital markets and flexible exchange rates destroy any room for manoeuvre for fiscal expansion if the state of confidence is low. The Keynesian theory of psychological crowding out points to this possibility, but in a situation of unemployment this kind of crowding out is based on irrational factors and may be overcome after a tricky start. However, in unfavourable internal and external circumstances psychological crowding out, an uncontrollable shift of certain micro-economic preferences, can be an effective barrier to full employment. Generally, countries with current account surpluses have substantial room for manoeuvre for expansionary fiscal policy. International cooperation would imply that surplus countries in particular should follow expansionary economic policies. But the demand for cooperation is as old as the existence of asymmetric relations: it might well be in the economic and political interest of a surplus country to follow restrictive policies and, unfortunately, this may even be in accordance with the preferences of the majority of its population. Isolated expansionary economic policies are, however, possible even without a surplus in the current account. Under certain circumstances a country can follow an expansionary fiscal policy in combination with a stable exchange rate and a deficit in the current account and without a restrictive monetary policy if it can use its brand-name capital to create private capital inflows. If agents trust in an economic policy which will defend the exchange rate even if it creates an internal crisis a huge current account deficit can easily be financed even in the long term. The 'fundamentals' in respect to exchange rate expectations are not to be found in a balanced current account, but rather in the expectation that in future the economic policy of a country will be to defend the exchange rate - or not, as the case may be. Besides, a system with institutionally fixed exchange rates can, to a certain extent, produce the expectations that countries will defend the convertibility of their currencies and in many cases this will increase the room for manoeuvre for expansionary fiscal policy.

It is not easy to develop a recipe for fiscal expansion in an uncooperative world economy. Of course it is possible to fight for a high quality of one's own currency in order to finance current account deficits without high interest rates. However, such a policy is generally only possible under certain circumstances and mostly only for leading currency nations. The most crucial point for countries with currencies with lower brand-name capital must be seen in a successful incomes policy which allows an internal expansion or even depreciation without intensive inflationary pressure and high interest rates. In the latter case, capital controls might still be useful to facilitate such a strategy without external instability.

NOTES

1 Recently the theory of psychological crowding out was rediscovered by leading German economists (cf. Fels and Fröhlich, 1987), who even saw a negative fiscal multiplier initiated by fiscal stimulation at work. In the tradition of Keynes it can be argued that after 1981 the German economic profession - together with the position of the Bundesbank and the passivity of the Schmidt-administration - created or at last deepened the confidence crisis in Germany. The thesis of psychological crowding out in West Germany after 1981 and the belief that the reduction of the budget led to higher growth even in the short run is not very convincing.
2 From this argument it follows directly that - apart from during a slump - fiscal expansion must have a medium-term time horizon to improve profit expectations.
3 In the standard Keynesian interpretation - the *IS-LM model* - investment and consumption goods are aggregated to 'goods', with the result that in this model government demand can easily substitute a lack of investment demand. In original Keynesian thinking, investment goods are - like bonds - assets and must be clearly separated from consumption goods (cf. Leijonhufvud, 1968). The specific aggregation of the IS-LM model is one reason for its over-optimistic view about fiscal policy.
4 As a result of the aggregation of investment and consumption goods the Mundell-Fleming model postulates that a restrictive monetary policy as the instrument to secure external balance can be overcompensated by expansionary fiscal policy to secure (internal) full employment.
5 For a more detailed analysis of fiscal policy since the 1970s see Herr and Spahn (1989).
6 By contrast in 1972-74 there was a clash between the unions and the Bundesbank. The Bundesbank made it clear that it would not accommodate high wage increases. When wage increases reached new peaks - by German standards - the Bundesbank deliberately created unemployment.

REFERENCES

Bliss, C., 'The Rise and the Fall of the Dollar', *Oxford Review of Economics*, Vol. 2 , 1985.

Davidson, P., 'Financial Markets, Investment and Employment', in J.A. Kregel, E. Matzner and A. Roncaglia (eds.), *Barriers to Full Employment*, London, Macmillan, 1988.

Deutschmann, C., 'Economic Restructuring and Company Unionism: The Japanese Model', *Discussion Paper IIM/LMP 86-17*, Wissenschaftszentrum Berlin für Sozialforschung, 1986.

Dornbusch, R., 'Unemployment: Europe's Challenge of the '80s', *Challenge*, September, October 1986.

Dornbusch, R., 'Exchange Rate Economics', *The Economic Journal*, Vol. 97, 1987.

Dornbusch, R. and Frankel, J., 'Flexible Exchange Rate System: Experience and Alternatives', in S. Borner (ed.), *International Finance and Trade in a Polycentric World*, London, Macmillan, 1988.

Emminger, O., *D-Mark-Mark, Dollar, Währungskrisen. Die Erinnerungen eines Bundesbankpräsidenten*, Stuttgart, Deutsche Verlagsanstalt, 1986.

Fels, G. and Fröhlich, H.-P., 'Germany and the World Economy: A German View', *Economic Policy*, Vol. 4, 1987.

Fleming, J.M., ' Domestic Financial Policies under Fixed and Floating Exchange Rates', *IMF Staff Papers*, Vol. 9, 1962.

Hahn, F., 'Reflections on the Invisible Hand', *Lloyds Bank Review*, April, 1982.

Herr, H. and Spahn, H.-P., 'Staatsverschuldung, Zahlungsbilanz und Wechselkurs. Außenwirtschaftliche Spielräume und Grenzen der Fiskalpolitik', *Studien zur monetären Ökonomie*, Regensburg, Transfer, 1989.

Hicks, J., *Causality in Economics*, London, Oxford University Press, 1979.

Keynes, J.M., *A Treatise on Money*, London, Macmillan, 1930.

Keynes, J.M., *The General Theory of Employment, Interest, and Money*, London, Macmillan, 1936.

Klein, B., 'The Competitive Supply of Money', *Journal of Money, Credit and Banking*, Vol. 6, 1974.

Kregel, J.A., 'Budget Deficits, Stabilization Policy and Liquidity Preference: Keynes' Post-War Policy Proposals', in F. Vicarelli (ed.), *Keynes' Relevance Today*, London, Macmillan, 1985.

Leijonhufvud, A., *On Keynesian Economics and the Economics of Keynes*, London, Oxford University Press, 1968.

Levine, S.B. and Taira, K., 'Japan's Industrial Relations: A Social Compact Emerges', in J. Harvey, M. Thompson and W. Daniels (eds.), *Industrial Relations in a Decade of Economic Change*, Madison, Industrial Relations Research Department, 1985.

Middleton, R., *Towards the Money Economy: Keynes, the Treasury and the Fiscal Policy Debate of the 1930s*, London, Methuen, 1985.

Minsky, H.P., 'Financial Interrelations, the Balance of Payments, and the Dollar Crisis', in J.D. Aronson (ed.), *Debt and the Less Developed Countries*, Boulder, Westview Press, 1979.

Mundell, R.A., *International Economics*, New York, London, Macmillan, 1968.

OECD, *Why Economic Policies Change Course*, Paris, 1988.

Riese, H., *Theorie der Inflation*, Tübingen, Mohr, 1986.

Sachs, J., 'The Dollar and the Policy Mix: 1985', *Brookings Papers on Economic Activity*, 1985.

Sachs, J. and Wyplosz, L., 'France under Mitterrand', *Economic Policy*, Vol. 2, 1986.

Sachverständigenrat, 'Wachstum und Währung', *Annual Report 1978-79*, 1978.

Scharpf, F., *Sozialdemokratische Krisenpolitik in Europa*, Frankfurt, Campus, 1987.

Schulmeister, S., 'An Essay on Exchange Rate Dynamics', *Discussion Paper FS I 87-8*, Wissenschaftszentrum Berlin für Sozialforschung 1987, 1987.

Schumpeter, J.A., *Theorie der wirtschaftlichen Entwicklung*, Berlin, Duncker & Humblot, 1926.

Soskice, D., 'Industrial Relations and Unemployment: The Case for Flexible Corporatism', in J. A. Kregel, E. Matzner and A. Roncaglia (eds.), *Barriers to Full Employment*, London, Macmillan, 1988.

Tobin, J., *Asset Accumulation and Economic Activity*, London, Oxford University Press, 1980.

8. Monopolistic International Policy Co-ordination by DM-Appreciation: An Alternative to Flexible Exchange Rates and EMS-Harmonisation[1]

Heinz-Peter Spahn

This chapter will broach three topics: first, the instability of foreign exchange markets under the regime of flexible exchange rates; second, some problems of and reform proposals for the European Monetary System; and third, a scenario in which German monetary policy takes the lead in a future system which may be characterised as policy co-ordination by market forces.

1. FOREIGN EXCHANGE MARKET INSTABILITY

The instability in foreign exchange markets can still most easily be demonstrated by looking at the path of the D-Mark-dollar exchange rate. Since 1985, this rate has dropped from 3.50 to 1.60, risen to 2 marks per dollar in mid-summer 1989 and then started to decline again. For many years now, most economists have agreed that exchange rate movements can hardly be explained by referring to the so-called economic fundamentals. Nevertheless, the devaluation of the D-Mark against the dollar in the first half of 1989 came as a surprise for many observers, including the German central bank. It argued (1989) that the currency of a country with a huge current account surplus should be appreciating rather than depreciating.

Indeed, a current account surplus usually indicates monetary stability, i.e. comparatively low inflation. As a consequence, owners of financial wealth who are interested in protecting the real value of their assets should direct capital flows towards the country in question.

Capital imports should then strengthen the tendencies of revaluation which are already at work because of the export surplus. However this is not the way the process works in reality. Countries with a strong currency are often interested in maintaining an export surplus because of its positive effect on employment and try to stabilise a corresponding net capital export by means of interest rate policy.

On the other hand - imagine a two-country model of West Germany and the United States - the economy with a current account deficit needs a higher rate of interest to maintain the inflow of foreign capital. We may further assume that both countries would like to keep the exchange rate constant in order to avoid the deflationary or inflationary effects of revaluation and devaluation, respectively. Thus we may arrive at a temporary equilibrium which, however, will most probably be instable. The fundamental reason for instability is the flexibility of exchange rates itself and the knowledge of this flexibility. To elucidate this hypothesis of instability four points can be made.

First, an analysis of foreign exchange market behaviour and trading patterns has shown a tendency for cumulative exchange rate movements. Professional market agents can profit by following trading rules, irrespective of the 'true' equilibrium value and irrespective of the actual movement heading to or leading away from this 'true' value. Therefore trading mechanisms tend to aggravate initial disturbances, because - contrary to early monetarist beliefs - destabilising speculation is profitable (cf. Schulmeister, 1987; Dornbusch and Frankel, 1988).

Second, the more fundamental point is that the true equilibrium value of the exchange rate is unknown, for the following reason: over the medium and long term the real sector of the economy has to adjust even to a 'wrong' exchange rate. Overvaluation brought about by capital movements, for example, enforces an adjustment process of prices, wages, productivity, structural change and so on, so that a reallocation of resources makes a wrong rate right in the end. To be sure, this process entails substantial adjustment costs. But if there is no equilibrium rate which can be deduced from real factors and relative prices, any rate can represent a temporary equilibrium. We cannot judge whether an ongoing exchange rate movement is directed towards a 'fundamental' equilibrium or not (cf. Bliss, 1986; Dornbusch, 1987a).

Third, the previous argument can be taken even further. The 'true' equilibrium exchange rate is unknown because it does not exist. The irony here is that exchange rate instability is the consequence of the validity of a basic neoclassical belief - that the *level* of prices is irrelevant in the long run and that, to this extent, money is neutral. It is precisely for this reason that an institution is needed to stabilise the level of prices and price expectations. Otherwise, as any price level can settle down as an equilibrium, all economic contracts would be subject to severe uncertainty and economic activity would stay far below the optimum level. It should be clear that contract-making on the labour and asset markets in particular would be hampered as here the time element plays an important role.

If applied to an international monetary system, the above argument turns the exchange rate into an absolute price. Although from a formal perspective it is the relative price of two currencies, it reflects the indeterminateness of the two price levels involved. Therefore an equilibrium exchange rate is not predetermined by real forces. In order not to destroy the confidence of international wealth holders (see below) monetary policy often acts to stabilise any *level* of the exchange rate, because any *rate of change* in the value of money - no matter whether measured in home goods or foreign currency - can upset financial markets (cf. Sievert, 1988, p. 29; Stadermann, 1988, p. 127).

Fourth, the previous points must be combined with the assumption of rational expectations. It follows that owners of financial wealth - in order to avoid capital losses - will form exchange rate expectations which depend on the rate's actual movement. A devaluation feeds the expectation of further devaluation and vice versa. A flexible exchange rate will tend to destabilise the capital balance, whereas the price mechanism may work in the balance of the current account. But because of the relative weight of capital movements the exchange rate overshoots, which will disturb trade flows as well.

We conclude that a temporary equilibrium of the exchange rate - or rather a non-movement - can be characterised as a knife-edge equilibrium. A certain equilibrium value exists as long as it prevails and it moves the very moment the actual rate starts to move. Thus the foreign exchange market is difficult to stabilise by means of monetary policy: 'realistic', i.e. manageable interest rate differentials are at times too small to neutralise an expected rate of depreciation or appreciation.

Two further points should be emphasised. First, the initial disturbance may not at all be of primary order and importance. Just think of small exogenous shocks, fluctuations in trade or prices: 'white noise' in the language of econometrics. Second, and more importantly, the direction of the exchange rate movement is independent of the status of the balance of payments. The dollar may depreciate or appreciate, although there is no change in the current account and other 'fundamental' factors, including the famous budget deficit. Or, from the West German point of view, net capital exports may fall short of or exceed an initially given current account surplus so that the D-Mark starts appreciating, as from 1985 to 1987, or depreciating, as from 1988 up to mid-1989.

The consequence is that the German strategy of export-led growth suffers from severe problems in the regime of flexible exchange rates. The first problem is a movement towards real appreciation choking off the export dynamic. In this case the central bank has always resorted to expansionary monetary policy. But the results were mixed. To a large extent, market agents reacted by holding the additional money and increasing their accumulated stocks of financial assets. In the medium-run the by-product of this liquidity trap then aggravated the second type of problem. The turn to depreciation in 1980 and 1988 took place all of a sudden. Price increases were not only driven by exchange rate devaluation, but were also fuelled by market agents running down their financial stocks accumulated just previously (cf. Spahn, 1988, pp. 177-9).

To sum up, there are two sources of instability in the foreign exchange market. First, the flexibility of exchange rates itself, because it gives rise to capital uncertainty and speculation. Second, the practice of financing large imbalances in the trade account with equally large imbalances in the capital account. White noise fluctuations which are relatively small with respect to the overall volume of transactions thus have a leverage impact on the exchange rate. It is this instability which is behind the search for alternative institutions and regulations governing the foreign exchange market.

2. THE EUROPEAN MONETARY SYSTEM

The general alternative to market instability quite naturally consists of steps towards co-ordination and cooperation. Under this heading the European Monetary System has achieved the advantages of a return to fixed exchange rates. However, because there is no 'free lunch', countries have to pay for these advantages by giving up at least some, and sometimes a considerable amount of national autonomy in economic policy decisions.

Proposals for future economic policy co-ordination within the European Communities have been discussed intensively for many years. The whole 'project' seems to be moving from the current state of affairs - which is described as a loose cooperation among partners with unequal economic and political power - towards a true model of integration (cf. Delors *et al.*, 1989). At the moment it is not yet clear whether this tendency gives occasion for optimism or pessimism.

The costs of the common market and the joint policies project as such should not be underrated. The centralisation of decision making and the execution of a common macro-policy at European level will entail the need for corresponding micro-policies at regional level. Some countries will ask for compensation if they are prepared to agree to a course of monetary and exchange rate policy which undermines the competitiveness of home industries. We will therefore witness the rise of even larger bureaucratic institutions engaged in collecting and redistributing funds, in granting ever rising subsidies, according to a politico-economic rent seeking process with numerous interest groups.

What, on the other hand, are the benefits? It is argued that the opening up of a large common market will produce substantial welfare gains due to the effects of economies of scale. However, the aforementioned rise of subsidy payments goes along with the assumption that misallocation of resources is expected to persist. Last but not least, wealth is not necessarily linked to the size of an economic system: Switzerland is a fairly small country.

Most probably the various proposals for monetary policy co-ordination in Europe stem from a vague discontent with the consequences of the 'hardline' course of the Bundesbank. Some countries may hope that a future common monetary policy - pursued by the new institution of a European central bank - will counteract the extreme German preference for price stability. On the other hand, it is highly questionable whether West Germany as the leading country in the EC will agree to the creation of a common European currency with only average quality, because the long-run success story of the West German economy has been based on a hard currency.

Furthermore, a future European currency has to hold its own in competition with the dollar and the yen; and the recent history of currency competition in the era of large capital movements shows that weak currency regions aiming for a 'soft' budget constraint sooner or later have to pay with higher rates of interest and terms-of-trade losses.

The general critique of the current 'rules of the game' in European monetary policy emphasises its asymmetric features. Countries which are more inflation prone than others and which more often run into current account deficits are forced to employ restrictive policies, whereas surplus countries in practice can avoid departing from their course of monetary stability. Thus the mechanisms of the EMS seem to show a deflationary bias. Some countries at least feel themselves hampered in pursuing a more expansionary policy.

The reproach that the regulatory effect of the EMS is biased, however, seems to be beside the point. Every monetary production economy needs an institution providing an anchor of stability for prices and price expectations. In a closed system this job is - and should be - done by the central bank. In an open system one country has to take over the stabilising function. We should bear in mind that the Bretton-Woods system finally broke down precisely because countries with a stable monetary system were forced to import inflationary pressures from abroad.

The central problem within the EMS is not the restrictive policy stance of the Bundesbank which - according to the critics - has to be moderated by means of harmonisation. If there really were a turnaround of West German monetary policy, other countries would not gain anything in the end; their internal conditions for maintaining monetary stability are comparatively poor and a vicious circle of inflation and depreciation is no way to support international competitiveness. These countries would end up where they started in the early 1980s with high inflation and a need for economic stabilisation. It should be recalled that during the following years these countries accepted and profited from the course of the Bundesbank because they were able to 'export' their responsibility for austerity policies to Frankfurt (cf. Giavazzi and Pagano, 1988).

Rather, the central problem within the EMS is West Germany's traditional attempt to combine its hard currency, i.e. price stability, with real undervaluation of the D-Mark allowing for a more or less permanent export surplus. From the perspective of the other European countries this is a contradictory market constellation. This becomes clear if the actual situation is contrasted with two alternative scenarios.

In the first one, the German export surplus is accompanied - and caused - by a weak D-Mark. Then the deficit countries would not have to fear capital outflows which normally result from the impact of current account deficits on exchange rate expectations. In the second one, Germany keeps its hard currency, but - to consider an extreme case - accepts net imports. In this case the foreign preference for the D-Mark, i.e. the flow of funds into D-Mark assets serving as stores of value, are accompanied by net exports to Germany.

In general, both scenarios promise to be compatible with a balance of payment equilibrium. The current state of affairs, on the other hand, sometimes suffers from a cumulative flow of funds into the D-Mark stemming from the capital and current accounts. If the aim is to stabilise the working of the international monetary system, it seems that a solution can only be found if West Germany changes the course of its economic policy.

3.   A POLICY OF REVALUATION OF THE D-MARK

It seems obvious that only the second alternative, i.e. a policy of D-Mark appreciation, could represent a feasible strategy for Germany (cf. Riese, 1989; Herr, 1989). What form should such a strategy take?

In the short run an appreciation can be achieved by the central bank running down its accumulated stocks of foreign reserves. At present, the non-institutional system of international reserve holding is characterised by hierarchical order depending on the status of the currencies involved. In simple terms the situation is as follows. The central bank issuing the dominant currency, i.e. the dollar, holds no reserves because the dollar *is* the reserve. The central bank which comes next in the hierarchy, say the Bundesbank, has to accept the leadership of the United States and therefore holds dollars, but no currencies of a lower quality. The other European central banks hold dollars *and* D-Mark.

If a central bank which is placed somewhere in this hierarchy feels strong enough to attack the position of a bank with a higher ranking it can decide to give up holding the currency in question. Thus the Bundesbank may sell its dollar assets. However this option is rather limited, because no one can seriously assume that the D-Mark would be able to substitute the dollar as the world currency. In a period of currency competition each central bank should be equipped with adequate foreign reserves for 'funding' the confidence in its currency. Therefore, in general, the Bundesbank has to keep its dollar reserves.

A feasible long-run strategy could consist of eliminating the trade surplus by means of interest rate policy and its impact on the exchange rate. As long as the trade balance is in surplus, short rates should be increased thereby lowering short-run capital exports - mainly those of West German commercial banks. The exchange rate is not absolutely fixed as the target rate clearing the trade balance is a variable depending on all factors of the net export function. In the final equilibrium, we have trade flows summing up to zero and, of course, zero net capital exports.

If West Germany pursued such a policy, a kind of monopolistic international policy co-ordination would evolve. Two specific features of this scenario stand out.

First, it would be a monopolistic constellation as the hegemonic position of the D-Mark - with respect to monetary affairs - would be acknowledged. In particular, German economic policy has to realise that the consequence of the hard currency option would be the reduction of the export surplus, or - in case of strong capital imports - even a deficit in the trade balance. Second, this type of policy co-ordination can be reached without a tedious institutional process of joint decision-making in economic policy. The basic agreement is possible because the ensuing market constellation is in accordance with the interests of the countries taking part in the system. Germany gets price stability, while other countries can afford stronger growth because their former balance of payment restriction is alleviated.

Maybe it is useful to mention that the scenario sketched above resembles the constellation of the gold standard with England holding the dominant position. The pound was the leading currency and England acted as the world's banker. Foreigners kept their short-term financial assets as deposits in London, and London extended long-term credits to foreign countries. Just like any commercial bank, England gained from the spread between the short and the long rate of interest. The bank's profit - so to speak - consisted of interest payments which could be consumed in the form of net imports. Thus an equilibrium was reached with a negative English trade balance, but with a current account which was nearly balanced due to interest payments.

Currently, Switzerland is in a similar position. The safe haven quality of its currency area provides for relatively low rates of interest. As a consequence of its overvalued currency Switzerland has a negative trade balance. Furthermore the rate of inflation is low because of the external strength of the Swiss franc. It is interesting to note that Switzerland nevertheless manages to combine price stability with full employment.

Thus the hard currency option not only leads to welfare gains due to an improvement in the terms of trade; the labour market does not necessarily suffer from overvaluation - at least, if we take a long-run perspective which is only appropriate if we are considering alternative regimes of macro-policy co-ordination. It has to be conceded however that in the short run the proposal of a strategic revaluation of the D-Mark does not appear to be a way to full employment. That is why German governments - and sometimes the Bundesbank as well - have always opposed an appreciation of the D-Mark in the past.

But, as mentioned above, the results of this behaviour have been mixed. In the 1960s the continued undervaluation of the D-Mark fostered labour demand so that bottlenecks on the labour market appeared. These supply constraints were only postponed by the strategy of importing foreign workers. But in the end the process of wage inflation could not be avoided. The monetary history of West Germany is characterised by many sequences of *postponed* D-Mark revaluations which each time made a stabilisation crisis necessary in the end.

A further consequence of the undervalued D-Mark was the strengthening of a relatively large export sector which made West Germany's economic performance vulnerable to world market shocks. In the coming years, labour shortages - at least in specific sectors - cannot be ruled out, even if the overall rate of unemployment remains high. A renewed strategy of importing foreign workers is surely not appropriate given the obvious social and political problems associated with such a policy.

A better way seems to be a consequent policy of high quality production (see Streeck's contribution, Chapter 2, above). The West German economy should extend the strategy already pursued of engaging in markets for 'intelligent' products, leaving low productivity, low paid jobs to the developing countries. In principle, this is a policy of structural change in West Germany, and not a Keynesian demand policy.

However, it is important to emphasise a further point. If the plea for a more expansionary German economic policy is substituted by a rule for D-Mark appreciation, two barriers to full employment can be removed at the same time. First, because of the reduction of balance of payment problems in other countries they will be able to pursue a more expansionary policy stance - provided they employ an incomes policy to control inflation. In addition, as a consequence of these favourable conditions for growth in other countries, West Germany in turn can profit from an increase in foreign demand. Second, if an overshooting of D-Mark appreciation should occur, West Germany will then be forced to employ expansionary fiscal and monetary policies (cf. Drèze *et al.*, 1987). By contrast, in the present system other countries are compelled to restrict their economic growth in case of global disequilibrium. Thus some of the deflationary bias of policy co-ordination under the present regime would be removed.

Just like any 'blueprint', the proposal of strategic DM revaluation is susceptible to criticism. The first obvious question is: How to appreciate if - as mentioned above - the foreign exchange market, at times at least, will not alter its preferences just by means of a recommended slight increase of short-term interest rates? An occasion for revaluation of the DM will arise in case of a dollar crisis. The Bundesbank should then not resort to its 'traditional' policy of supporting the dollar but accept a - perhaps smoothed - process of DM appreciation instead.

With respect to the EMS the 'rules of the game' could be altered to allow for a steady increase of the DM exchange rate to be announced in advance, an option which was already discussed in the 1960s. The targeted rate of nominal appreciation could serve as a guide for the formation of expectations in the market process and would therefore take over the function which is now (not that successfully) fulfilled by the targeted growth rate of the money supply.

A policy of raising short-term interest rates in Germany which might be necessary to bring about a revaluation of the DM will not be restrictive for all other countries participating in the DM area, at least in so far as these countries are no longer obliged to follow the West German monetary policy stance in order to keep their exchange rate fixed to the DM. In this context one may doubt whether the other EC countries in fact would subscribe to a nominal depreciation of their currencies as this would deprive them of the instrument of an overvalued currency as part of their anti-inflation policy. On the other hand, since the mid-1980s some countries, e.g. France, have uttered their altered preference in favour of growth and employment and they might find other ways to dampen wage inflation. Of course, some countries will still prefer to fix their currency to the DM if they feel they need to do so (Austria has imported monetary stability in this way for many years).

Finally, it cannot be ruled out that DM appreciation may come about as a by-product of an internal stabilisation crisis when the Bundesbank should return to a restrictive stance in order to suppress the inflationary consequences of near full employment (which might be achieved within a decade in spite of the stream of immigrants from Eastern European countries and the former GDR). The West German authorities might then use a short-term event, a spell of anti-inflation policies, to make the way for a change in long-term strategy.

Another set of problems is centred around the internal consequences of a DM revaluation. If workers in the export industries are in danger of losing their jobs the unions might try to neutralise the effect of real appreciation by means of a concessionary wage policy. However, it is not a priori clear to what extent wage policy in general, and in West Germany in particular, will be affected by unemployment in the future. On past evidence, the response would not appear to be very marked.

A quite different argument in this context is that because of the high non-price competitiveness of West German products on world markets there will be no substantial reduction of exports (and jobs in the export industries) in case of a real appreciation of the DM. This argument surely should not be pushed too far, although it has to be recognised that terms-of-trade elasticity is most probably greater with respect to West German imports than on the export side. In turn, this would help to enforce the policy of DM appreciation as foreign employment could increase without an equally large loss of employment in Germany.

Finally, the 'hegemonic' German monetary policy might be criticised for political reasons. On the other hand, it is already a fact that Western Europe has developed into a 'Deutsche Mark Club' (Dornbusch, 1987b). In the current situation the costs and benefits stemming from the peculiar position of the DM are distributed very unevenly and the 'rules of the game' produce unnecessary barriers to increasing employment. Whereas traditional proposals - most often in the spirit of the post-Keynesian paradigm - opt for a removal of these barriers by loosening monetary restrictions, or build up new barriers, e.g. capital controls, to shelter desired political outcomes against market forces, this paper is based on the assumption - elaborated elsewhere (cf. Spahn, 1988) - that a market system cannot function properly and efficiently without such a hard 'monetary budget constraint'. But Germany should share the burden by adjusting its trade policy to the overall economic regime which is characterised by the position of the DM on the international financial markets.

4.   A FINAL SUMMING UP

The main advantage of this policy proposal is the reduction of tensions in the European Community which until now have resulted from the fact that West Germany has tried to maintain two features of economic policy which are not compatible - at least from the point of view of foreign countries: a strong position of the DM on the financial markets cannot coexist with the traditional German preference for maintaining large export surpluses.

The remedy is not to turn to an expansionary monetary policy in West Germany for this would deprive the European economy of an anchor of monetary stability. Rather, Germany should change its course in favour of a consequent policy of DM appreciation. Other countries will then be able to pursue more expansionary policies and the reduction of trade imbalances will enhance exchange rate stability. Finally, the realisation of terms-of-trade improvements by pursuing a hard currency option is the only appropriate economic policy strategy for a rich, mature creditor country like West Germany.

NOTE

1 The current version of this paper gained much from critical remarks and a lively debate at the WZB-conference on 'No Way to Full Employment?' (Berlin-West, 5-7 July 1989). In particular I would like to thank Robert Boyer, Christoph Deutschmann, Wilhelm Hankel, Stuart Holland, Jan Kregel, Jürgen Kromphardt, Peter Rosner, Fritz Scharpf and Michael Wagner for their helpful comments, although I did not conform to all their arguments. Inspiring discussions with Gerhard Michael Ambrosi, Hansjörg Herr, Hajo Riese and Albrecht Sommer are gratefully acknowledged.

REFERENCES

Bliss, C., 'The Rise and Fall of the Dollar', *Oxford Review of Economic Policy*, No. 2, 1986, pp. 7-24.

Delors, J., Wyplosz, C., Bean, C., Giavazzi, F. and Giersch, H., *Report on Economic and Monetary Union in the European Community*, EC, Brussels, 1989.

Deutsche Bundesbank, *Monthly Report*, June 1989.

Drèze, J. et al., *The Two-Handed Growth Strategy for Europe - External Autonomy Through Flexible Cooperation*, Centre for European Policy Studies, Brussels, 1987.

Dornbusch, R., (1987a), 'Exchange Rate Economics - 1986', *Economic Journal*, 97, 1987, pp. 1-18.

Dornbusch, R., (1987b), 'Prosperity or Price Stability', *Oxford Review of Economic Policy*, 3, 1987, pp. 9-19.

Dornbusch, R. and Frankel, J., 'The Flexible Exchange Rate System - Experience and Alternatives', in S. Borner (ed.), *International Financial Markets and Trade in a Polycentric World*, London, Macmillan, 1988, pp. 155-213.

Giavazzi, F. and Pagano, M., 'The Advantages of Tying One's Hands - EMS Discipline and Central Bank Credibility', *European Economic Review*, 32, 1988, pp. 1055-82.

Herr, H., 'Mercantilistic Strategies, Cooperation and the Option of the European Monetary System', *Discussion Paper FS I 89-2*, Wissenschaftszentrum Berlin für Sozialforschung, 1989.

Riese, H., 'Geldpolitik bei Preisniveaustabilität - Anmerkungen zur Politik der Deutschen Bundesbank', in H. J. Ramser et al. (eds.), *Beiträge zur angewandten Wirtschaftsforschung*, Berlin/Heidelberg, Springer, 1989, pp. 101-23.

Schulmeister, S., 'An Essay on Exchange Rate Dynamics', *Discussion Paper FS I 87-8*, Wissenschaftszentrum Berlin für Sozialforschung, 1987.

Sievert, O., *Außenwirtschaftliche Zwänge der Wirtschaftspolitik*, Kiel, Institut für Weltwirtschaft, 1988.

Spahn, H.-P., *Bundesbank und Wirtschaftskrise - Geldpolitik, gesamtwirtschaftliche Finanzierung und Vermögensakkumulation der Unternehmen 1970-1987*, Regensburg, Transfer, 1988.

Stadermann, H.-J., *Weltwirtschaft*, Tübingen, Mohr, 1988.

9. On 'Monopolistic Co-ordination' and Some International Consequences of German Unification[1]

Jan Kregel

1. THE TWO-SIDED NATURE OF FOREIGN BALANCES

Ever since the recognition that a positive trade balance increases domestic demand, and could thus substitute for a weak propensity to invest, export-led growth has become enthroned as the best way to pursue employment and growth policy in an integrated world, and economists seem to have lost sight of the other side of the argument. It is interesting, and perhaps not a little ironic, that the early Keynesians were acutely aware of the two-sided nature of the foreign balance. There is no better way to show this than to quote Joan Robinson, *Introduction to the Theory of Employment* (1937a):

But from the point of view of the world as a whole the foreign investment of one country is not investment at all. If one country increases its surplus of exports to the rest of the world, the rest of the world must increase its surplus of imports from that country to an equal extent, and there is an increase in unemployment in the rest of the world which offsets the increase of employment in that country. Moreover, as citizens of that country increase their holding of securities representing loans to the rest of the world, the citizens of the rest of the world are increasing their indebtedness to that country, and for the world as a whole there is no increase in wealth.

In an article written at about the same time she also noted that if any one country tried to expand by using the tactics suggested by the Fleming-Mundell analysis, attempting to use an increase in the rate of interest to attract foreign lending:

It is sometimes supposed that an increase in the prospective earnings of capital in one country will lead to an increased desire on the part of foreigners to lend to it... But this cannot occur when home and foreign speculators take an equally optimistic view of prospects, for if they do the price of securities will be driven up to such a point as to compensate for the improvement in their prospective yield, and no movement of funds will actually take place (Robinson, 1937b).

It is quite clear, as she also states, that it is the rate of interest that is the primary instrument available to control the difficulties associated with the use of the exchange rate as an instrument to affect growth policy. A large part of the problems facing the EEC at the macro level are associated with attempting to escape from this paradox.

In this respect, one can view Herr's contribution to this volume (see Chapter 7 above), based on the idea of the quality of international currencies, as being closely associated to the idea of international liquidity preference. The quotation given from Mrs Robinson, it should be noted, presumes that home and foreign speculators have equivalent opinions, or, one might say, a similar degree of preference over the currencies involved. When this is not the case, as Herr shows clearly it is not, some space is opened up to allow for capital movements such as would be required for a country seeking to grow to find international finance. At the same time this provides some scope for the use of fiscal policy to act directly on the level of employment.

2.   MONOPOLISTIC CO-ORDINATION: A ONE-SIDED APPROACH

It is also in this area that Spahn's contribution to this volume (see Chapter 8 above) lies. It attempts to answer an extremely difficult question: How a central bank in an increasingly interdependent world should act in order to assure that its money remains the dominant money domestically while some other currency dominates it internationally. In an open system with capital mobility this would suggest that the domestic money can only become co-equal with the world money, which then means that the country's monetary policy is dominated by the decisions of the country issuing the international money. There is only one way out of this dilemma, and that is to become *the* international money. This is what Spahn suggests for the DM, at least in so far as the EC area is concerned.

There are two problems that have to be faced in resolving this dilemma. The first is a practical one - how do we get there from here? The second is a more theoretical one: if the DM does become the dominant currency, at least in the EMS, what implications will this have for the overall macro environment that will result?

The initial problems result from the simple statement that part of the increased international instability is caused by

the practice of financing large imbalances in the trade account with equally large imbalances in the capital account (see Spahn, p. 185 above),

which seems to imply that there is some choice in the matter. Deficits have to be financed, and they can only be financed by capital account surpluses in the rest of the world - if they were not, they would not exist! The only choice is not to have the trade imbalances, but this implies reducing equilibrium to current account balance; the rough equivalent to international barter. This proposition can be put another way. If you want to sell abroad you have to provide credits to foreign buyers, if you want foreigners to be net purchasers of your goods, you have to provide net credits, i.e. foreign lending.

There can be no quarrel with the argument that West Germany and the world might both be better served by a reduction in the West German trade surplus. The proposal that Spahn makes to achieve this is to reduce West German credits to foreigners, which means reducing foreign deficits. If the reduction in the West German surplus was just equal to the reduction in the rest of the world's deficits with West Germany then on the aggregate level, the best that could be achieved would be no net change in aggregate demand.

However, the real problem lies in the method that is proposed: an increase in interest rates in West Germany to make it more attractive for West German investors to keep their money in Germany. Even if there is no interest rate effect on the level of West German spending, we should remember that during the early 1980s, high interest rates in the United States led to an increase in rates throughout the world, even in the presence of a sharp appreciation of the US dollar. It would certainly not be appropriate to press this analogy too far, but within the wider European community, DM rates probably exert a similar influence to that of the dollar worldwide. Austria, Holland, and Switzerland all follow policies of more or less perfect linkage to the DM, and recently France looks like it is trying to join this group, while Britain and Italy have very diverse conditions which nonetheless both lead to pressure for higher interest rates that increases in rates in West Germany would only exacerbate. It is also important to remember that the West German surplus originates increasingly from intra community trade rather than with the rest of the world. There seems to be little doubt that a move towards tightening in West Germany would lead to a general tightening all round Europe, irrespective of whether or not it is accompanied by a realignment of exchange rates within the EMS. The net result could only be contractionary in terms of the overall demand effects, and it is not clear that it would really have the desired effect on the current account balance.

The basic problem is a more general one, expressed in Mrs Robinson's dictum that foreign investment by a single country does not represent an increase in net investment for the world as a whole. The Spahn proposal, by attempting to deal only with the distribution of foreign investment (i.e. by reducing German foreign investment) risks bringing about a net reduction in European investment (since the rise in German rates is unlikely to bring about any offsetting investment within Germany), when what is required is a net increase. There is nothing inherent in reducing international imbalances that will increase overall investment, unless the decline in exchange rate variability has a positive effect on investment. There is little hard evidence to suggest that variability has had any direct impact on trade, so one must presume that the impact on investment is not large.

3. HOW TO PERSUADE WEST GERMANS TO INVEST MORE?

There is a much simpler way to resolve the problem: direct investment at home. It is true that investment has recently been increasing. The latest figures suggest for 1989 an increase of 27 per cent in domestic orders for machinery and plant and equipment, but foreign orders also went up by 24 per cent. Nevertheless, the overall figures have been extremely disappointing in the recent past and are not predicted to remain at current levels. Indeed, one of the reasons that has been suggested for the weakness of the DM is not so much the level of interest rates as the belief that West Germany is no longer making the investment necessary to keep it at the technological forefront of a Europe with a unified internal market (along with the impact of the investment withholding tax).

There seems to be no way out of the current paradox that does not involve some sort of expansion in West Germany relative to the rest of the European community. Or, to put the point another way, under the gold standard rules of the game, which are now presumed to apply within the EMS, the country with a surplus should have an expanding money supply and rising prices. West Germany is unwilling to accept either of these channels of adjustment. But they imply constraints. A country operating with a trade surplus at less than full employment has the possibility of using its surplus to finance expansion without increasing prices. There is unemployed labour, if there is no capacity, then increasing investment is the only way to resolve the problem. I do not want to suggest that this is easy - indeed, one of the most difficult problems for economic policy is to influence the rate of investment. But, it is much easier to work on it once it is recognised that this is the problem that has to be resolved, not the establishment of the hegemonic position of the DM.

From this point of view, the enlarged internal market may be looked at, as Giersch (1989) does, as a mammoth supply-side policy, cutting down on regulation, or in Keynesian terms as a policy to increase the marginal efficiency of capital employed within Europe. If West Germany will not consume more from abroad, the problem is to persuade West Germans to hold more capital goods and fewer DM, not to try to shift their preferences from EuroDM to domestic DM.

4.   GERMAN UNIFICATION: THE DOMESTIC SIDE

There has been a great deal of dispute over the likely economic consequences of the decision to move rapidly to monetary unification of the two Germanies. Initial optimistic reactions were soon replaced by growing pessimism over the cost to the West German government and by fears that conversion of East German savings deposits into DM at parity would lead to an increase in inflation and higher interest rates. After the East German election on 18 March 1990 financial markets once again turned optimistic and recovered levels of six months earlier by X Day, 1 July 1990, when formal monetary union took place. Since that time the estimates of the inflationary costs have diminished, but those concerning the cost to the German treasury have reached alarming levels. But, in all this discussion, the most striking characteristic of the analysis of the impact of monetary unification from the point of view of an outside observer has been its nearly total concentration on implications for the domestic economy. The analysis of the impact on monetary aggregates of the conversion of East-Mark into DM and the anticipated domestic inflationary impact dominated market attention at the beginning of the year, despite the fact that there was very little sound basis for this conclusion. At the same time, the direct expenditure costs to be borne by the West German goverment and the implications for the domestic economy did not initially attract much attention, but in the months following X Day this aspect has come to dominate discussion. The increase in the estimates of the direct costs, and the consequent increase in the estimates of required government borrowing and the increase in the goverment deficit are primarily the result of the uncertainty created by the temporal separation of the treaties initiating economic and political unification. Certain responses which were necessary for the efficient operation of the monetary union were only possible after political unification took place. In particular, the restructuring of East German state enterprise and the inflows of private investments required to complete monetary union could only take place once decisions had been taken on the legal ownership of state property, but these issues were part of the discussions of the treaty of political union. The more rapid the move to political unification, the lower the costs associated with the reconstruction of the productive structure of East Germany will be. Thus, although the focus of discussion has shifted, it remains within the sphere of the domestic consequences of the unification process.

Yet, throughout the 1980s, the growing integration of the world economy has acted to constrain the policy options available to the Bundesbank and to German goverment policy-makers. The G-5 commitments to stabilise the value of the US dollar and the role of the DM as the key currency in the exchange rate mechanism of the European Monetary System have meant that domestic German monetary policy has frequently been sacrificed to exchange rate policy. On the other had, goverment policy has been subject to continuous international criticism for being excessively restrictive and as retarding the recovery of the world economy in the first half of the decade. In particular, the performance of the German economy has been the mirror image of the United States economy, with increasing trade surpluses and declining goverment expenditure deficits representing excess saving reducing the world level of aggregate demand. The German trade surplus, which in the first half of the 1980s was with the United States, has been shifted to Germany's European Community trading partners in the last half of the decade (see Tables 9.1 and 9.2)

Table 9.1   Government Deficits in Selected OECD Countries

Country	1986	1987	1988	1989	1990
West Germany	-1.3	-1.8	-2.0	-0.3	-0.9
Belgium	-8.8	-7.0	-6.5	-6.2	-6.2
Denmark	3.1	1.8	0.4	0.5	1.1
France	-2.9	-2.5	-1.6	-1.7	-1.6
Italy	-11.4	-10.5	-10.6	-10.4	-10.9
Holland	-2.9	-6.2	-5.0	-4.5	-4.7
UK	-2.4	-1.4	0.8	1.7	1.8
USA	-4.4	-2.3	-1.8	-1.8	-1.7
Japan	-1.1	-0.3	0.5	0.4	0.4
EEC	-4.8	-4.2	-3.6	-3.0	-3.2

Source: European Commission

Much of the discussion of monetary union concerned the precise rate at which East German Marks would be converted to DM, with the goverment proposing full parity conversion and the Bundesbank proposing a 2:1 conversion. Despite the opposite impression that was given by the financial press, the divergence on this matter did not concern the inflationary impact of the conversion rate, for even full parity conversion is unlikely to have led to unacceptable inflationary consequences. The divergence of position was rather over the likely direct monetary contribution that would have to be financed by domestic borrowing by the West German goverment in the event of monetary union preceding political union, a problem which could have been minimised by either delaying monetary union, or, more preferably, by anticipating political union. In either case parity conversion would have been domestically more acceptable to the Central Bank.

In addition, full parity conversion would have had additional positive effects on the international environment of the German economy. If the conversion of East to West German Marks were to lead to some increase in expenditure by East Germans, the relevant question would then become what types of goods will be purchased, and, in particular, which types of goods not previously available to East German residents. It seems clear that any increased expenditure would not be primarily in food, lodging and other basic or necessary goods, which will presumably still remain cheaper in East Germany even as price subsidies are gradually removed and whose price will depend on domestic wage and production conditions. The most likely area of increased expenditure should be in those goods which epitomise the consumer society of the western industrialised countries, i.e. small household appliances and labour-saving, light consumer durables, domestic electronic goods, and then automobiles. All of these goods are likely to fall in price to East German consumers as they are sold freely in competitive markets.

But, West German production of these types of goods are of extremely high quality, and are generally positioned at the upper end of the price range with substantial price inelasticity of demand. East German buyers are unlikely to use their newly-acquired DM to purchase the most expensive, top of the line consumer durables. Instead it is more likely that they will exhibit high price elasticity of demand and be much more likely to purchase the cheapest, bottom of the line goods. The cheapest range of these type of goods are produced primarily by French, Italian, Spanish and East Asian firms. The increased expenditures are thus most likely to be directed, in the short term, to non-German imports, rather than to relatively higher priced German products.

There is no obvious reason why an increase in demand for these types of goods, spread across a number of different nations, and across highly competitive producers, should cause their prices to rise in terms of DM; indeed there is even less reason given the historical trend of nominal appreciation and real stability of the DM with respect to these countries' currencies.[2] Indeed, overall, West German import prices have been falling steadily in the recent past. Thus, on the side of prices there is little reason to suggest that had the conversion of East-Mark to DM taken place at parity, and even if the new DM were to bring a marked increase in the propensity to consume, there should have been any sharp or sustained inflationary pressure on the German domestic price level.

Table 9.2   Trade Balances (in billions DM)

Country	1985	1986	1987	1988	1989	Change
UK	8.8	14.8	17.2	22.4	24.7	15.9
France	14.7	15.2	16.1	18.2	24.0	9.3
Italy	4.6	4.8	6.9	11.4	14.6	10.0
EEC	31.6	51.4	62.3	80.8	94.2	62.6
USA	23.2	28.3	24.3	16.6	8.4	-14.8
Japan	-12.8	-15.3	-14.7	-15.3	-16.9	-4.4
Total	73.4	112.6	117.7	128.0	135.0	61.0

Source: *European Commission*

5.   GERMAN UNIFICATION: THE NEGLECTED INTERNATIONAL SIDE

On the other hand, in the event of an increase in spending, there should be an impact on the German trade surplus, which should decline relative to those countries where it has been increasing since 1985 (cf. Table 9.2). To the extent that increased East German consumption expenditures produce improvement in the overall Italian and French trade balances, the need for these countries to maintain high interest rates relative to the DM in order to attract capital inflows to offset their trade imbalances with Germany and keep their currencies stable relative to the DM within the EMS should be reduced. Any resulting reduction in Italian and French interest rates should also be expected to take pressure off the Bundesbank to keep interest rates high in order to keep the DM stable within the EMS. In these conditions the DM might be expected to strengthen against these currencies within the European Monetary System exchange rate mechanism, leading to reductions in import prices from these countries and further reinforcing the positive benefits of the expenditure created by the conversion of East-Mark for DM.

This double benefit from an increase in expenditures on imports suggests that a purely domestic analysis of the impact of monetary union ignores an important aspect - the impact on international trade imbalances, on interest rate patterns and differentials, and on international investment capital flows. If it is true that real interest rates in Europe are generally too high, and the DM too weak, because countries such as Italy and France with higher structural inflation and growth rates use tight monetary policy and high interest rates in order to keep the exchange rates of their currencies fixed relative to the DM in the approach to Phase 1 of the Delors Plan for European Monetary Union, then a reduction in trade imbalances should allow these countries to achieve their growth and exchange rate objectives with lower interest rates.

The reduction in intra-European trade balances will also be beneficial if it reverses the recently initiated process in which currency overvaluation in countries with excessively high interest rates produces a continuous decline in international competitivity, making the excessively high interest rates relative to the DM even more necessary in order to attract capital inflows to offset declining trade balances.[3] Reducing these countries' need for increasing capital inflows will allow them to rely on sales of goods rather than the sale of excessively cheap financial liabilities, which should have the effect of stemming outflows or even increasing capital flows into Germany, strengthening the DM and reducing import prices further.

Looked at in a European context, an increase in demand for imported consumption goods in Germany may provide a desirable alternative to tighter monetary policy in order to strengthen the DM and reduce, not increase, domestic inflation in Germany.

There are other reasons which have been evoked as necessitating a higher interest rate, when unification is considered from a purely domestic standpoint. The most common of these is that since East German industry has to replace its own productive structure in order to be able to compete in a market economy, it will have to import capital goods from West Germany. But, with capacity utilisation near 90 per cent of normal for the manufacturing sector as a whole in West Germany, any increase in demand is presumed to place pressure on prices. Aside from the fact that increasing capital goods prices need have no direct effect on the cost of necessary goods and thus no immediate effect on wage rates, this argument also looks rather different if viewed from an international perspective. While it is certainly the case that capacity utilisation is historically high in capital goods-producing industries (higher than the 90 per cent figure for manufacturing as a whole), it is also the case that the capital goods industries represent the major export sector of the West German economy. One of the justifications for the German export surplus in the last half of the 1980s is that it is due to the burst of investment in other European countries due to their preparation for the opening of the unified internal EEC market in 1993. Indeed, the German government has argued that no policy action would be required to correct the surpluses, since they were purely temporary and would disappear as this short investment boom drew to a close. It is most likely that the initial reconstruction expenditures in East Germany will be in replacement of social overhead capital and infrastructure such as roads, railways, telephone and satellite communications and so forth, all of which are essential preconditions for the profitable production and distribution of industrial goods for the European market. None of these types of investment is likely to require substantial additional capital goods and most of them are relatively labour intensive investments.

Only after these basic facilities are in place will the second impact of expansion of investment in plant and equipment be possible. But here again, plant must be constructed before equipment can be installed. It must also be assumed that the housing stock must be improved and enlarged. Thus on both counts it is likely that it will be the construction industry which will feel the initial increase in demand over the coming two years. There appears to be excess capacity in construction, and it is likely that there will be a great deal of excess labour in the East.

All this suggests that capital goods producers should have some leeway to adjust capacity to meet the needs of reconstruction and that the need for capital goods in the East should arrive at just about the time that foreign demand is officially expected to be falling off. There is no reason why redirecting these capital exports to East Germany should have any direct impact on capacity or on capital goods prices.

Again, in the event of redirecting exports for internal use in East Germany there should be a beneficial effect on payments imbalances, for Germany has large surpluses in trade in capital goods with both France and Italy. As soon as exports would be reduced and/or capital would be redirected to domestic investment, the same potentially positive influence on the exchange rate will be produced which was foreseen above as a consequence of increased imports of consumption goods.

6. UNIFICATION AND THE DEMAND FOR SAVINGS

There is a more sophisticated form of this argument which says that the financial needs of reconstruction will put additional pressure on the world's demand for decreasing supply of private savings provided by German and Japanese families. East Germany would thus have to pay higher interest rates in order to attract the capital necessary for reconstruction. Aside from the dubious theoretical basis of this argument, in the case of East German reconstruction the argument does not seem to be valid for the internal distribution of saving in a unified Germany. The excess saving of the West German households is the accounting mirror image of the current account surplus, or the outflows of capital from West Germany to international financial markets. The redirection of capital goods to the East is thus the same thing as a reduction in excess savings, an increase in domestic investment and a reduction in capital outflows. The German capital account balance now shows a deficit of well over 100 billion Marks, around 5 per cent of GDP. The current federal government deficit is around 1 per cent, leaving a net savings surplus of around 4 per cent of GDP. Half of this surplus, redirected to the former GDR, would represent a 25 to 50 per cent share of investment in 1989 GDR national income, irrespective of any internally generated East German savings. This argument would also benefit from the international aspects indicated above due to any subsequent reaction of reduced imbalances leading to declines in European interest rates and the strengthening of the DM.

Thus while it is true that reconstruction will require capital, it is by no means evident that higher real interest rates will be required to attract it.

Internal sources should be more than adequate to satisfy even the most rapid recovery. It is of course true that the financing may require increasing German goverment borrowing, but this is simply the other side of the reduction in the savings surplus. On the other hand, any assessment of the overall effect must include the effect of reconstruction in increasing incomes in the former East German economy, as well as the contribution of what should be an approximately 1 to 1.5 per cent increase in the West German growth rate due to unification; this latter effect alone should amount to more than 20 billion DM in 1990.

It thus appears that the unification process might be more rapid and successful if it does lead to net increases in expenditure in a unified Germany. It is not the supply of capital that is the really binding constraint. Rather, the most important element will be to assure that there are factors capable of justifying this increase in net expenditure. On the side of families, there are a number of reasons which suggest that spending is unlikely to increase substantially, irrespective of the conversion rate. There are a number of reasons - rising prices of East German necessaries, the possibility of purchasing and owning housing, positive real rates of return to savings, the increasing threat of unemployment, etc. which suggest that there will not be an enormous increase in expenditures on West German goods or imported goods from the conversion of accumulated East German savings deposits to DM.

It will thus be necessary to ensure that expenditures take place in terms of capital expenditures in the East. This is a question of ensuring adequate incentives to investment in East Germany. In addition to the essential social overhead investments already mentioned, which are primarily the responsibility of the Länder, but will have to be financed by West Germany, this is a question of the introduction of efficient Lander administration, the adoption of existing West German property and contract law, the determination of property rights and the expectation of adequate rates of return to investment.[4] However, none of these issues was resolved in the monetary unification treaty, but have been postponed to the treaty of political unification. The absence of clear agreement on the contents of the political treaty settling these issues represents a clear disincentive to rapid increases in private capital expenditures. The longer the reconstruction of East German state enterprises and new direct investments are postponed, the easier it will be to supply the East German market from capacity created in West Germany. Thus, the most pressing domestic issue is the rapidity and the content of political unification. For only when this is agreed will the positive international benefits that might arise from increased spending become possible.

7. FAVOURABLE INTERNATIONAL CONSEQUENCES

The emphasis on the domestic aspects of German monetary unification has thus far given excessive importance to the highly unlikely inflationary consequences of monetary unification and tended to ignore the potentially more positive benefits arising in Germany through the possible reduction of international trade imbalances. The conversion of the existing stock of savings, even if completely financed by West Germany and fully used to increase the propensity to consume, should not be expected to lead to any appreciable impact on prices, nor should the increase in the demand for capital put undue pressure on available capital resources. Indeed, the arguments presented above suggest that an increase in either consumption or investment spending is likely to have beneficial consequences for domestic and international financial markets. From this point of view the greatest risk is that the agreement for monetary unification is neither sufficiently attractive to stem the flow of immigrants from East to West, nor capable of giving sufficient guarantees of rights to private property to generate an inflow of new private direct investment into the East. If such a risk materialised, it would produce the collapse of those parts of the East German economy which might have made a contribution to national income under free market conditions.

On the other hand, if looked at in narrow terms of monetary policy and the ability of the Bundesbank to defend the integrity of the DM, then the plan will be more beneficial the more it leads to reductions in trade and payments imbalances within the EEC. For it is this, not changes in consumer demand or wages or prices, which will allow interest rates in the rest of the EEC to fall and capital flows into the unified Germany allow the DM to strengthen as a consequence.

This is a result which can only provide positive benefits to the overall process of EEC integration. From the point of view of the high growth, high inflation countries it will lessen economy. As a consequence, they will have to forego less growth, introduce less stringent monetary and less restrictive fiscal policy, have lower interest rates and unemployment rates in order to keep their currencies tied to the DM in an EEC monetary union in which realignments have been seemingly eliminated. Since the economic costs to these countries of a unified EEC should thus be lower with a unified Germany based on rapid reconstruction of the East, the rest of the EEC should be more willing to accept a larger, and economically stronger, German state as an EEC partner. However, the longer political unification is delayed, the more costly and the more difficult will be the successful integration of the two economies. This is the result of the lower incentive to invest and consume and thus the slower reduction in the trade and payment imbalances, and the growth and interest rate differentials between Germany and the rest of the EEC which goes together with a slower process of political unification.

NOTES

1   This paper is a collection of arguments presented at several lectures. Sections 1 to 3 are from my comment on Herr's and Spahn's contributions (see Chapters 7 and 8, above) at the conference 'No Way to Full Employment?' (in Berlin, 5-7 July, 1989). Sections 4 to 6 collect remarks from a seminar presented at the Wissenschaftszentrum Berlin für Sozialforschung, 14 May, 1990 (subsequently published as 'German Monetary and Economic Unification: Are Financial Markets Asking the Right Questions?' in *Banca Nazionale del Lavoro Quarterly Review*, September 1990) and from the Laws Lecture ('Some Implications of European Economic Integration for the United States Economy') which I presented as Alcoa Visiting Professor at the College of Business Administration of the University of Tennessee, Knoxville (translated and published as 'Zum Verhältnis von deutscher, westeuropäischer und gesamteuropäischer Integration' in M. Heine *et al.* (eds.), 1990). I am indebted to Dr Doris Cornelsen, Dr Dieter Hiss, Prof. Dr Lutz Hoffmann and Prof. Dr Egon Matzner for discussions clarifying a number of inaccuracies and errors in the seminar presentation. I am grateful to Nathaniel Land for providing statistical support.

2   It is also highly likely that given the current structure of East German production and on the presumption that wage rates do not rise rapidly, that these are also precisely the areas in which the East will start its industrial production for they do not require either high technology or large capital investments. One might thus expect that in about five years Germany will be a strong competitor in precisely those areas where the Mediterranean basin countries such as Spain, Italy and France are currently strong. In this sense the East may fill a 'gap' in the German export basket which will eventually require a substantial currency realignment between the DM and the southern tier.

3   For 1985 (the most recent date for which OECD Series C trade figures were available to us) over 12 per cent of German exports in both SITC categories 6 and 7 (manufactured goods and machinery) went to France, yielding surpluses of 1 and 4.5 billion dollars respectively. For Italy the figures are 7.3 and 6.5 per cent with a deficit of 75 billion dollars for SITC 6 and a surplus of 2.4 billion dollars for SITC 7. By comparison, for the US the percentages were 7.2 and 14.5 and the balances 1.7 and 7.5 billion dollars. As can be seen from Table 9.2, since 1985 most of the overall surplus with the US has been transferred to the EEC, so the figures for France and Italy have probably roughly doubled.

4   It is perhaps necessary to make a distinction between finance and industry. Both will require the social overhead investments, but the financial system is more dependent on the communications links, and less on the behaviour of wages. Given the rapidity with which German banks have set up branch offices in the East, even before the legal provisions under which this might be done have been settled, suggests that the first unification will be in terms of the financial sector. The recent agreement of Deutsche and Dresdner banks with Kredit bank supports this. The real problems will be in attracting industrial investors to the East, *de facto* the banking system is already unified.

REFERENCES

Giersch, H., 'Europe's Prospects for the 1990s', *Economic Papers of the Directorate-General for Economic and Financial Affairs*, Commission of the European Communities, Brussels, No. 76, May 1989.

Heine, M., Herr, H., Westphal, A., Busch, U. and Mandelaers, R. (eds.), *Die Zukunft der DDR-Wirtschaft*, Reinbek, Rowohlt, 1990.

Robinson, J., (1937a), *Introduction to the Theory of Employment*, London, Macmillan, 1937.

Robinson, J., (1937b), 'The Foreign Exchanges', in *Essays in the Theory of Employment*, London, Macmillan, 1937, note 4.

10. Employment Growth and the Speed of Industrial Innovation

Gerhard Hanappi and Michael Wagner

Technical progress is a major source of economic and social well-being. Its benefits are not, however, spread evenly among industries, regions, and occupations as frequently the structural adjustment accompanying technical progress imposes substantial costs in terms of income and wealth. This is true in particular for major dislocations of jobs, which entail far-reaching shifts of employment opportunities for a substantial part of the working population (cf. OECD, 1985; for West Germany, Matzner and Wagner, 1990).

Quite apart from the moral problem of striking a just balance between overall productivity growth and the selective incidence of adjustment costs, there is the difficulty identifying the quantitative dimensions of the trade-off (for a recent exercise cf. Blazejczak, 1989).

It is this issue to which this chapter hopes to make a contribution. More specifically it addresses two questions: *First*, how do policy measures which increase the share of resources devoted to technical advance affect the distribution of employment opportunities among workers offering their labour services? *Second*, how does the impact of growing funds (deployed for the purpose of technical advance) interact with other public policy instruments?

Both questions are dealt with at the macro-level. The empirical test case is West Germany, not least because it contributes substantial resources to overall technical progress in the OECD area.

1. INVESTMENT IN TECHNICAL PROGRESS

There are several measures for the effort an economy makes to enhance its standard of technical competence. Spending on R&D is one among several variables indicating the amount of resources devoted to technical advance both at the firm and at the national level.

To the extent that R&D is determined by economic considerations, it has been suggested that it ought to be treated as a specific form of investment (For competing indicators cf. Dosi, 1988 and for the investment approach cf. Schmookler, 1971).

Such a view is expressed in an equation which makes spending on R&D (IRD) a function of output (Y) and relative factor prices. Note that the first argument, the 'accelerator', can be interpreted as an indicator of the expected profit rate, if the latter depends on the ratio of capacity utilisation. Taking interest rate r as the price of finance, w as the real wage rate and transforming into logs yields:

$$\ln IRD_t = a + b(\ln Y_t - \ln Y_{t-1})$$
$$+ c(\ln r_{t-1} - \ln w_{t-1})$$
$$+ d[b(\ln Y_{t-1} - \ln Y_{t-2})$$
$$+ c(\ln r_{t-2} - \ln w_{t-2})]$$

There are competing theoretical arguments on the signs the parameters are expected to take. If IRD conforms to regular investment in equipment then b and c should be positive. However, if one subscribes to Schumpeter's view on 'innovation', then $b < 0$ and $c > 0$ seems more appropriate. For $b < 0$ captures the notion that firms look out for innovation opportunities during slumps; they increase their efforts to achieve technical advance in order to create new products and gain access to so far untapped markets (For a treatment of R & D as 'regular' investment, cf. Frühstück and Wagner, 1989 and for a Schumpeterian view Kleinknecht, 1984.)

The estimates of the function for IRD lend support to a Schumpeterian configuration for West Germany during the period 1970-1988:

$$\ln IRD_t = 7.0225 - 0.998 (\ln Y_t - \ln Y_{t-1})$$
$$(28.73) \quad (2.42)$$
$$- 0.217 (\ln r_{t-1} - \ln w_{t-1})$$
$$(12.30)$$
$$+ [0.998(\ln Y_{t-1} - Y_{t-2})$$
$$- 0.217(\ln r_{t-2} - \ln w_{t-2})]$$

This result is subject to the restriction that $d = 1$. This assumption can be justified by the argument that firms take a long-term view on investment in R&D; they attach the same weight to recent as to current experiences (cf. Dosi, 1988).

The sensitivity of investment in R&D with respect to relative factor prices entails that rising interest rates exert a depressing influence on innovation activities. This is a point to which we will return later.

2. DEMAND FOR LABOUR AS A FUNCTION OF INNOVATION

In order to evaluate the impact of R&D on employment, IRD is aggregated into a 'stock of knowledge'. This stock (KRD) is built up by investment (IRD). The stock of know-how enters the production function along with the regular stock of capital (adjusted for the degree of utilisation) and labour:

$$\ln Y_t = a \ln(cu_t . K_t) + b \, KRD_t + c \, L_t.$$

Estimating this equation under the restriction $a + c = 1$ generates the following results:

$$
\begin{aligned}
a &= 0.285 \ (14.25) \\
b &= 0.191 \ (14.25) \\
c &= 0.715 \ (9.59)
\end{aligned}
$$

This functional form (together with the parameter restriction) assigns a specific role to R&D as a factor of production; the stock of know-how creates increasing returns to scale. A recent industry-specific estimate for West Germay has been presented by Blazejczak, Erber and Horn (1990).

Inverting the production function leads to a demand for labour equation in which KRD serves as a substitute to labour services. Stepping up the accumulation of know-how causes an increase in labour productivity; the demand for labour falls off.

The labour-saving bias of enhanced technical know-how does not, however, translate fully into cuts in employment. There are several compensating mechanisms among which the trade balance deserves special attention. Whenever labour productivity increases, our estimated price equation indicates that domestic prices tend to fall, shifting the terms of trade in favour of exports. (Evidence for West Germany is provided by the Meta Study, documented in Schettkat and Wagner, 1990.)

3. WAGES AND PRICES

Price formation in West Germany is dominated by markets in which firms follow a mark-up price-setting policy. Prices thus depend on wage costs and the prices of imported commodities and services. Moreover, firms take labour productivity into account when determining the magnitude of the mark up. An OLS-estimation of equation 20 (see Table 10.2) yields parameters which are correctly signed and are within reasonable orders of magnitude. Changes in output prices are quite sensitive to changes in wage growth. An increase in labour productivity exerts a moderating pressure on inflation.

Wage formation in West Germany depends crucially on its collective bargaining context. Generally, agreements are reached in which the pace of wage increases is made contingent on price rises and labour productivity growth. An excess supply of labour (i.e. unemployment) restrains union demands for wage rises. The specific national parameter values for equation 21 (OLS-estimate) (see Table 10.2) match the expectations of standard labour market theory.

4.   THE CURRENT ACCOUNTS AND MONEY MARKETS

The stock of know-how affects the current account through various channels, notably through its influence on the terms of trade. Furthermore there is an impact on non-price competitiveness. The more know-how is embodied in commodities and services exported, the larger is the share the exporting country gains in world trade.[1]

This is captured in the following export equation:

$$\ln EXP_t = a \ln TTX_t + b \ln Y_t + c\, KRD_t.$$

Exports depend on world output and terms of trade and technical know-how. On theoretical grounds one would expect $a < 0, b > 0, c > 0$. This is indeed the case for West Germany over the period 1970-1988 (For similar results cf. Blazejczak, Erber and Horn, 1990. For a sceptical view on the 'productivity-export perfomance' link cf. Marin, 1988.)

Disequilibria in the trade balance induce movements on capital markets. The capital account depends on differences between domestic and foreign interest rates and on expected variations of the exchange rate. The US long-term interest rate was used as indicator for the 'external' rate of interest; it carries a significant parameter with the correct sign. Expectations of the exchange rate are formed in the simplest possible way, i.e. last years change is assumed to continue. This parameter has the correct sign, but, perhaps due to the oversimplified expectation hypothesis, is insignificant.[2]

In order to refine the working properties it is necessary to model an intervention rule for the central bank. This is a difficult task, not least because observed changes in reserves always include some intervention already undertaken. This forces the model-builder to estimate the parameters of the intervention rule together with the parameters of the other behavioural equations of the foreign exchange market. Hence one would expect poor significance as is the case with our intervention rule. The first of the two parameters reflects 'leaning against the wind behaviour' of the central bank, the second parameter expresses the bank's concern about the level of its foreign exchange reserves. Both estimated parameter values fall within the range delineated by Driskill and McCafferty (1985) as being reasonable.[3]

The foreign exchange market is linked to the money market. There, the domestic interest rate is endogeneously determined, allowing for temporary deviations from international interest rates which explain the direction of international capital flows. The interest rate which clears the money market, the 'target rate', serves as centre of gravitation for the actual rate. Sudden jumps of more than 25 per cent per period up or a fall below a level of 5.5 per cent are excluded in our model in accordance with restrictions imposed by institutional arrangements (cf. Hanappi, 1989).

The underlying money demand function is of the conventional type, showing significant influence by GDP and the interest rate. Money supply is assumed to react solely on a change of the stock of foreign exchange. The last assumption is clearly a short cut intended to prevent the model from being overloaded with questions of monetary policy rules. The estimates of this equation carry correct signs and are significant.

Putting the trade balance, capital account and domestic money markets together, it is interesting to note how investment in R&D creates need for adjustment. *Ceteris paribus* an increase of KRD causes a favourable shift of the trade balance, inducing an inflow of capital, which lowers interest rates, stimulating further investment in R&D. This positive feedback loop is checked by an acceleration of GDP growth precipitating a deterioration of the trade balance triggering off rises in the rate of interest which limit further investment in R&D. The net effect of these two countervailing forces depends on the parameter values of the model.

5. THE MODEL TANDEM-M

The equations representing investment in know-how, the production function and the interactions between the current account and capital markets are parts of a larger model developed by the authors (Tandem-M). Apart from some of the features already discussed, Tandem-M is a fairly standard macro-economic model of an open economy being similar in structure to the model developed by the DIW, one of West Germany's leading economic research institutes. (A detailed account of Tandem-M is given in Frühstück, Hanappi and Wagner, 1990. The DIW-Langfristmodel is described in Blazejczak, 1986.)

The basic building blocks of the models are the goods market (Y, C, IR, EXP, IMP, G), the labour market (LS, LD, U), the foreign exchange market (FE, CAA, FEP) and the money market (MS, MD, r). Tandem-M treats foreign growth, import and export prices, foreign interest rates, domestic labour supply, and domestic utilisation as exogenously given. All other variables are determined endogenously.

The interaction between goods and labour markets, on the one hand, and foreign exchange and money markets, on the other hand, allow for an interesting dynamic behaviour of Tandem-M. This is made use of in the following simulation exercises which should help to evaluate the employment impact of different scenarios of innovation promotion policies in West Germany.

Regarding the dynamic properties of Tandem-M it might be useful to mention that a simplified core model (Tandem-T, cf. Frühstück, Hanappi and Wagner, 1990) exhibits the following properties. Though dynamic stability cannot be determined in general, it is possible to identify ranges of parameter values which guarantee stable behaviour of the system. The simulation version of Tandem (M8906) operates under binding lower limits for the nominal rate of interest (liquidity trap) and for the US dollar/DM exchange rate. The rate of interest cannot fall below 5.5 per cent (which is supposed to be the long-term historical floor of interest rates in West Germany), whereas the US dollar/DM rate is assumed to stay above the 1.5 ratio.

Given these constraints, Tandem-M generates trajectories staying within reasonable limits up to the year 2010, which serves as terminal point for our exercise. There is, however, a persistent disequilibrium in the current account. The German surplus rises from about 3 per cent of GDP in the year 1988 to about 5.5 per cent in 2010. This trend certainly will cause worries among German trading partners, which might create exogeneous pressures for a downward adjustment of the current account surplus of West Germany.

Table 10.1 List of Variables of Tandem-M

Endogenous:

C .... private consumption
CAA .... capital account
CUA .... current account
EXCH .... exchange rate
EXP .... exports
FE .... foreign exchange (stock)
FEP .... foreign exchange market policy intervention
G .... government expenditure
IMP .... imports
IR .... investment (regular)
IRD .... investment in research and development
K .... capital stock
KRD .... capital stock in R&D (technical knowledge)
L .... employment
M^D .... money demand
M^S .... money supply
P .... GDP deflator
r_t .... interest rate
r^T .... target interest rate
TTM .... terms of trade for imports
TTX .... terms of trade for exports
U .... unemployed persons
w .... wage rate
Y .... national income

Exogenous:

cu .... capacity utilisation
L^S .... labour supply
p^M .... import price index
p^X .... export price index
r^* .... interest rate of the world
Y^* .... GDP of export partners

Table 10.2 Tandem-M Equations

Goods market

Equilibrium condition:

[0] $\quad Y_t \qquad = C_t + IR_t + IRD_t + G_t + EXP_t - IMP_t$

Behaviourial equations and technical relations:

[1] $\quad \ln Y_t \qquad = a_{1,1} \ln (cu_t K_t) + a_{1,2} \ln KRD_t + a_{1,3} \ln L_t$

[2] $\quad \ln C_t \qquad = a_{2,1} + a_{2,2} \ln Y_t$

[3] $\quad \ln IR_t \qquad = a_{3,1} + a_{3,2} (\ln Y_t - \ln Y_{t-1}) - a_{3,3} (\ln r_{t-1} - \ln w_{t-1})$

[4] $\quad \ln IRD_{Dt} \qquad = a_{4,1} + a_{4,2} (\ln Y_t - \ln Y_{t-1}) + a_{4,3} (\ln r_{t-1} - \ln w_{t-1}) + a_{4,4} (a_{4,2} (\ln Y_{t-1} - \ln Y_{t-2}) + a_{4,3} (\ln r_{t-2} - \ln w_{t-2}))$

[5] $\quad \ln EXP_t \qquad = a_{5,1} \ln TTX_t + a_{5,2} \ln Y^*_t + a_{5,3} KRD_t$

[6] $\quad \ln IMP_t \qquad = a_{6,1} \ln TTM_t + a_{6,2} \ln Y_t$

[7] $\quad \ln G_t \qquad = a_{7,1} \ln Y_{t-1}$

[8] $\quad K_t \qquad = K_{t-1} + IR_t - a_{8,1} K_{t-1}$

Definitions:

[9] $\quad KRD_t \qquad = KRD_{t-1} + IRD_t$

[10] $\quad TTX \qquad = P_t / (P^X_t \cdot EXCH_t)$

[11] $\quad TTM \qquad = P_t / (P^M_t \cdot EXCH_t)$

Labour market

Disequilibrium:

[12] $\quad U_t \qquad = L^S_t - L^D_t$

Behaviourial equations and technical relations:

[1.1] $\quad \ln L^D_t \qquad = (\ln Y_t - a_{1,1} \ln (cu_t K_t) - a_{1,2} \ln KRD_t) / a_{1,3}$

Foreign exchange market

Disequilibrium:

[13] $\quad FE_t - FE_{t-1} \qquad = CUA_t + CAA_t + FEP_t$

Behaviourial equations:

[14] $\quad CAA_t \qquad = a_{14,1} (r_t - r^*_t) + a_{14,2} (EXCH_t - EXCH_{t-1})/EXCH_{t-1}$

[15] $\quad FEP_t \qquad = a_{15,1} EXCH_t + a_{15,2} FE_{t-1}$

Definition:

[16] $\quad CUA_t \qquad = EXP_t - IMP_t$

Money market

Equilibrium:

[17] $\quad M^S_t \qquad = M^D_t$

Behaviourial equations:

[18] $\quad \ln M^D_t \qquad = a_{18,1} \ln Y_t + a_{18,2} \ln r_t$

[19] $\quad \ln M^S_t \qquad = a_{19,1} \ln FE_t$

Wages and prices

Behaviourial equations:

[20] $\quad \ln P_t \qquad = \ln P_{t-1} + a_{20,1} \ln P^M_t + a_{20,2} (\ln w_t - \ln w_{t-1}) + a_{20,3} ((\ln Y_{t-1} - \ln L_{t-1}) - (\ln Y_{t-2} - \ln L_{t-2}))$

[21] $\quad \ln w_t \qquad = \ln w_{t-1} + a_{21,1} (\ln L_t - \ln L^S_t) + a_{21,2} (\ln P_{t-1} - \ln P_{t-2}) + a_{21,3} ((\ln Y_{t-1} - \ln L_{t-1}) - (\ln Y_{t-2} - \ln L_{t-2}))$

Figure 10.1 Main Circuits in Tandem-M

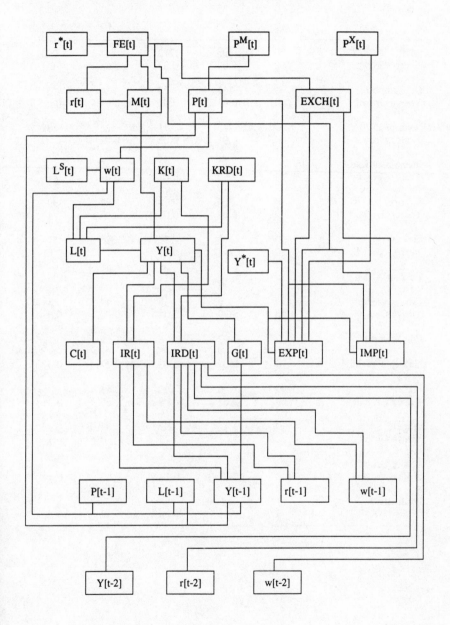

Table 10.3 Scenario 1 (Difference to Base Run)

	89	90	91	92	93
GDP	0	-195	272	843	-1 004
Yearly Growth	0	-0.02	0.03	0.04	-0.1
Consumption	0	-166	-23	524	-108
Yearly Growth	0	-0.02	0.02	0.06	-0.07
Investment Reg.	0	-45	21	125	-138
Yearly Growth	0	-0.01	0.02	0.04	-0.09
Investment R&D	16 883	7	-2	-7	56
Yearly Growth	38.15	-27.9	-0.02	-0.01	0.15
Exports	0	506	114	687	-390
Yearly Growth	0	0.09	-0.06	0.09	-0.17
Imports	0	498	-197	536	574
Yearly Growth	0	0.1	-0.13	0.13	0.01
Current Account	0	8	311	151	-964
Gov. Expend.	-16 883	0	-35	49	151
Yearly Growth	-4.96	5.23	-0.01	0.03	0.03
Employment	0	-92	6	-69	-19
Unemployment Rate	0	0.37	-0.02	0.27	0.07
Prices	0	0	0.1	0.3	0.5
Yearly Growth	0	-0.03	0.13	0.09	0.21
Wages	0	-12	89	89	232
Yearly Growth	0	-0.03	0.27	0	0.37
Yearly Growth of Real Wages	0	-0.01	0.14	-0.09	0.14
Productivity (1980=100)	0	0.45	0	0.42	0.02

Figure 10.2 Scenario 1

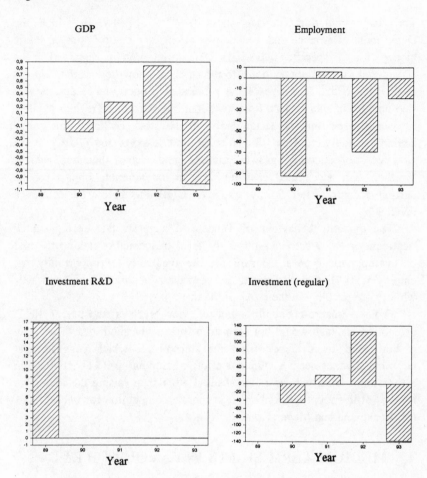

6.   THE SHORT-TERM R&D PROMOTION PACKAGE

The first simulation exercise starts from a scenario in which the Department of Science and Technology allocates a one-off sum of public money for a specific industrial R&D promotion package. This is considered as a temporary boost to the stock of know-how at the disposal of German firms. The size of the promotion programme is designed to step up current spending on R&D by about one-third of its regular level.

Such a speed-up of accumulation in the stock of know-how raises labour productivity. This stimulates, at first, exports and GDP growth. However, productivity growth induces real wage increases which, together with accelerated growth, have an unfavourable impact on the current account. After four years, even GDP falls below the reference level.

The dynamic behaviour of Tandem-M suggests that such a shock treatment of R&D activities raises the level of inequality (taking the rate of unemployment as a measure for the inequality of opportunity for employment). Those who manage to keep their jobs receive higher wages while more people join the ranks of the unemployed.

From a macro-economic point of view such a short-term R&D promotion package would not seem to be a terribly good idea. This view is buttressed by evidence from the micro-level which suggests that technical advance needs continuous efforts. Stepping up R&D activities on a short-term basis will bear little fruit. Rather than raising the long-term level of efficiency it will only spur corporate competition for public funds (cf. Beckmann and Meyer-Krahmer, 1986).

7.   MEDIUM-TERM SHIFTS IN FAVOUR OF R&D

The second scenario depicts the consequences of a permanent increase of public funds available for industrial investment in R&D. It is assumed that this additional provision of public money is balanced by cuts in other expenditure items, thus leaving total government spending unaffected during the first year. The underlying rule states that the additional public promotion package for R&D should be equal to 1 per cent of GDP in the previous year (For a more complex design of such a scenario cf. Blazejczak, 1986.)

Table 10.4 Scenario 2 (Difference to Base Run)

	89	90	91	92	93
GDP	0	-195	271	-635	2 589
Yearly Growth	0	-0.02	0.03	-0.05	0.19
Consumption	0	-166	533	-2 945	1 604
Yearly Growth	0	-0.02	0.07	-0.35	0.46
Investment Reg.	0	-45	167	-800	556
Yearly Growth	0	-0.01	0.07	-0.35	0.48
Investment R&D	16 883	17 050	17 254	17 270	17 392
Yearly Growth	38.15	-0.35	0.85	0.55	-0.1
Exports	0	506	502	1 662	1 614
Yearly Growth	0	0.09	0	0.19	-0.02
Imports	0	498	871	-1 269	1 053
Yearly Growth	0	0.1	0.07	-0.39	0.42
Current Account	0	8	-369	2 931	561
Gov. Expend.	-16 883	-17 043	-17 314	-17 092	-17 524
Yearly Growth	-4.96	-0.01	-0.02	0.03	-0.05
Employment	0	-92	-86	-182	-130
Unemployment Rate	0	0.37	0.34	0.71	0.51
Prices	0	0	0.1	0.1	0.2
Yearly Growth	0	-0.03	0.11	0	0.11
Wages	0	-12	76	76	176
Yearly Growth	0	-0.03	0.23	0	0.25
Yearly Growth of Real Wages	0	-0.01	0.13	0	0.13
Productivity (1980=100)	0	0.45	0.43	0.9	0.78

Figure 10.3   Scenario 2

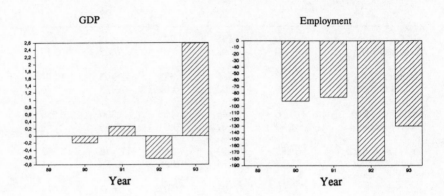

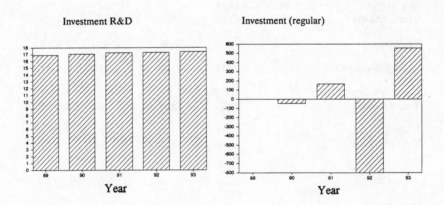

Table 10.5 Scenario 3 (Difference to Base Run)

	89	90	91	92	93
GDP	41 201	-17 385	15 608	21 145	30 448
Yearly Growth	2.44	-3.39	1.92	0.31	0.5
Consumption	30 740	-6 837	3 548	9 743	19 200
Yearly Growth	3.19	-3.8	1.06	0.63	0.91
Investment Reg.	8 308	-12 030	402	-2 342	-79
Yearly Growth	2.85	-6.97	4.39	-0.99	0.81
Investment R&D	15 637	15370	13 372	12 756	14 787
Yearly Growth	35.33	-1.03	-2.76	-0.62	3.32
Exports	-1 110	-10 060	350	645	252
Yearly Growth	-0.19	-1.49	1.76	0.05	-0.06
Imports	15 798	14 772	2 402	5 967	11 068
Yearly Growth	2.98	-0.26	-2.24	0.62	0.86
Current Account	-16 908	-24 831	-2 052	-5 321	-10 816
Gov. Expend.	3 426	10 941	338	6 308	7 357
Yearly Growth	1.01	2.16	-3.01	1.71	0.27
Employment	787	-415	236	234	450
Unemployment Rate	-3.12	1.64	-0.92	-0.91	-1.74
Prices	0.4	0.2	0.9	1.2	1.6
Yearly Growth	0.26	-0.15	0.56	0.19	0.39
Wages	103	-66	410	410	652
Yearly Growth	0.28	-0.45	1.27	0	0.58
Interest Rate	1.7	2.12	1.27	0.76	0.46
Yearly Growth of Real Wages	0.02	-0.31	0.69	-0.19	0.18
Productivity (1980=100)	-1.08	0.93	-0.09	0.24	0.1

Figure 10.4 Scenario 3

GDP

Employment

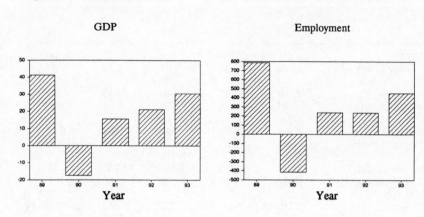

Investment R&D

Investment (regular)

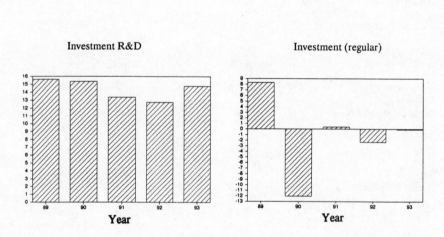

Such a strategy would raise labour productivity considerably. Exports could run substantially above their level in the base run, pushing the current account into an even more favourable position. Unions will benefit from the extra rises in real wage rates, which accompany the speed up of GDP growth.

There is a price to be paid for such benefits. Employment falls off on this track of accelerated innovation; unemployment rises relative to the base run. In this sense the moving into a faster lane of know-how accumulation amounts to a scenario favourable to social élites. It is part of a path toward a 'two-tiers society'.

On a technical level it seems interesting to note that the shifts in the trade balance and the current accounts do not trigger off noticeable adjustments in the rate of interest. The neutralisation of the notional expansionary fiscal stimulus of increased investment in R&D via cuts in other public expenditure items is sufficient to avoid major reactions on money markets. This keeps investment in equipment on its regular path (apart from the deviation caused by dynamic adjustment).

8.   INNOVATION-LED EMPLOYMENT GROWTH

The third scenario illustrates the proposition that a socially balanced innovation strategy might want to redistribute the gains from enhanced know-how. This is brought about by combining an expansionary fiscal stance with additional funds for R&D. Rather than neutralising the demand push of growing investment in R&D (as is the case under scenario 2), the government just tops up its regular budget with the extra R&D promotion package. Under such circumstances the notional gains in productivity are consumed by an expansion of employment. Thus there are hardly any additional rises in real wages.

This scenario seems to be quite attractive from the point of view of a trade-off between equity and efficiency. Growth of GDP is stronger than under scenario 2 and at the same time there is a reduction of the rate of unemployment by about 1.5 percentage points (over a period of 4 years). The speed-up of inflation is rather moderate.

In contrast to scenario 2, there is a noticeable feedback through the current account and interest rates. The current account deteriorates (relative to the base run) causing a rise of the rate of interest via the money markets. The initial response of interest rates is quite remarkable; after one year the interest rate is already about 2 percentage points higher than in the base run. This has a short-term dampening effect on regular investment and GDP. After two more years this depressive impact levels out.

Such an innovation-led growth programme amounts to a 'two handed approach towards European recovery' (cf. Blanchard, Dornbusch and Layard, 1986). The supply-side is taken care of through additional funds for R&D, whereas the demand side conditions are met by increased public spending and growing income spent on consumption.

9.   CONCLUDING REMARKS

The simulation exercises with Tandem-M suggest that West Germany could avail itself of the opportunity of a programme of 'innovation-led employment growth'. To achieve the goals set it would not have 'to beggar its neighbours' or dispense with its independent (and rather restrictively inclined) monetary authorities. In fact such a policy would serve as a stimulus for most trading partners, since imports would grow while the trade balance surplus would shrink.

Such a strategy has to be based on a firm commitment: temporary stimuli will not do. On the contrary, a short-term acceleration in the accumulation of know-how entails adjustment costs with little permanent benefits. However, continuity in provision of extra public funds for R&D is not sufficient either, because it raises the level of inequality; an even larger share of German labour supply would remain under-utilised, while the employed would enjoy higher real wage rates (compared to the base projection).

The scenario of 'innovation-led employment growth' asks only for a once and for all increase of the share of public spending in GDP by 1 per cent. There is no further relative growth in public spending. At the same time, the rate of unemployment would drop visibly. The successful implementation of such a programme would also require an institutional reform (as suggested in Chapter 11, below); it might even amount to a transition to a new growth regime (cf. Boyer, 1988).

NOTES

1   'The paper suggests that trade may be caused by technical changes and developments that influence some industries and not others; because particular technical changes originate in one country, "comparative cost differences" may induce trade in particular goods during the lapse of time taken for the rest of the world to imitate one country's innovation. It is claimed that for various theoretical reasons such a model may be better suited to explain substantial parts of world trade than some alternative models, but the main aim is to add to rather than replace the range of explanations available' (cf. Posner, 1961, p. 323).

2 'The movement of international capital depends on investment opportunities as reflected in interest rates and on anticipated changes in the exchange rate' (cf. Dernburg, 1989, p. 107).

3 'Of course, a wide variety of intervention rules conceivably could be relevant, but we focus on a linear rule that reflects concern for both exchange rate variance and reserve stock variance. Specifically we assume that the change in the stock of foreign assets held by the central bank is negatively related to the current exchange rate and to their foreign asset holdings last period, ...' (cf. Driskill and McCafferty, 1985, p. 85).

REFERENCES

Beckmann, G. and Meyer-Krahmer, F. (eds.), *Technologiepolitik und Sozialwissenschaft*, Frankfurt, Campus, 1986.

Bhandari, J.S. (ed.), *Exchange Rate Management under Uncertainty*, Cambridge, MIT Press, 1985.

Blanchard, O., Dornbusch, R. and Layard, R. (eds.), *Restoring Europe's Prosperity: Macroeconomic Papers from the Centre for European Policy Studies*, Cambridge, MIT Press, 1986.

Blazejczak, J., *Das DIW-Langfristmodell. Modellbeschreibung*, Berlin, DIW, 1986.

Blazejczak, J., 'Beschäftigungspolitik durch verstärkte Innovationsanstrengungen?', *DIW Wochenbericht* 4, 1989, pp. 46-51.

Blazejczak, J., Erber, G. and Horn, G. A., 'Sectoral and Macroeconomic Impacts of Research and Development on Employment', in E. Matzner and M. Wagner (eds.), *The Employment Impact of New Technology*, Aldershot, Avebury, 1990.

Boyer, R., 'Formalizing Growth Regimes', in G. Dosi, Ch. Freeman, R. Nelson, G. Silverberg, L. Soete (eds.), *Technical Change and Economic Theory*, London, Pinters Publishers, 1988.

Dernburg, T.F., *Global Macroeconomics*, New York, Harper & Row, 1989.

Dosi, G., 'Sources, Procedures, and Microeconomic Effects of Innovation', *The Journal of Economic Literature* XXVI, 1988, pp. 1120-71.

Driskill, R. and McCafferty, A., 'Exchange Market Intervention under Rational Expectations with Imperfect Capital Substitutability', in J.S. Bhandari (ed.), *Exchange Rate Management under Uncertainty*, Cambridge, MIT Press, 1985, pp. 83-95.

Frühstück, W. and Wagner, M., 'Tandem. Simulationen zum Funktionskreis Innovation-Wachstum-Beschäftigung', in R. Schettkat and M. Wagner (eds.), *Technologischer Wandel und Beschäftigung. Fakten, Analysen, Trends*, Berlin, De Gruyter, 1989.

Frühstück, W., Hanappi, G. and Wagner, M., *Tandem. Innovationsaktivitäten im wirtschaftlichen Funktionsgefüge der Bundesrepublik Deutschland*, Berlin, De Gruyter, 1990.

Hanappi, G., 'The Stages of Industrial Capitalism', in M. Di MAtteo, R. Goodwin and A. Vercelli, *Technological and Social Factors in Long-Term Fluctuations*, Heidelberg, Springer, 1989.

Kleinknecht, A., 'Observations on the Schumpeterian Swarming of Innovations', in Ch. Freeman (ed.), *Long Waves in the World Economy*, London, Francis Pinter, 1984, pp. 48-63.

Marin, D., 'Trade and Scale Economics', *EVI Working Papers* 88/332, 1988.

Matzner, E. and Wagner, M. (eds.), *The Employment Impact of New Technology. The Case of West Germany*, Aldershot, Avebury, 1990.

OECD, *Main Science and Technology Indicators*, Paris, OECD, 1985.

Posner, M.V., 'International Trade and Technical Change', *Oxford Economic Papers*, Vol. 13, 1961, pp. 323-41.

Schettkat, R. and Wagner, M. (eds.), *Technological Change and Employment. Innovation in the German Economy*, Berlin, De Gruyter, 1990.

Schmookler, J., 'Economic Sources of Inventive Activity', in N. Rosenberg (ed.), *The Economics of Technological Change*, Middlesex, Penguin, 1971, pp. 117-36.

PART 4:

TOWARDS A CONTEXT
ENHANCING FULL EMPLOYMENT

11. Policies, Institutions and Employment Performance

Egon Matzner

1. INSTITUTIONAL REFORM: DE-REGULATION OR RE-REGULATION?

In the 1970s and the 1980s the belief was widespread in both the political and the scientific arenas that by positive political intervention neither the performance of market economies could be improved nor unemployment be reduced.[1] The mood of the time was in favour of laissez-faire to be realised by negative political intervention, i.e. de-regulation and, in the end, a minimum of intervention by a minimalist state. According to protagonists of laissez-faire policies like F.A. Hayek or M. Friedman, such a strategy, whatever it produced, was the best possible.

Meanwhile, new evidence and experience have accrued which allow a re-assessment of the role policies and institutions play in economic performance. The contributions to this volume present an attempt at such a reassessment. Three conclusions can be drawn:

First, policies[2] and institutions (including regulations) do matter. Both matter in the positive and/or negative. Their influence will be in the negative if they do not respond to changing circumstances (e.g. of competition, of skill or of income levels).

Second, institutions (including regulations) and policies cannot be completely replaced by laissez-faire. For markets need to be supplemented by institutions and policies to function in a way that is not self-destructive. This perception of institutions (including markets) and policies is based on theoretical and empirical analysis. It can be supported by historical research, which has shown that laissez-faire and political non-intervention have never existed in industrial societies and liberal democracies (cf. Brebner, 1966).

Third, it is the very task of political, social and economic research to explore the changing institutional and political preconditions which promote the functioning of markets in a socially acceptable way.

In tackling this task we have organised our reasoning in three steps:

In a *first* step (section 2) we establish, by way of analysis, that institutions and policies are indispensable for the functioning of markets and hence for coping with the unemployment problem.

In a *second* step (section 3) we will present evidence on the influence of policies and institutions on the quantity and quality of jobs supplied and demanded. On this basis preliminary conclusions will be drawn on the comparative, institutional and political (dis)advantages which may influence a country's economic performance and its development of employment opportunities.

In a *third* step (section 4) *context-making* will be suggested as a way to internationally competitive production and full employment.

2. POLICIES, INSTITUTIONS AND MARKETS

Notions like 'political' and 'institutional' are often used in a very broad sense. In this wide sense the word 'political' can be used to signal individual decisions and actions (or abstaining from them) the effects of which transgress the individual sphere and which thereby obtain a social dimension. Delineated in this way almost all human activities could be termed 'political'.

The notion 'institutional' too can have a very broad meaning. 'Institutional' refers not only to organisations, but also to regulations, rules, routines, habits and even conventions (like the use of language). Thus social reality is constituted to a great extent by 'institutions'. They form an ensemble of social configurations in which only a subset of individual decisions and actions emerge as a result of 'rational choice'. The relation between institutionalised behaviour (or behaviour moulded by institutions) in the broad sense and deliberately chosen behaviour could by analogy be compared to the relation between solid and liquid matter. We do not know of a state of nature in which liquidity exists without being embedded into solid matter. In a similar way, deliberate behaviour of individuals is embedded in a social fabric of institutions. Just as fluid matter - although unwillingly - cuts into solid matter, so the social fabric is changed by continuous action.

Price-Guided and Institution-Supported Behaviour

For the purpose of our argument we have to employ, however, a narrower definition of 'institutional' and 'political'. In the context of economic performance and of problems of unemployment both of these notions are regarded as rival to 'competition' and 'free markets'. Such a view is widespread and corresponds even to conventional wisdom. It is a judgement which has to be rejected for good reasons. To arrive at that end, it is useful to have a closer look at the two phenomena. Markets can be understood as social events, in which goods and services are traded between sellers and buyers. In an ideal market, individuals compete with each other over the prices of well-defined products. Both production and supply, as well as demand and use (consumption) of goods and services react to (changes in) prices and income of factors of production, which, in turn, result from competitive processes. In the standard theory of the market process an optimum of output and welfare is achieved by an unregulated supply of and demand for factors of production and commodities, provided that economic agents follow the 'economic calculus'. Free entry into and exit out of markets as well as freely-moving prices and incomes, solely constrained by competition, can be considered as features of market economies. The deliberate and rational choice made by economic agents results in a form of *price-guided* behaviour that is based on the 'economic calculus'. Such a *price-guided* rational choice is juxtaposed to a kind of economic behaviour shaped and constrained by institutions, e.g. organisations (like a producer cartel or a trade union), regulations (such as abstaining from selling beer on Sunday afternoons), habits (such as allowing absence from labour in the case of urgent family obligations in rural societies), rules of thumb (such as an established mark-up on direct costs or renegotiation of wages, if productivity and profit margins exceed an established level), etc. *Institution-supported* (change of) behaviour can be regarded as the essence of socially or politically determined choice.

Price-guided as well as *institution-supported* behaviour figure as the two pure and theoretical opposites in a continuum. In reality, the two opposites mix to the extent that it invalidates a perception of reality in terms of the two opposites. The 'market', for instance, (both as an ideal and as a real type) also has to be perceived as an institution (cf. Hodgson, 1988, pp. 172-8). To a significant extent, competition, too, is dependent on the contextual factors, i.e. the societal 'capsule' within which competition takes place (cf. Etzioni, 1988, p. 199); economic behaviour is only rarely purely price-guided; it too is embedded in a social fabric of ties (cf. Granovetter, 1985). On top, even prices are often set according to established 'rules of thumb' following 'focal points' (Scherer, 1971, pp. 179-82). Even 'prices can be perceived... as 'conventions'...', as was argued by Shackle (1972, p. 227). And, as was shown by Kregel (1988), even the Stock Exchange in New York, which most people would consider as the nearest approximation to a market with perfect competition, is not governed by Walrasian auctioning towards equilibrium prices, but by prices which are influenced by regulations defined at the discretion of the association of traders and sanctioned by the authority. It has been convincingly argued that the efficiency of a market economy depends on the existence of non-market institutions. It was shown that a system of pure markets, based on completely specified property rights, is logically inconsistent (cf. Arrow, 1975, pp. 22-24). Deductive *logic* thus demands the existence of non-market institutions. There are also important *anthropological* reasons which explain the emergence of institutions. As they guide the individual in selecting information out of an often complex reality, they bring a regularity into individual behaviour. Institutions contribute in this way to the co-ordination of individuals' activities in society. Finally, there are specific *economic* reasons which have influenced the spontaneous emergence as well as the conscious creation of institutions which are typical of modern industrial societies.

The *first* of them has been highlighted by Keynes. It is the crucial role which *uncertainty* exerts in a monetary production economy. This uncertainty can have both a creative effect (to strengthen one's competitiveness because rewards are high but uncertain) as well as a destructive impulse (to reduce one's investment in the future, if returns are highly uncertain). Institutions may reduce this uncertainty. They thus tend to bring again regularity into individual and collective behaviour. If successful, they can introduce an element of stability into the expectations on future outcomes, which enhances positive individual decisions and actions, in particular with respect to investment.[3]

A *second* economic reason for the emergence of institutions in modern economies refers to the way in which potentially abundant information is transformed into usable knowledge (cf. Hayek, 1945). Habits or rules of thumb are examples of such institutions. They allow economising on the collecting and processing of information (or on 'transaction cost'). Action is thus based on what has been called 'thoughtless rationality' (Etzioni, 1988, p. 166).

A *third* feature of modern economies may, in the future, call for institutional response. It is the speed of transactions specific for the 'age of microelectronics' that is particularly relevant in financial markets.

According to standard theory, increasing speed should stabilise market processes. In practice, however, with the increasing speed of transactions, made possible by technology and de-regulation, the volatility of prices (especially exchange rates, cf. Schulmeister, 1987) has increased and the planning span has decreased. Institutional constraints which reduce short-term speculation and support agents to plan for a longer time-horizon may thus be a desirable policy option.

A *fourth* basic feature of market economies is their inherent tendency to provide an insufficient amount of public goods which are often crucial for successful economic performance: hence non-market-institutions, for instance, are needed for the supply of education, training and R&D.

We can therefore conclude that institutions are indispensable for a socially acceptable functioning of market economies. The specific way in which institutions matter, whether they assist or constrain initiatives, cannot, however, be deducted from theoretical considerations alone. Whether institutions (or markets) effectively support or constrain economic performance and employment, has to be evaluated also on the basis of empirical evidence.

Limits of and Scope for Institutional Reform

Institutions can be perceived (see Chapter 1, Introduction above) as the embodiment of accumulated knowledge, helpful in coping with recurrent problems in society. However, changing societies can be assumed to give rise to new as well as modified problems.[4] Although mutual adaptation processes spontaneously take place, in many circumstances they will remain either insufficient or socially unacceptable.

High unemployment, too, has been explained by institutional and political deficiencies such as 'Euro-sclerosis' or overregulation. As a consequence, institutional reform (i.e. improving the functioning of markets by de-regulation) has been insistently proclaimed as a way to achieve full employment (cf. Fels and Fürstenberg, 1989).

Institutional reform can indeed contribute to full employment; and though de-regulation and/or political non-intervention need not be excluded from the *political agenda* of employment enhancing reform, institutional adaptation of old and designing as well as establishing of new institutions also have their proper place.

Institutional reform has been rightly marked as a high risk project. It is time-consuming and of indeterminate outcome (cf. Scharpf, 1986). In spite of that, it will remain an important part of the *political agenda*. Even if there are always limits to institutional reform, it is also true that there are limits to abstaining from reform: at some stage, the cost of not carrying out reforms becomes greater than its 'uncertain' benefits. In recent years, de-regulation of the banking system in the USA has led to the colapse of savings and loans firms, which, in turn, threatens the whole financial system. There was a need for quick government intervention and for a kind of re-regulation. Still the estimated damage will exceed by far the costs of the Vietnam War.

Institutions may change spontaneously or as a result of purposeful action. This change influences individual decision-making. It either encourages or discourages certain decisions. This is why institutional change is *political* in its very character: whether as the result of *purposeful* political actions or as the tacit acceptance of its *spontaneous* emergence. The focus of this paper is on institutional reform which is strived for by conscious policies, and that is an important item of the *political agenda*.

A political agenda basically consists of two categories of political actions. Included in the *first* category are all political actions directed towards the change or upholding of the available set of instruments. The *second* category comprises all political actions aimed at the whole set of institutions, both their change and/or the protection against change.

The *set of instruments* and the *set of institutions* together form an important part of the *third* category which we call the *socio-economic context*. The first two categories of political action and their direction towards reform or stability form a repertoire of four possible combinations of political actions (see Table 11.1).

Table 11.1 Political Repertoire Matrix

| | | Set of instruments | |
		stability	reform
Set of insti-tutions	stability	office holder I	technocrat II
	reform	III reformer	IV context-maker

The four possible combinations of political actions differ greatly as to the scope and depth of their consequences. It is therefore difficult to imagine that one single politician is able to represent and pursue all the possible combinations of the repertoire. It is rather more likely (as has been shown by Kirsch and Mackscheidt, 1986) that the different combinations have to be represented by quite different political personalities. Following the taxonomy suggested by Kirsch and Mackscheidt, the combination I (both stable set of instruments and set of institutions available) can be represented by office holders of various political leanings. They only differ by how they apply the existing instruments. Combination II (reform of box in a stable set of institutions) calls for the 'technocrat'. Combination III represents the programme of the 'reformer'; combination IV calls for the 'context-maker'. Technocrat, context-maker and reformer can be of a more élite or of a more egalitarian orientation. Both the context-maker and the reformer can act either as statesmen or demagogues, depending on whether their policies change the social context in favour of universal, emancipatory relations between individuals or in favour of discriminating categories of individuals by demagogically exploiting anxieties (Kirsch and Mackscheidt, 1986). It is obvious that in reality *policy-makers* do not represent these four possibilities in their pure form. These categories are analytical abstractions. But they do point to important 'subjective' elements in the political process. Therefore, 'real life'-politicians can be identified as roughly corresponding to one or more of the four characters.

The history of the last decades gives, without doubt, credence to this typology. It therefore provides us with a better understanding of political theory and practice. It was convincingly argued by Kirsch and Mackscheidt that Down's *economic theory of democracy* deals with only one type of politician - namely the 'office holder', the representation of the average voter, while the 'statesman' and the 'demagogue' (in our case: the context-maker and the reformer) are beyond a Downsonian calculus of political costs and benefits. And yet, at times, both political characters prove to be highly important and occasionally successful.

The categorisation proposed is of relevance in political analyses. In evaluating the performance of political parties and their chances of success, the character of the personalities representing the political agenda has to be taken into account. The performance of a party which is directed in its intention by an 'office holder' has to be distinguished from a party directed by a 'context-maker'. This, however, is often neglected in political analyses which are based implicitly on the model of Downsonian 'office holders'. Innovative 'political entrepreneurs' such as the 'context-maker' and the 'reformer' can indeed succeed practically. They can succeed even though their chances of success would be non-existent from the point of view of a Downsonian 'office holder'. This also tends to be overlooked in the political analysis of the unemployment problem (cf. Scharpf, 1988).

3.   ON COMPARATIVE INSTITUTIONAL ADVANTAGE

Employment is strongly dependent on the volume of output and its growth. In order to have such growth in an open economy, the output has to be internationally competitive. According to classical economic theory, competitiveness in trade results from specialisation which would bring comparative cost advantages. Specialisation would be determined by the relative scarcity of factor endowments. Classical competitiveness results from the pursuit of self-interest by economic agents in competitive markets. In the original formulation of the theory of comparative cost advantage, institutional factors are left aside entirely. (An institutional setting with private property, the labour contract, free markets and their protection are implicitly assumed.)

If one is prepared to recognise that *price-guided* activity is the Siamese-twin to *institution-supported* activity, and, that, in the same way, institutions define the scope of markets and the weight of price signals, institutions themselves gain, alongside costs and prices, their proper place in determining competitiveness. While in classical trade theory a given set of products with a heavy content of natural resources, capital and/or labour is assumed, in a modern dynamic context neither factor endowments, technology and the set of products, nor institutions - and hence comparative cost advantage - can be regarded as predetermined. Natural resources have only a small role in establishing comparative advantage. Comparative advantage is regarded as 'man-made'. As was stressed by Pasinetti (1988), competitiveness in trade is increasingly contingent on knowledge and its use - a rediscovery of a main tenet of Austrian economics highlighted in the planning controversy by Hayek (1945). The institutional setting, in which knowledge both in its explicit and tacit form is accumulated, diffused and used, gains paramount importance. It determines if and how goods and services both old and new are produced competitively. Cost and prices are therefore but one element of competitiveness, which, however, are becoming less and less *economically* significant. Econcomic success has increasingly become dependent on innovation of product, organisation and technology. All that runs counter to the assumption of *constancy* contained in traditional theories of trade.

Competitiveness at the micro-level, in its turn, is in the long run a necessary but insufficient condition for also solving the employment problem. To reduce unemployment, the productive capacity has to be sufficiently large and, in addition, to be utilised. *Effective output* in terms of cost, prices, quality and structural adaptability has to be matched by *effective demand*. This demand is not created endogeneously in domestic and international markets; it has to be created deliberately by monetary and fiscal, as well as by active labour market policies. The extent to which a matching of conditions of effective supply, as well as of labour market-policies lead to full employment, is strongly influenced by *effective institutions*.

It has already been a basic tenet in Adam Smith and the English classical political economy (cf. Robbins, 1978) that institutions are a decisive factor of economic performance. They have been rediscovered as significant by a branch of standard theory, the 'new institutional economics' (as developed by Coase, Alchian, North *et al.*).[5] With few exceptions (e.g. Williamson, 1985) their approach appears to perceive institutions as mainly constraining variables which depend on relative prices (cf. North, 1989). (As was shown by Parrinello, 1990, not even the influence of institutions on relative prices, e.g. in the production function, is fully recognised.) The enabling function of an institution is even less appreciated. Given this strong bias to neglect the productive side of institutions, it appears to be worth summarising the evidence for the potentially positive role of institutions in enhancing the conditions of effective supply, as well as the effective labour market and demand policies.

Institutions and Effective Supply

What are the factors making for success in internationally contested markets? Our international comparative studies provide us with an understanding of some 'success stories' and the factors behind them. They point to interdependencies between the creation and application of new technology, the strategies of firms, the organisation of work and production processes, industrial relations and the provision of skills, as well as the functional and spatial division of work and tasks, as Chapters 2 and 3 have amply shown. The studies referred to deal with the building industry and the car as well as the iron and steel industries. Investigations were done on the micro- and meso- (i.e. branch and regional) levels. In some cases the macro-level was also included, as, for example, trade unions cannot be conceptually reconstructed 'from the bottom', since they are not the result of a spontaneous voluntaristic 'logic of membership' (cf. Schmitter and Streeck, 1981). From this empirical evidence we can draw some important conclusions; in some cases even conceptualisation could be derived. In this section they can be summarised briefly as follows:

1. *Diversified quality production* of products with a low price and high income elasticity of demand, was found to be a response to stagnant markets for mass products (see Sorge and Streeck, 1988 and Streeck, Chapter 2, above). We discerned some internal (in terms of technology, organisation, qualification, industrial relations) and external (in terms of supportive policies by the public sector and non-governmental bodies) preconditions for launching such a strategy. The stock of industrial skills and knowledge seems of special relevance. Its quantity and quality is enhanced by institutions that permit a mutual interpenetration of learning and work; institutions in which both the requirements of the firms and the interests of the trainees are represented jointly. The enterprise is a place of learning - in particular of tacit knowledge. Social contexts that enhance this learning provide increasingly comparative advantages. Qualification should not be too narrowly defined. They should allow for an overlap with the specialisation specific to the job that is acquired by 'learning by doing'. Institutions which provide such skills appear to be superior to those market solutions that were proposed by representatives of the 'deregulation school' and that, for instance, are practised, for example, in the United States.

2. *Industrial relations* (see Streeck, Chapter 2 above). Strong evidence indicates that there are forms of organisation of workers' and employers' interests which enhance competitiveness by allowing technological and organisational restructuring in exchange for recurrent training, job security, as well as relatively high wages which have been found to be compatible with stable unit cost. Clear evidence shows that co-operative industrial relations - under the challenge of international competition - enhance a high rate of adaptation and innovation and hence stimulate a rapid rise in productivity.

3. *Regional networks* of functionally autonomous firms amount to a highly significant institutional factor for an effective regional output (see Grabher, Chapter 3 above). This is clearly shown in Baden-Württemberg's 'success story' (cf. Sabel *et al.*, 1987). The insufficient existence of such networks in old industrial regions (dominated by one

single industry, e.g. steel) explains to a large extent the decline of such regions.

It could be shown that institutions mediate interaction within and between productive units as well as with their environment. Institution-supported interaction, in particular in education and vocational training, is a factor promoting competitiveness with respect to both quality and price. Institution-supported interaction can thus be important for adaptability and responsiveness of economic behaviour. It is thus a constitutive element of effective supply.

While the 'de-regulation school' regards trade unions as a form of 'institutional rigidities' hampering adaptation to new market conditions (cf. Fels and Fürstenberg, 1989), evidence shows that they can play a positive role in the process of structural change. In co-operation with the management, West German unions, for instance, are instrumental in developing a long-term perspective for the workforce. This, in its turn, favours long-term investment in skills as well as organisational and technological innovation. Contrary to the belief of the 'de-regulation school', trade unions which co-operate in the process of structural change tend to provide a clear institutional advantage.

An improvement of *effective supply conditions* is a way in which the successful producer can cope with the sales problem in the zero-sum-situation of stagnating markets. However, effective supply conditions, when dominant in an economy, also allow a more expansionary monetary and fiscal policy since additional demand can be met more easily by additional supply. If effective supply conditions also include incomes policies, the economy is less prone to inflationary pressure which, in its turn, relaxes the balance of payment constraint still further.

Institutions and Effective Labour Market Policies

Active labour market policy has been criticised on 'efficiency terms' by some supply-side economists who therefore suggested its abolition (cf. Soltwedel, 1989). Nonetheless, the record of countries pursuing active public employment policy in a determined way compares favourably with those who more or less abstain from such a policy. This can be seen from Table 11.2 in which the unemployment rate and the public spending for labour market programmes as well as the share of expenditure for active measures of employment promotion and for income maintenance are collected for OECD countries.

Table 11.2 Rate of Unemployment and Public Expenditure for Labour Market Policy (per cent of GDP) in 1987

	Rate of Unemployment	Total Expenditure	Active Measures	Income Maintenance
Austria	3.7	1.48	0.41	1.07
Belgium	11.2	4.35	1.10	3.25
Denmark	7.9	5.03	1.14	3.89
France	10.6	3.07	0.74	2.33
Germany	7.9	2.34	0.99	1.35
Italy	11.0	1.27	0.46	0.81
Netherlands	12.6	3.99	1.08	2.90
Sweden	1.9	2.66	1.86	0.80
UK	10.4	2.57	0.89	1.68
USA	6.2	0.83	0.26	0.59

Source: OECD Employment Outlook 1988, Tables 1.7 and 3.1

Comparing Sweden's figures with those of West Germany and the United Kingdom, at least four interesting observations can be made.

First, Sweden, as is known, puts great emphasis on active employment programmes. More than double the amount is allocated to active labour market policy as compared to income maintenance. Nonetheless, the sum spent for both types of programmes (measured as share of the GDP) only slightly exceeds that which is spent by West Germany. It is about the same as the share of the GDP spent in the United Kingdom on labour market programmes. *Second*, in West Germany the rate of unemployment is three times higher and in the United Kingdom more than five times higher than in Sweden. As a result, both West Germany and the United Kingdom are trapped into spending a much higher share on income maintenance than on active employment programmes. *Third*, in most countries that have a higher rate of unemployment than in Sweden, *public expenditure* for income maintenance (as a percentage of the GDP) is higher than Sweden's total labour market expenditure. It should be added that the social costs of unemployment are not fully reflected in public expenditures, particularly in countries with high unemployment like in Southern Italy, or in the United States, where income maintenance schemes cover only a fraction of the unemployed. (Income maintenance is provided there by family support, charity or crime.) *Fourth*, account must be taken of the fact that unemployment, particularly long-term unemployment, results in a cumulative process of *deskilling*. This, in its turn, adversely affects the *effective* supply conditions and, thus, tends to constrain the possibilities of future expansion. Once a high level of unemployment is reached, most of the public expenditure for labour market programmes is absorbed by income maintenance schemes. This mechanism can therefore be perceived as an institutional dimension of *hysteresis*. Looking at unemployment from such a perspective, the income maintenance schemes which are given preference in most countries are a public contribution to both waste and the disinvestment of knowledge and skills (cf. Soskice and Carlin, 1990, p. 254). By giving priority to active employment programmes, Swedish labour market policies have, on the contrary, succeeded in expanding their stock of skills and knowledge.

The causes of both low and high employment are certainly complex. The case of Sweden, however, can be regarded as further evidence against the 'policy-ineffectiveness hypothesis'. Whatever its formulation may be, it is not valid if full employment is pursued as a priority target in an appropriate socio-economic context. This requires a determined and continuous policy of intervention which instils certainty with economic agents, that this policy pattern will be maintained also in the future.

Findings from comparative international research suggest that Sweden's successful labour market perfomance can be attributed to that land's comparative institutional advantage. The Meidner-Rehn model of labour market policy can, as a matter of fact, be regarded as one of the most successful examples of institutional reform, or, put in our terms, of the making of an unemployment-reducing context:

1. In a six country comparison we have analysed the financing systems of active and passive labour market policy (including the external income maintenance schemes) in Austria, France, West Germany, the United Kingdom, the United States and Sweden. *Institutional (in)congruence* was found to be a major factor in explaining the differences in the size and effectiveness of national labour market policy (see Schmid and Reissert, Chapter 4, above). Effective implementation of labour market policy is facilitated, if the institutional set up and its financing system is congruent with the political targets, e.g. to give priority to programmes of active employment promotion. In the case of incongruence, labour market policy becomes ineffective. One other conclusion might be drawn from the study: institutions filter information and constrain actions. In this sense, they can be regarded as 'predetermined decisions' (Schmid and Reissert, p. 83, above). This

largely explains the differences in the volume of total public expenditure for labour market policy as well as the relative size of active to passive programmes.

2. Another important factor determining the extent to which the targets of programmes can be met are *implementation structures*. This is because the execution of policies involves a great number of intermediary services such as planning, consulting, organisation, information processing or controlling. The effectiveness of complex programmes depends on the interaction in a network of key actors. In the case of labour market policy, employers, trade unionists, functionaries in business organisation, in the labour market and local authorities as well as in the educational system have to be included. Studies have shown that the success of well designed public labour market programmes depends on the availability of an effective implementation structure. Approximately half of their success is owed to it. Similar results were obtained in programmes aimed at promoting the establishment and the growth of small businesses by Hull and Hjern (1987). Institutional and tax factors as well as the provision of a child-care infrastructure account for both the higher rate of participation of Swedish women in the labour market and their higher birth rate compared to women in West Germany (cf. Gustafsson, 1985).

3. *Impact of flexibilisation* (de-regulation). Supply-side economists hold higher flexibility as an important condition for increasing employment. In 1985, following such a de-regulation proposal, West Germany introduced the Employment Promotion Act. It facilitates the conclusion of fixed-term employment contracts that do not provide legal protection against unfair dismissals and redundancy. In an analysis of data from representative surveys of firms, employees and placement officers at the Federal Employment Agency concerned, it was found (see Büchtemann, Chapter 5, above) that this measure (a partial de-regulation of dismissal protection) had, however, not markedly increased the propensity of employers to hire labour. Trade unions originally had strongly opposed this measure of de-regulation. They feared that 'good' employment contracts with regulated protection would be substituted for jobs unprotected against lay-off. But these fears, too, proved unfounded. Despite this evidence, supporters of the 'de-regulation school' still regard the impact of the Employment Promotion Act as a great success (Walter, 1989, p. 412).

In the area of labour market and social policies, too, clear evidence can be found that policies and institutions 'matter'. It is a political decision which channels resources either into income maintenance of the unemployed or into the training of the otherwise unemployed. It is a political decision, too, whether the direction of funds is supported or constrained by the institutional conditions under which labour market and social policies have to be implemented. De-regulation, in its turn, does not necessarily lead to the results expected by its advocates. 'Rigidities' in the West German labour market did not prevent an adaptation as speedily as that of its de-regulated American counterpart (see Appelbaum and Schettkat, Chapter 6, above). The skill-enhancing German institutions, however, contribute to a great extent to Germany's competitive advantage over the US economy.

Institutions and Effective Demand

In sections 2 (on effective supply) and 3 (on effective labour market policy) institutional conditions were described which are favourable to (potential) employment growth: conditions of a diversified quality production such as co-operative industrial relations, non-market institutions for providing occupational skills, or institutional congruence, and effective implementation structures. The significance of these conditions for the promotion of production and employment is of paramount relevance. Nonetheless, very often this is still overlooked in policy programmes inspired by Keynesianism. On the other hand, 'supply-siders' of all complexions tend to belittle the fact that the best ('effective') supply of goods does not guarantee their being sold, as long as effective demand is insufficient. As is well established in Keynesian theory, effective demand is not automatically provided in a market economy. In a market, private decisions - which to a great extent determine economic performance - are taken in a *socio-economic context* representing a prisoners' dilemma (cf. Matzner *et al.*, 1979; Maital and Benjamini, 1980) and which produces an 'endogenous business cycle' (Kalecki, 1971). 'Effective demand failure' and increasing unemployment resulting from it can be prevented, either by a collectively 'concerted action' or an 'aggregate actor' or both (cf. Rürup and Sesselmaier, 1989). In any case, adequate policies and institutions are needed which are capable of rule-making (or influencing of rules), of habit forming, of creating tax/expenditure schemes, or of making monetary policies in those cases where the aggregated outcome of individual actions do not provide jobs for all who seek one. For a long time, institutions have been recognised as stabilising factors, examples of which are trade unions and collective bargaining systems (cf. Kregel, 1980), mandatory unemployment insurance as well as progressive income-tax systems (the last two examples were notably suggested by Friedman, 1965, as 'automatic stabilisers'). There are indeed still good reasons for stabilising public interventions both of an automatic type, and, as these tend to remain insufficient, also of a discretionary type. The case for public intervention cannot be ruled out by the mere fact of frequent 'public decision failure'.

Before stabilising public intervention can be suggested, one decisive question, however, has to be answered: Is a traditional policy of (expansive) demand management still feasible, given the free international mobility of money and capital which has become possible since the post-Bretton Woods era? Such a question has been raised even by those economists and social scientists who fully accept the 'instability hypothesis' of Keynesian economics. Some authors have come to the conclusion that, under the changed circumstances, a national expansionary monetary and fiscal policy is no longer feasible. Such a 'Keynesian' version of the 'policy-ineffectiveness theorem' has been based on two empirically observable phenomena: the *renaissance of the rentier* and the *external* constraints that have been created by the international competition between national currencies.

The *renaissance of the rentier* - counter to Keynes's plea for his euthanasia - followed from the policies against inflation at the end of the 1970s. The breakdown of the Bretton Woods system, price shocks, accommodating wage agreements, expansionary monetary and fiscal policies ended in an escalation of the public debt. This in return has prompted strong anti-inflationary policies and a corresponding rise of interest rates. All these have been factors in this post-modern 'euphoria of the rentier' at the dawning of a 'casino society'. The *entrepreneur* - the key figure in the process of production of *material* wealth - has been assigned dashing relevance; while the opposite is true for the *speculator* - the key-figure in *financial* transactions. This evolution has been fostered by the de-regulation of national and international financial markets. Nowadays, the rentier/speculator is continuously seeking to reallocate his international portfolio of assets and in this he is assisted by computer programmes. In these activities, interest rates, exchange rates as well as their actual and expectational evaluation are critical input data. Thus, a permanent 'beauty contest' of assets and of currencies has been established, where the speculator is continuously guessing the 'average' opinion. Contrary to the prediction of neoclassical theory, prices in stock and currency markets have become more volatile the more the conditions of markets have been de-regulated (cf. Goldberg and Schulmeister, 1988).

   More or less in line with the growth of international financial
transactions the *external constraints* for expansionary fiscal and monetary
policies have clearly become tightened; and this to an extent that, in the
view of some authors, traditional Keynesian full employment policies have
become more or less impossible. Yet they arrive at this conclusion for
different and sometimes diametrically opposed reasons. (The subsequent
argument closely follows Bhaduri and Matzner, 1990, pp. 50-1.) The
conventional argument made popular by the Mundell-Fleming model
(Mundell, 1961; Fleming, 1962) deals with the *ineffectiveness* of fiscal
policy in a world where free movement of financial capital keeps domestic
interest in line with a given international rate. In the Mundell-Fleming
model a fiscal expansion increases effective demand. This raises the
transaction demand for money. If monetary policy remains
unaccommodating, it increases the domestic interest rates beyond the
international rates. In a small open economy this prompts the inflow of
international financial capital. That again leads to the *appreciation* of the
domestic currency and, as a consequence, exports are reduced and
imports are stimulated. As a result, the aggregate effective demand is
depressed and the original expansionary impulse is largely neutralised. In
the extreme case, the appreciation of the domestic currency may fully
'crowd out' the initial fiscal expansion.

   The essential point of the Mundell-Fleming argument about the
ineffectiveness of fiscal policy is its prediction that the home currency
would *appreciate* as a result of fiscal expansion. The expansionary fiscal
effect would be neutralised by a reduction in the level of trade surplus due
to currency appreciation. But it is on this very point that the Mundell-
Fleming model can rightly be questioned by even those economists who
would otherwise agree that fiscal policy is largely powerless in today's
open economies. For most policy-makers and economists in Europe today
would presume that as a consequence of fiscal stimulation the home
currency would tend to *depreciate*, as aggregate demand is stimulated
through fiscal expansion. In the absence of *effective supply conditions*,
higher aggregate demand means higher import with little or no increase in
export and that worsens the balance of payments. This depresses the
exchange rate of the domestic currency. But what makes fiscal expansion
a *dangerous* policy is the speculative capital flight that may be set in
motion by (actual or expected) depreciation. Capital mobility under
current conditions basically means that an increasing amount of
speculative 'hot money' could flee from the home currency, forcing it into
a speculative spiral of uncontrollable depreciation, simply on the basis of
news (or the expectation) of a fiscal expansion. Given the current

conditions of flexible exchange rates with high capital mobility, this threat of massive capital flight makes fiscal policy not so much *ineffective* as *unpredictably dangerous*. Thus, both economists who believe that a fiscal expansion would be ineffective due to currency *appreciation* (such as in the Mundell-Fleming model) and as those who fear spiralling currency *depreciation* due to massive capital flights, perceive a binding external constraint on fiscal expansion to fight unemployment. The high degree of capital mobility brought about by the integration of international capital markets underlies this paradoxically common view.

Abstract reasoning alone does not tell us all about the *scope* which has remained for national fiscal and monetary expansion even under the current circumstances. This problem has therefore also to be investigated empirically. Various studies have shown that in OECD countries fiscal (and monetary) policy has been probably the most important causal variable for explaining the differences in the rates of unemployment (cf. McCallum, 1986; Drèze *et al.*, 1987). Our own study also shows that the scope for expansionary policies varies between countries, depending on whether they have a surplus or deficit in the current account (see Herr, Chapter 7, above). Surplus countries are usually in a strong, competitive position and this also implies a comparatively low wage/price pressure. In these countries, there is usually scope for fiscal expansion by means of expenditure growth and/or reduction in tax rates as well as for an expansionary monetary policy. For Tobin (1982), expansionary policies belong even to the 'adjustment responsibilities' of surplus countries: a strong currency like the D-Mark would allow a policy of lower interest rates, as the differential to countries with higher interest rates is compensated by the greater confidence in the mightier and more stable currency. Such a monetary course could counter the speculative pressure for still further appreciation and it would relieve the monetary pressure on deficit countries. An expansionist course would also gradually reduce the surplus in the current account; and this, too, would relieve the situation of deficit countries (see Kregel, Chapter 9, above). Those, in their turn, can cope under such a relaxation of the external constraint in a more co-ordinated way with the causes of the external imbalance such as too low a pace of structural adaptation and/or too high a rate of inflation (cf. Soskice, 1990).

These considerations and findings concerning the role of fiscal and monetary policy after the end of the Bretton Woods era can be summarised in three points:

1. There is sufficient theoretical and empirical evidence for rejecting both the neoclassical and the Keynesian versions of the 'policy-ineffectiveness theorem'. Even under the changed circumstances there is still scope for fiscal and monetary expansion, though certainly to a lesser extent and not at all times as stated earlier on (see Herr, Chapter 7, above). If a surplus country, such as West Germany, refrains from expansion then it is not because it could not expand, but because it has political preferences. (West) Germany puts greater value on DM stability and on 'monopolistic international policy co-ordination' than on full employment and on a reduction of international imbalances.[6] Nonetheless, effective demand will now be increased as a result of the expenditure needs of German unification. It will reduce the German surplus and thus relax the external constraints for deficit countries (see Kregel, Chapter 9, above). But this *de facto* change of fiscal policy does not follow either from the intentions of the Bundesbank or of the German government.

2. Expansionary fiscal and monetary policies are a pre-requisite for fully exploiting the chances of favourable conditions of effective supply and of employment-enhancing, labour market policies. Effective supply conditions require a macro-foundation by effective demand and vice versa. This 'two-handed-approach' differs from the original version suggested by the Bruxelles Study (cf. Drèze *et al.*, 1987) in an important way. It recognises the potentially positive role of institutions including regulations for production and employment.

3. Our 'two-handed-approach' does not confine supply-side policy to de-regulation measures. On the other hand, programmes which increase effective demand must be complemented by those that improve supply conditions. Such a policy can clearly be regarded as superior. Active labour market policies evidently have to be part of it; as would be a programme of 'innovation-led employment growth' based on increased public expenditures. Such a programme is an additional attempt to combine both demand and supply measures for the stimulation of production and employment (see Hanappi and Wagner, Chapter 10, above).

Comparative Institutional Advantage: Argument and Evidence

Attempts to clarify the role of institutions in determining economic performance by a qualitative evaluation are nowadays bound to be viewed with suspicion. Economists have become accustomed to considering the quantification of phenomena and the measurement of 'cause' and 'effect' as the ultimate aim, and as the test of a 'truly scientific' approach. Such an epistemological yardstick has already been rejected by Georgescu-Roegen:

To conclude, however, that in this clash between our intuition and the edifice constructed with numbers our intuition alone errs is the highest form of non sequitur (Georgescu-Roegen, 1971, p. 68).

And, indeed, parameters estimated in functional relations between prices, costs, incomes, assets, etc. may be seen as nothing more than *epiphenomena* (cf. Matzner, 1982, p. 41; Solow, 1986, p. 533). Lastly, they are generated in a setting of institutions, most of the time ignored in modern economic thinking. In social and economic life such institutions are the enabling and constraining elements. Because institutions do not lend themselves as easily to measurement as prices, the institutional base of social activities tends to be neglected in social and economic studies. The argument on which the significance of institutions, therefore, has to be based, can rarely, or only indirectly, be substantiated by quantitative data. We have to argue from historical and logical evidence; and seen from that angle, it is evident that a market is an institution whose functioning is dependent on other institutions. Historical experience and logical reasoning prove that it would be impossible to de-regulate in the sense of abolishing all institutions except the market. The wealth or poverty of an economy's institutional endowment is highly relevant to its economic performance.

Experience also shows that the differences in the institutional endowments between countries correlate with differences in unemployment, growth, productivity, price level, public expenditure, current account, etc. Given the intricate balance between effective supply conditions, effective labour market and social policies as well as effective demand policies, it is not possible to express institutional effectiveness in terms of statistical coefficients. And, yet, the contributions to this volume plausibly show that, for example, Sweden's comparatively low unemployment, the United States' comparatively low competitiveness and West Germany's high competitiveness go together with differences in institutions and policies.

Although in the 1980s most OECD countries pursued de-regulation policies, their scope and impact differed greatly. De-regulation probably went farthest in the United States and in the United Kingdom. This was particularly the case in the labour markets and the reduced role of the trade unions. In neither case did de-regulation lead to a substantial improvement in competitive employment. West Germany's competitive strength, however, could be increased not least through comparatively strong and co-operative trade unions. West German labour markets have not been de-regulated to any significant extent. Industrial performance seems to suffer equally from the absence of strong trade unions and from non-cooperative trade unions: in both cases the supply of essential public goods is reduced. These public goods - such as education or 'on-the-job training' are of peculiar relevance for industrial competitiveness.

The experience of one decade of de-regulation in the United States has been disillusioning. Nonetheless, this policy is still being proposed as a 'supply-side agenda for Germany and Europe' (by Fels and Fürstenberg, 1989). But it is exactly the American experience which should prevent us from taking the wrong steps. What has followed from *America's New Beginning: A Program for Economic Recovery* (White Paper, US Congress, 1981)?

After 1982, the Reagan administration did, indeed, follow a highly expansionist fiscal policy. This increased output and led to a quantitative growth in employment. The case of the USA after 1982 has demonstrated that even a deficit country can grow by fiscal expansion, provided its currency is regarded as sufficiently safe. Reagan's programme of de-regulation was fully implemented in at least two key areas of the economy: in the financial and in the labour markets. In the *financial markets* this led to an outburst of destabilising speculation and 'hostile take-overs'. Long-term investment in capital and the development of skills and productivity suffered as a consequence. In that sense, 'de-regulation' has hardly moved the United States towards greater efficiency. In the savings sector of the banking system, de-regulation caused an outright crisis, the solving of which will require public expenditures greater than those for the Vietnam War. De-regulation in this field had to be abandoned. Instead, there is 're-regulation' again on the agenda.

In the *labour markets*, de-regulation mainly promoted downward flexibility of wages. Lower wages reduced the incentive for skilling of employees and also lowered the incentive to improve productivity. Finally, it increased dramatically the number of contingent (female) workers in the low productivity sectors (cf. Appelbaum, 1988). This, in turn, had a negative impact on the current account, as employment growth hardly increased the production of exportable goods or services.

As far as the 'supply-side' is concerned, the American experience can only serve as a strong caveat against a dogmatic de-regulation policy. The recent history of the United States, however, contrary to what the advocates of a 'supply-side agenda' intend, does support arguments for an expansion of effective demand. But experience also points to a basic pre-requisite of such a policy, a strong competitive position in international trade. On that account, it is better suited for countries with a structural surplus such as West Germany or Japan.

4.   THE CONTEXT-MAKING APPROACH

The Political Agenda

Policies and institutions influence economic performance and employment on the micro-, meso- and macro-levels. The influence can sometimes be negative. As was shown, it can be positive, too. In the latter case, the pursuit of private interest is taking place in a political and institutional environment in which the enabling effects exceed the constraining ones. In such a case, when the market conforms to the postulated targets, interference with its operation would be harmful and self-frustrating.

However, the high and persistent unemployment which prevails in many countries clearly indicates that the pursuit of private interests in the markets does not automatically lead to a socially-acceptable outcome. What counsel should be given in such instances?

First, it is necessary to test the existing economic and social policies and institutions as to their effectiveness and efficiency. This then might help us to discern, design and implement a *socio-economic context* for private action. Private action is both to be enhanced and constrained and finally so co-ordinated as to create a socially-acceptable performance of economic agents. The function of the political agents and the state have therefore to be conceived as a clearly positive one. For the time being, context-making by political and institutional reform (see Table 11.1 and p. 237 above) does run counter to the 'mood of the time' as expressed in scientifically established proposals (cf. Drèze *et al.*, 1987; Fels and Fürstenberg, 1989) or political programmes (e.g. by the OECD, the IMF or even the EC). Though not confirming this 'mood of time', context-making in our sense would confirm the tradition of the theory of economic policy as established by English classical political economists such as Hume, Smith, Malthus, Ricardo, Bentham or the Mills for which

(the *invisible* hand) is the hand of the law maker, the hand which withdraws from the sphere of the pursuit of self-interest those possibilities which do not harmonize with the public good. ... And they (the English classical political economists) do believe that ... the pursuit of self-interest, unrestrained by suitable institutions, carries no guarantee of anything except chaos (Robbins, 1978, p. 56).

Keynes's proposals, too, did, in principle, correspond to this tradition of classical political economy. Of course there is a difference in content. But this is due to the fact that economic and social circumstances had changed in the course of the century, lying between the classical period of political economy and Keynes. In the half century which has passed since the death of Keynes, circumstances have changed again, a fact, by the way, which Keynes himself had foreseen (cf. Guger and Walterskirchen, 1988). The *political agenda* of the state has now to be redefined in order to foster the making of an adequate *socio-economic context*. This is once again an urgent scientific and political task.

Elements of an Employment Enhancing Context

We have defined the 'socio-economic context' as the ensemble of elements which influence a social situation *and* its logic from which decisions, actions and their outcomes ensue. As a fully-fledged theory of context-making still has to be developed (for a first attempt cf. Unger, 1987), we have to confine ourselves for the time being to naming those factors which guide and frame self-interested, individual behaviour in our society.

A *first* factor are *signals* that emanate as relative prices, costs and incomes from the market processes. These signals allow the individual to estimate the pay-off attributed to his/her chances and efforts.

A *second* factor that guides behaviour is bound to *institutions* (and the *technologies* available) - both in their explicit as well as implicit form. Institutions in their turn influence the market signals (and vice versa).

A *third* factor is provided by the *policy instruments* which again influence market signals and institutions.

Fourthly, individual and *collective world views* and their *moral dimension* (Etzioni, 1988) have to be taken into account as crucial factors in guiding individual and collective behaviour.

Like institutions or other social phenomena, a *socio-economic context* can result from purposeful action or it might emerge spontaneously. The end of the Bretton Woods era amounted to an almost complete change of context: institutions lost their purpose, prices which were fixed became flexible, policy instruments became obsolete, world views and motives altered from the atelier perspective to the casino perspective, the dominance and prominence went from production to finance. Was this change of context the result of purposeful action or did it emerge with nobody ultimately deciding about it? Obviously nobody was in charge.

There are, however, also important changes of context which are man-and woman-made: Few will question that Mrs. Thatcher did change the socio-economic context in Great Britain drastically within ten years. Few will doubt that 'EC 92' is a huge project of context-making. Perestroika, too, was originally intended as a large-scale project of context-making. Then why not imagine and suggest the making of a context which enhances full employment?

The contours of a context conducive to full employment can be drawn by sketching (1) institutional changes and (2) changes in tax-expenditure instruments, which, in their turn, could bring about the necessary changes in market signals - the first of the four elements regarded essential for the making of a context.

(1) *Institutional changes* have been perceived as important for improving *effective supply conditions*. These institutional changes can promote the social and political conditions of diversified quality production (see Streeck, Chapter 2, above); they may create regional networks for the reindustrialisation of old industrial regions (see Grabher, Chapter 3, above). Depending on the actual circumstances, such a problem could be supplemented by other changes: as for instance by a ceiling on the voting power of large shareholders in order to prevent 'hostile take-overs'.

Institutional reform could also substantially improve the *conditions of effective labour market policies*. Sweden, for instance, has effectively sought to combine a tax-finance scheme with active labour market policies (see Schmid and Reissert, Chapter 4, above). Depending on the circumstances, a further reduction or a flexibilisation of working time could also be part of a programme for full employment.

Finally, *institutional reform* could also improve the *conditions of effective demand policies*; and this, primarily, by introducing international monetary policy co-ordination. An example for such effective co-ordination is provided by the European Payments Union (EPU). In the EPU both deficit and surplus countries shared responsibilities for balancing the current account. (This is an idea suggested by Keynes 1943.) In the further reform and evolution of a European Monetary Union next to the target of monetary stability the target of full employment could be made binding for the central banks or, finally, for a European Federal Bank. A central bank's performance then would be judged not just by rates of inflation, but also by rates of unemployment.

(2) *Changes in instruments. Effective supply conditions* could be improved by reducing taxes and social contributions based on wage income (as suggested by Drèze *et al.*, 1987).

Effective demand policies could encompass measures to reduce the profitability of merely speculative financial transactions. One could, for instance, envisage the introduction of a tax on speculative transactions across the border (TOSTAB, see Bhaduri and Matzner, 1990, and for even more drastic measures Steindl, 1990). Of course taxation of sales of shares, too, should have been maintained where it already existed, as in Germany before 1991, or could be introduced if not yet implemented. The context could for instance also be changed favourably by ecologically superior, new, capital goods which should be substituted for environmentally damaging old ones. This could be stimulated by an accelerated depreciation of old capital goods which thus would lose in profitability (Spahn, 1988, p. 139).

Germany certainly has the scope for fiscal and monetary expansion which could be further increased by introducing TOSTAB. This room for manoeuvre could be used for the stimulation of an innovation-led growth (see Hanappi and Wagner, Chapter 10, above). It could be supported by a programme of active labour market policy based on an institutional reform of the financing system (see the suggestions by Schmid and Reissert, Chapter 4, above). The Eastern part of the new, united German state urgently needs to improve its infrastructure as well as a wholesale renewal of its capital equipment. The great number of people which has to be deployed in the process of transformation will exert political and social pressure for economic expansion and a redistribution of taxes and welfare outlays which the German political and social establishment, in all likelihood, will not be able to resist. It is for this reason that, for the future, a more expansionary German economic policy, which one could call *unification Keynesianism*, is to be expected. It will use the existing and still extendable scope for expanding effective demand; and it will help in establishing effective demand in the region of the former GDR. At the same time it will also reduce Germany's surplus in the current account with EC countries and thus promote the scope for more expansionary policies on a worldwide level (see Kregel, Chapter 9, above).

Context-Making: More than a National Task

Our ideas for the making of a context to encourage employment and competitive production are not meant as a blueprint for political action.

They are intended as suggestions as to the directions to be taken for concrete action. In this sense, the context-making approach is significant in promoting competitive production and employment in the advanced industrialised countries. This appears to be particularly pertinent for the redirection of those countries whose economies have suffered from *comparative institutional disadvantage* by competitively misplaced deregulation such as Great Britain or the United States. The positive perception of institutions is also of great importance for the design and implementation of policies and institutions which could enable the European Single Market to function in an efficient and socially-acceptable way.

However, the ideas on which the context-making approach is based have by far the greatest significance for the transformation of former centrally-planned economies. The rapid transition to a capitalist market economy is rightly perceived as a promising way to an improvement of the deplorable economic conditions in Central and Eastern Europe. But it is again often forgotten that the functioning of a market depends on enabling and restraining institutions and policies. As a consequence, it would be an especially urgent task to shape a proper socio-economic context in the former Communist nations. This is necessary, if the desired social outcome of private action is to be achieved. Unfortunately, it is still not widely realised that central planning failed primarily on account of the *non-use* of knowledge, and even the widespread *punishment* of its use characteristic of the Communist regime. Only he will recognise the importance of effective institutions who perceives them as accumulated knowledge so needed in post-Communist societies.

And yet, it seems as if, this time without political dictatorship, the engineers of change become once again victims of an ideology.

NOTES

1 The author is particularly grateful to Thomas Nowotny for his suggestions to improve the present version of this text. An earlier version which was discussed at the conference 'No Way to Full Employment?' in July 1989, benefited from comments by Wolfgang Blaas, Robert Boyer, Georg Fischer, Wilhelm Hankel, Geoff Hodgson, Stuart Holland, Peter Kalmbach, Jan Kregel, Jürgen Kromphardt, Dieter Mertens, Jan Odhnoff, Peter Rosner, Fritz W. Scharpf, Peter Skott, David Soskice, Josef Steindl, and Ewald Walterskirchen (see the full documentation of the conference edited by Matzner, 1989). The author alone is responsible for the errors and mistakes which remain.
2 This is evident also in the narrow sense of governmental policies. It was shown that 'left' governments coincide with lower rates of unemployment and vice versa (cf. Rothschild, 1986).
3 It was suggested to perceive an individual's choice of occupation of (re-)skilling as a process which is similar to an entrepreneur's decision about investment in capital (cf. Ginsberg, 1985, pp. 75-8).

4 This argument is taken from Schumpeter's essay on 'The Crisis of the Tax State' (1954) which is still to be regarded essential for the understanding of institutional change. (For an account of the range of intellectual and political positions in Austrian economics on this point see Prisching, 1989.)
5 The new boom of institutional economics was already foreseen by Myrdal in the early 1970s as a result of what Myrdal called the irrelevance of mathematical models for understanding the most important economic problems of our time (cf. Myrdal, 1973).
6 The Bundesbank obviously has a strong preference for 'monopolistic international policy co-ordination' by maintaining the superior quality of the D-Mark. A member of its board recently stated:

First, we have to stick to the policy stance which has established the D-Mark as an anchor of stability. *Second*, all European central banks which have not yet done so, have to be brought to follow this policy by strengthening their cooperation (Thomas, 1990).

The playwright Heiner Müller gave an acid account of the German attitude towards the D-Mark:

The D-Mark *is* the German identity. If the D-Mark is in danger, Germans will run havoc (Müller, 1990).

There are not many in the German establishment who oppose 'monopolistic co-ordination'. One of them is former Chancellor Helmut Schmidt who, as co-editor of *Die Zeit* and as author, insistently argues for a trade-off between monetary stability and full employment as well as for a *bargained* co-ordination of European monetary policy within the framework of a European Monetary Union (cf. Schmidt, 1990). The policy stance preferred by the (West) German establishment has, however, a long tradition. It is in its core similar to the plans which where made during the Second World War after the military defeat of Germany had become certain (cf. Giordano, 1989, chapter on 'The Triumph after Defeat').

REFERENCES

Appelbaum, E., 'The Growth in the US Contingent Labour Force', *Discussion Paper FS I 88-7*, Wissenschaftszentrum Berlin für Sozialforschung, 1988.

Arrow, K. J., 'Gifts and Exchanges', in E. S. Phelps (ed.), *Altruism, Morality and Economic Theory*, New York, Harper & Brothers, 1957.

Bhaduri, A. and Matzner, E., 'Relaxing the International Constraints on Full Employment', *Banca Nazionale del Lavoro Quarterly Review*, No. 172, March 1990.

Brebner, J. B., 'Laissez-Faire and State Intervention in Nineteenth-Century Britain', in E.M. Carus-Wilson (ed.), *Essays in Economic History*, Vol. III, London, Arnold, 1966.

Davidson, P. and Kregel, J. A. (eds.), *Macroeconomic Problems and Policies of Income Distribution*, Aldershot, Edward Elgar, 1990.

Drèze, J., Wyplosz, C., Bean, C., Giavazzi, F. and Giersch, H., *The Two-Handed Growth Strategy for Europe: Autonomy Through Flexible Cooperation*, Brussels, Centre for European Studies, 1987.

Etzioni, A., *The Moral Dimension. Towards a New Economics*, New York, The Free Press, 1988.

Fels, G. and Fürstenberg, G. M., (eds.), *A Supply-Side Agenda for Germany. Sparks from the United States*, Berlin, Springer Verlag, 1989.

Fleming, J.M., 'Domestic Financial Policies Under Fixed and Under Floating Exchange Rates', *IMF Staff Papers*, Vol. 9, 1962.

Friedman, M., 'A Monetary and Fiscal Framework for Economic Stability', in M. Friedman, *Essays in Positive Economics*, Chicago, University Press, 1965 (first published 1954).

Georgescu-Roegen, N., *The Entropy Law and the Economic Process*, Harvard University Press, 1971.

Ginsberg, E., *Understanding Human Resources*, Boston, University Press of America, 1985.

Giordano, R., 'Vom Triumph der Niederlage' (The Triumph after the Defeat), in *Wenn Hitler den Krieg gewonnen hätte*, Hamburg, Rasch & Röhrig, 1989.

Goldberg, M. and Schulmeister, S., 'Technical Analysis and Stock Market Efficiency', *Discussion Paper FSI 88-9*, Wissenschaftszentrum Berlin für Sozialforschung, 1988.

Granovetter, M., 'Economic Action and Social Structure: The Problem of Embeddedness', *The American Journal of Sociology*, Vol. 91, No. 3, 1985, pp. 481-510.

Guger, A. and Walterskirchen, E., 'Fiscal and Monetary Policy in the Keynes-Kalecki Tradition', in J. A. Kregel *et al.* (eds.), 1988.

Gustafsson, S., 'Institutional Environment and the Economics of Female Labor Force Participation and Fertility. A Comparison between Sweden and West Germany', *Discussion Paper FS I 85-9*, Wissenschaftszentrum Berlin für Sozialforschung, 1985.

Hayek, F.A., 'The Use of Knowledge in Society', *American Economic Review*, Vol. 35, No. 4, 1945.

Hodgson, G. M., *Economics and Institutions. A Manifesto for a Modern Institutional Economics*, Cambridge (UK), Polity Press, 1988.

Hull, C. and Hjern, B., *Helping Small Firms Grow. An Implementation Approach*, Kent, Croomshelm, 1987.

Kalecki, M., 'The Mechanism of Business Upswing' in M. Kalecki, *Selected Essays on the Dynamics of the Capitalist Economy 1933-1970*, Cambridge, University Press, 1971 (first published 1937).

Keynes, J. M., 'Proposals for an International Clearing Union' in J. K. Horsefield (ed.), *The International Monetary Fund 1945-1965*, Vol. 3: *Documents*, Washington DC, 1969 (first published 1943).

Kirsch, G. and Mackscheidt, K., *Staatsmann, Demagoge, Amtsinhaber*, Göttingen, Vanderhoeck & Ruprecht, 1986.

Kregel, J. A., 'Markets and Institutions as Features of a Capitalist Production System', *Journal of Post Keynesian Economics*, Vol. III, No. 1, 1980.

Kregel, J. A., 'Innovation in Financial Markets', *Banca Nazionale del Lavoro*, No. 166, December 1988.

Kregel, J. A., Matzner, E. and Roncaglia, A., *Barriers to Full Employment*, London, Macmillan Press, 1988.

McCallum, G., 'Unemployment in the OECD Countries in the 1980s', *The Economic Journal*, Vol. 96, December 1986.

Maital, S. and Benjamini, Y., 'Inflation as Prisoner's Dilemma', *Journal of Post Keynesian Economics*, Vol. 2, No. 4, 1980.

Matzner, E., *Wohlfahrtsstaat und Wirtschaftskrise. Entwurf eines zeitgemäßen Musters staatlicher Interventionen*, Frankfurt, Campus, 1982.

Matzner, E., 'No Way to Full Employment?', *Discussion Paper FS I 89-16*, Vol. II, 1989.

Matzner, E., Blaas, W. and Schönbäck, W., 'Die Entwicklung des Staatsanteils. Eine funktionsanalytische Betrachtung', in C. C. Weizsäcker (ed.), *Staat und Wirtschaft*, Schriften des Vereins für Socialpolitik, N.F., Vol. 102, Berlin, Duncker & Humblodt, 1979.

Müller, H., 'Quotation' *Die Zeit*, No. 24, 1990, p. 56.

Mundell, R. A., 'Flexible Exchange Rates and Employment', *Canadian Journal of Economics and Political Science*, Vol. 27, November 1961.

Myrdal, G., 'How Scientific Are the Social Sciences?', *Journal of Social Issues*, Vol. 28, 1973, pp. 151-70.

North, D. C., 'Institutional Change and Economic History', *Journal of Institutional and Theoretical Economics*, Vol. 145, pp. 238-45, 1989.

Parrinello, G., 'Social Norms, Fluctuations and Money in the Analytical Representation of the Production Process', *Discussion Paper FS I 3-90*, Wissenschaftszentrum Berlin für Sozialforschung, 1990.

Pasinetti, L., 'Technical Progress and International Trade', *Empirica*, No. 1, 1988.

Prisching, M., 'Evolution and Design of Social Institutions in Austrian Theory', in J. J. Krabbe, A. Nautjes and H. Vissen (eds.), 'Austrian Economics: Roots and Ramifications Reconsidered - Part 2, *Journal of Economic Studies*, Vol. 16, No. 2, 1989.

Robbins, L. C., *The theory of economic policy in English classical political economy*, London, Macmillan, 1978 (first published 1952).

Rothschild, K. W., "Left' and 'Right' in Federal Europe', *Kyklos*, Vol. 39/3, 1986, pp. 359-76.

Rürup, B. and Sesselmaier, W., 'Anforderungen an die heutige und zukünftige Beschäftigungspolitik', *Mitteilungen des Institutes für Arbeitsmarkt und Berufsforschung*, Vol. 1989, pp. 139-62.

Sabel, C. F., Herrigel, G., Deeg, R. and Kazis, R., 'Regional Prosperities Compared: Massachusetts and Baden-Württemberg in the 1980s', *Discussion Paper FS I 87-10b*, Wissenschaftszentrum Berlin für Sozialforschung, 1987.

Scharpf, F. W., 'Grenzen der institutionellen Reform', *Discussion Paper FS I 86-5*, Wissenschaftszentrum Berlin für Sozialforschung, 1986.

Scharpf, F. W., 'A Game-Theoretical Interpretation of Inflation and Unemployment in Western Europe', *Journal of Public Policy*, Vol. 7, pp. 227-57, 1988.

Scherer, F. M., *Industrial Market Structure and Economic Performance*, Chicago, Rand McNally, 1970.

Schmidt, H., *Die Deutschen und ihre Nachbarn*, Berlin, Siedler Verlag, 1990.

Schmitter, P. and Streeck, W., 'The Organization of Business Interests'', *Discussion Paper FS I 81-13*, Wissenschaftszentrum Berlin für Sozialforschung, 1981.

Schulmeister, S., 'An Essay on Exchange Rate Dynamics', *Discussion Papers FS I 87-8*, Wissenschaftszentrum Berlin für Sozialforschung, 1987.

Schumpeter, J. A., 'The Crisis of the Tax State', *International Economic Papers*, Vol. 1954 (first published in German: *Die Krise des Steuerstaates*, Graz, Universitätsverlag, 1918).

Solow, R. A., 'Unemployment: Getting the Questions Right', *Economica*, Supplement to Vol. 53, 1986, pp. 523-34.

Soltwedel, W., 'Labour Market Rigidities and Deregulation', in G. Fels and G.M. Fürstenberg (eds.), 1989.

Sorge, A. and Streeck, W., 'Industrial Relations and Technical Change: The Case for an Extended Perspective', in R. Hyman and W. Streeck (eds.), *New Technology and Industrial Relation*, Oxford, Blackwell, 1988.

Soskice, D., 'Reinterpreting Corporatism and Explaining Unemployment: Coordinated and Non-Coordinated Market Economies', in R. Brunetta and C. della Ringa (eds.), *Institutions and Cooperation: Labour Relations and Economic Performance*, London, Macmillan, 1990.

Soskice, D. and Carlin, W., 'Medium-Run Keynesianism: Hysteresis and Capital Scrapping', in P. Davidson and J. A. Kregel (eds.), 1990.

Spahn, H.-P., 'Comment to Guger and Walterskirchen' (1988), in J. A. Kregel *et al.*, 1988.

Steindl, J., 'Comment to Bhaduri and Matzner', 1990.

Thomas, K., 'Quotation' in R. de Weck, 'Die Unvernunft des D-Mark Nationalismus' ('The Irrationality of the D-Mark Nationalism'), *Die Zeit*, No. 42, 1990, p. 1.

Tobin, J., 'A Proposal for International Monetary Reform', *Eastern Economic Journal*, Vol. 88, 1978, pp. 153-9.

Tobin, J., 'Adjustment Responsibilities of Surplus and Deficit Countries', in James Tobin, *Essays in Economics, Theory and Policy*, Cambridge (MA), MIT Press, 1982.

Unger, R. M., *False Necessity*, Boston, Harvard University Press, 1987.

US.Congress (1981), *America's New Beginning: A Program for Economic Recovery*. A White Paper presented on 18 February, 1981, Washington DC.

Walter, N., 'Supply-Side Economics: Struggling for Rebirth', in G. Fels and G. M. Fürstenberg (eds.), 1989.

Williamson, O. E., *The Economic Institutions of Capitalism, Firms, Markets, Rational Contracting*, New York, The Free Press, 1985.

Index